MILTON STUDIES
XIV

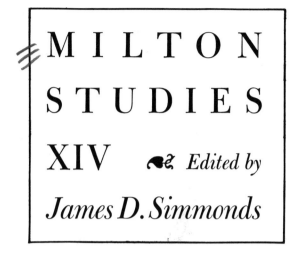

MILTON STUDIES

XIV *Edited by*

James D. Simmonds

UNIVERSITY OF PITTSBURGH PRESS

MILTON STUDIES

is published annually by the University of Pittsburgh Press as a forum for Milton scholarship and criticism. Articles submitted for publication may be biographical; they may interpret some aspect of Milton's writings; or they may define literary, intellectual, or historical contexts—by studying the work of his contemporaries, the traditions which affected his thought and art, contemporary political and religious movements, his influence on other writers, or the history of critical response to his work.

Manuscripts should be upwards of 3,000 words in length and should conform to the *MLA Style Sheet*. Manuscripts and editorial correspondence should be addressed to James D. Simmonds, Department of English, University of Pittsburgh, Pittsburgh, Pa. 15260.

Milton Studies does not review books.

Within the United States, *Milton Studies* may be ordered from the University of Pittsburgh Press, Pittsburgh, Pa. 15260.

Overseas orders should be addressed to Feffer and Simons, Inc., 100 Park Avenue, New York, N.Y. 10017, U.S.A.

Library of Congress Catalog Card Number 69-12335
ISBN 0-8229-3174-5 (Volume I) (out of print)
ISBN 0-8229-3194-X (Volume II)
ISBN 0-8229-3218-0 (Volume III)
ISBN 0-8229-3244-X (Volume IV)
ISBN 0-8229-3272-5 (Volume V)
ISBN 0-8229-3288-1 (Volume VI)
ISBN 0-8229-3305-5 (Volume VII)
ISBN 0-8229-3310-1 (Volume VIII)
ISBN 0-8229-3329-2 (Volume IX)
ISBN 0-8229-3356-X (Volume X)
ISBN 0-8229-3373-X (Volume XI)
ISBN 0-8229-3376-4 (Volume XII)
ISBN 0-8229-3404-3 (Volume XIII)
ISBN 0-8229-3429-9 (Volume XIV)
US ISSN 0076-8820
Published by the University of Pittsburgh Press, Pittsburgh, Pa. 15260
Copyright © 1980, University of Pittsburgh Press
Feffer & Simons, Inc., London
Manufactured in the United States of America

CONTENTS

MILTON STUDIES

XIV

THE POLITICS OF POETRY:
FEMINISM AND *PARADISE LOST*

Joan Malory Webber

Editor's Note: Joan Webber, Professor of English at the University of Washington, completed this essay a few days before her untimely death in a mountain-climbing accident. Her literary executor, Joseph A. Wittreich, submitted the manuscript to Milton Studies *and has seen it through the press. Aside from a few minor stylistic corrections, it is printed here as Professor Webber left it at her death.*

I N T H E highly delicate investigation of the relationship between politics and poetry, epic makes an obvious, though exhausting, field of inquiry. Traditionally, epic is described as a mingling of history with myth. Whatever this formula may actually mean, its effect is always that we are pulled in two ways, between a concern for the facts of the story (where was Troy? and when?) and a response to the universality of its symbols (Troy is any dying civilization). In epic we cannot have the one without the other: if Troy does not mean something, it does not matter where it was; if we do not know its actual history, we cannot be sure that our way of using the symbol is legitimate. Our uncertainty and ignorance in these matters are reflected in criticism's disarray.

One of the most blatant problems concerns the political orientation of the genre. We have a tendency to think of epic history (or politics), as well as myth, as conservative of a cultural past. Yet these materials may just as easily be instruments for social change. In fact, every major Western epic is revolutionary with respect to human consciousness.[1] Most significant poetry can make some analogous claim, but the epic purports to summarize its own culture, praise it, and at the same time subvert it, pointing the way to something higher.[2] Obviously an epic is not a tract, or a piece of socialist realism: even Milton, when he wrote *Paradise Lost*, had given up present hope for communal action, concluding that minds must change themselves before the world can change. The political poet's task is neither to man the barricades nor utterly to transcend his own time, but to speak through, challenge, and

3

transform the political materials and symbols of his time so as ideally to facilitate communal fostering of human possibilities, or to enable the individual person to resist the moribund or tyrannical state.

In its deceptively Homeric simplicity,[3] its apparent Christian moralism, its obvious personal involvement, and its relative nearness to our own time, Milton's epic poetry is conducive to easy stereotyping that allows us to approach it with distorting preconceptions. The difficulty of suspending disbelief when entering Milton's world should give us pause. We think of him as a poet of the past, yet in the great division that we make between the medieval and the modern age, Milton has to be considered a modern. To read him is to confront the central realities of our own culture, and we tend to react against some of those realities without recognizing that Milton himself is doing the same thing.[4] Studying the story of Adam and Eve, one is led to Milton's divorce tracts or *Areopagitica*, and from there to more modern documents on divorce and free speech. Then we attack Milton with weapons which he himself gave us the power to create by being among the first to recognize these issues.[5] With regard to cultural context, Milton's poetry puts us in a particularly difficult position. Because he himself was among those who first saw and helped to define the problems of our age, it is hard to put his ideas into historical perspective or to establish an aesthetic threshold to allow disinterested enjoyment of his art. He does not represent an antiquated part of our culture, as many unwary readers suppose. He anticipates our whole culture, with all its self-defeating conflicts, and asks us to choose change. Yet he speaks from a time that was itself a most unclear, ungainly, and mutilated mixture of ancient and modern ways, when nothing that we have now, including our problems, could have been taken for granted.

Despite the three hundred years between then and now, Milton almost makes possible an understanding of what it would be like to read a modern epic. Nothing else in our literature prepares us for the naive intensity of many readers' involvement in this poem. Almost everyone is either for or against *Paradise Lost* (or both at once); many see their own causes reflected or distorted in it. Its wholeness defeats argument, a fact which in itself breeds discontent. And so, because his issues are so contemporary, we find an easier course in detaching them from the poem and from the historical literary contexts which may not justify Milton, but do explain him.

In this essay, I wish to examine the role of women in his epics, from the particular perspective of Sandra K. Gilbert's recent analysis of the charge that *Paradise Lost* is misogynistic and patriarchal.[6] I choose this topic because it is politically far-reaching. Milton did not select our myth of origins only because he was a Christian concerned with the problem of evil. He believed that successful marriages (which he called fit conversations) are crucial to individual happiness, to the well-being of the state, and, indeed, to the right understanding of the world. Furthermore, Western epic is a genre notable for its extensive, significant attention to women characters. Yet, as women consider the poem, disagreement increases as to its value for them, based on interpretations of Milton's attitude, or the attitude expressed in the poem, toward women's place in life, and the nature of the system of growth and meaning that defines "women's place."[7]

Gilbert's essay, typifying the opposition, argues that "because the myth of origins that Milton articulates in *Paradise Lost* summarizes a long misogynistic tradition, literary women from Mary Wollstonecraft to Virginia Woolf have recorded anxieties about his paradigmatic patriarchal poetry." She believes that the poem tells the story of woman's secondness and otherness, her consequent fall and exclusion from heaven and poetry, her alliance with Satan, Sin, and Death. Hence women readers have allayed anxieties by "rereading, misreading, and misinterpreting *Paradise Lost*."[8] In developing her argument, Gilbert lumps together women's reactions to Milton with their reactions to patriarchal poetry in general, and she implies that their responses are to ideas that really are in the poem.

Paradise Lost certainly is a story of otherness, and of alienation. In explaining the ways of God, or perhaps in coming to terms with them, Milton shows that in his mind alienation is a necessary risk, and perhaps even a necessary fact, of Creation. But to think of the story as featuring Eve's particular alliance with evil is surely to distort the myth, and to ignore the historical context (not of misogyny, but of revolution) from which the poem came. It may well be that in trying to adjust the perspective for a more accurate political reading, I will sometimes appear to be submitting the cause of women to that of humanity: that is a familiar and often justifiable charge against men who would rather consider any other rights than those of women. Yet the opposite risk is to let the literature of our common humanity be needlessly sacrificed. In this instance, it must be remembered that we are dealing with the seventeenth century, when almost no politically radical woman could or would have dissociated herself from men regarding the issues of religious and secular freedom which were then being fought out. Furthermore, Milton's sense of the direction in which humanity has to move is generally one which prepares the way for feminist thinking. When he did raise issues involving women's importance and women's rights, he was awkwardly and imperfectly breaking ground.

Gilbert does not acknowledge either the seventeenth-century or the epic context of *Paradise Lost*, or the context of Milton's own life and writings. As opposed to critics like Barbara Lewalski, whose findings she appears to think are "academic,"[9] she sets out to consider not only "Milton's own intentions and assertions" but also the "implications of Milton's ideas for women."[10] At best such a separation of language from effect indicates a deep distrust of, or lack of concern for, Milton's use of words. And because Gilbert limits her territory to *Paradise Lost*, together with familiar platitudes about Milton's domestic life, she cannot adequately examine what his ideas and their implications are. More perhaps than most, revolutionary poets have to be read as a whole. The context of Milton's life and works has everything to do with every part of his writing. The prose tells us how to read the poetry.[11] Most important of all, *Paradise Lost* precedes and is incomplete without *Paradise Regained*.

Margaret Fuller wrote in 1846 that Milton was one of the fathers of her own age, a true understander of liberty, justice, marriage, and education, a father whose achievement still far outdistanced that of America, his child.[12] No doubt revolutionary fathers are as hard to accept as any other kind, but at least their inclination is to force rejection of patriarchy and conservative patriarchal systems, not to espouse them. When he wrote *Paradise Lost*, Milton was a fifty-two-year-old ex-convict who had narrowly escaped execution for opposing the restoration of Charles II at a time when most of his compatriots were changing their politics or taking shelter. The poem Milton had once intended to write was the old story of King Arthur. In choosing to write *Paradise Lost* instead, he could not and did not merely shift from one sort of patriarchy to another. We do not, of course, have his own explanation for the change. But it is apparent that he was abandoning a story that features one-man rule, an aristocratic society, and sex roles so stereotyped that their validity had already been challenged in poetry that Milton knew well.[13] The form and content of biblical epic, in Milton's handling of them, are layered with complexities and implications that exploit and overturn their traditions, while using them to orient and enlighten the knowing reader.

As a rewriting of the Bible in the late seventeenth century, *Paradise Lost* had to satisfy orthodoxy or fall under censorship.[14] In a superficially convincing way it appears as a bulwark of conservatism. Yet, even to read the Bible in English had not long before been an uncertain right.

The orthodox King James Bible owed everything to Tyndale's formidably influential translation, with its pugnacious marginalia emphasizing political interpretation and application. Milton's primary tenets, stressed over and over throughout his revolutionary prose, are self-control, self-knowledge, and internal freedom, in total opposition to what he calls external things. Since for him it was absolutely impossible that God could ordain any law contrary to human good, the external authority of the Bible always supports the inner promptings of the human spirit, even when, by our lights, he has to wrench the text to make this happen.[15] A double tension of this sort, between external control and inner conviction in Milton's own life, and between his inner convictions and some of the doctrines set forth in the Bible, informs all his involvement with the Bible, both in poetry and in prose.

The form of *Paradise Lost* is not only biblical; it is also epic. And, as previously indicated, Western epic traditionally undermines itself, providing criticism of the culture it is supposedly designed to admire. Just as Homer's poems implicitly criticize the Greek religious system, so do Milton's attack the Christianity of his peers. Moreover, in the Renaissance, the Bible itself was considered to be an epic: for translators like Tyndale it was the epic story of the chosen people, of whom the English nation was the contemporary realization. The fusion of Bible story with epic form very much increased the historical pertinence of Milton's poem, as at the same time the two elements radicalized each other. The Bible is famous for its denial of the decorum and aristocratic focus that epic had preserved,[16] and the history of biblical interpretation had long served as a tool for reinterpretation of epic. Epic, on the other hand, in its own history demonstrates cultural relativism; and in its character it shows how to undercut the reigning culture while seeming to praise it. *Paradise Lost* takes every advantage of its complex tradition's capacity to appear to be doing one thing while actually achieving something else.

At least one further significant element in this history ought to be mentioned. Foxe's *Book of Martyrs*, second only to the Bible as a best-seller of the age, had long promoted that idea that the Bible is the epic story of the chosen people of whom the English are the contemporary representatives.[17] Like the Bible, Foxe stressed the value of the lives of ordinary men and women, and, by recording the tortuous changes of religion that took place throughout the sixteenth century, increased the Puritan sense that individual conscience is more trustworthy than any reigning monarch. The failure of the revolution necessitated one more shift in emphasis: the chosen people themselves had broken their commitment. In *Paradise Lost* Milton says that true heroism requires patience, martyrdom, and loneliness.[18] No reigning monarch, no one leader or party, can be trusted, only the just, self-knowing solitary being.[19] Such a belief has obvious appeal to all men and women who find themselves victimized, and at once suggests one reason why women, who have always had to work by indirection and in isolation, still find value in the poem.

Renaissance artists were very fond of "turning pictures," optical illusions which change foreground with background in a seemingly arbitrary way, to emphasize completely different scenes from different perspectives.[20] It is thus, I think, with the limited Old Testament God of Book III of *Paradise Lost*, a figure who may be ironically modeled after Homer's Zeus,[21] and who has appeared to many readers, including Gilbert, as the autocratic designer of the conservative politics of heaven.[22] Surrounding this figure, as background or foreground, is a much ampler idea or power, a force for life that is neither anthropomorphized nor sexed, and to which even the God of Book III defers by giving the scepter and the power to his Son, who is to bring all creation into this greater unity, when "God shall be all in all" (III, 317–41). This is the bright and fluent source imagined in terms of light and fountain at the beginning of Book III:

> Hail holy Light, offspring of Heav'n first-born,
> Or of th' eternal Coeternal beam
> May I express thee unblam'd? since God is Light,
> And never but in unapproached light
> Dwelt from Eternitie, dwelt then in thee,
> Bright effluence of bright essence increate.   (III, 1–6)

All precedence and place here become mysterious. Between Satan's extensive maligning of his anthropomorphized God, and Milton's own portrayal of such a limited and inimical figure, is this luminous Being completely surpassing or encompassing the realm of ordinary human meaning. The syntax makes it possible to conceive of this Being as a God beyond God, certainly beyond rational expression. To the extent that any version of deity is anthropomorphic, one might say that he is not yet deity in this sense.

The God who is a character in Book III and elsewhere in *Paradise Lost*, self-justifying, dictatorial, and judgmental as well as splendid, roughly corresponds to the Christian idea of God in the Old Testament.[23] No doubt seventeenth-century readers accepted such a figure more easily than we do today. But Milton does not accept him, nor is this God satisfied with himself. He is in process toward full realization of the higher state imagined in the images of light. The only way to achieve that condition is by abnegation of title and rank. In illustration of that necessity, God gives the power and the scepter to his Son, but it is anticipated that at the end the scepter will simply become unnecessary: all life will be one with God. While the language, that "God shall be all in all," is biblical, and while the Bible is ordinarily understood to demonstrate that the more primitive Old Testament view of God yields to the New Testament sense of a God possessed of the more "feminine" qualities of love and mercy, this dramatic presentation of the change is Milton's own.

Although the words "Father" and "Son" refer to important concepts in the poem, the reality is very far from being simply a male patriarchal system, and not only because it is unusual for the patriarch to surrender his power voluntarily, foreseeing the end of all rule. The Son is begotten of the Father, out of time and out of any known sexual meaning. He then serves the Father as means of creation and separation, and also as a force for unity. Milton did not believe in the Holy Ghost as a distinct and equal part of a Trinity.[24] The Spirit, who seems interchangeable with God, the Son, and the Muse, is a symbolic, androgynous creative power. The extensive language of fertility and creativity everywhere in the poem prevents a conclusion that heaven is simply asexual. Nor is it the case, as Gilbert claims, that the female is excluded from heaven.[25] Wisdom and Understanding, for example, are female powers that existed in heaven before all Creation (VII, 1–12), although not necessarily named and bounded. Ordinarily, however, the descriptions of reproduction and creativity are so expressed as to prevent the sexes from falling into contraries. Both male and female muses are invoked. The angels "can either sex assume, or both; so soft / And uncompounded is thir Essence pure" (I, 424). When Adam questions Raphael about sex in heaven, Raphael blushes and declares, without reference to male or female characteristics, that sex is superior there because flesh presents no impediments (VIII, 618–29). Male and female are aspects of Creation, like light and dark, which grow more distinct the farther they are removed from heaven. And as heaven itself, in God's evolving process, moves closer to unity, its gradations may be expected to fall away with time.

In an interesting essay which Gilbert cites, Northrop Frye discusses the applicability to Milton's poetry "of the two great mythological structures" of our heritage—one, ruled by a male father-god, which dominates our culture from "the beginning of the Christian era down to the Romantic movement," and the other, centered on a mother-goddess, which has more frequently been influential in modern times. Frye traces in Milton a basic adherence to the father myth, the conception of a male creator superior to created nature, and the assumption that in all natural things male reason is superior to female imagination, even though that creative imagination is what the poet requires. Nature can be led upward toward the divine, or downward with the demonic: Eve, as representative of nature, has affinities both ways. But Frye also indicates, quite apart from Eve's partial association with the demonic, that she is given an unusual amount of independent power in the poem. "The father-myth is an inherently conservative one; the other is more naturally revolutionary, and the revolutionary emphasis in Milton shows how near he is to the mythology of Romanticism."[26]

Frye's essay rightly indicates that, rather than merely contributing to a long tradition of Christian misogynism, as Gilbert believes, Milton drew upon a much deeper, more primitive set of oppositions which Western culture had for thousands of years colored in a way that now seems prejudicial to women. Milton is obviously not only reworking this tradition but preparing it for its demise in the anticipated final unification of all things in God. Yet it is important in his poetry; it represents to him the way in which life has chosen to work itself out, for good and for ill. It is also an essential part of the epic line within which he is working, and so something needs to be said of it and of the problems which it presents for women readers.

As a great deal of our literature and mythology shows, the human mind, conscious or unconscious, has a strong tendency to group all experience, all phenomena, into opposites: up-down, day-night, sun-moon, reason-imagination, strength-softness, creating-nurturing, heaven-earth, and male-female.[27] Although most people who discuss the subject are quick to point out that the terms *male* and *female* are intended symbolically rather than literally (Jung believed that each person contains both elements), still women through the ages have always been associated with these "female" characteristics. Further, since men have been the thinkers and the writers, the female characteristics have often acquired connotations both of otherness and of evil, as men have projected their fears and fantasies upon the other sex. These patterns are extremely clear in the treatment of women in epic poetry.[28] On the one hand, there are women who guide and inspire, although their roles are externally passive compared to those of men, who seek, wage war, conquer, and find. Such women are Penelope, Beatrice, and Gloriana. On the other hand, there are witch-women, who seek to beguile, seduce, distract, and corrupt, such as Circe, Armida, and Duessa. All other epic women, with a very few exceptions, belong somewhere on the spectrum between these extremes. In some very real sense, men are associated with process and women with goals: women can deceive because they know, and compel because they are. Some epic writers, particularly those who include warrior women in their stories, raise women to a position of greater equality of function, but men and women are almost always seen as fundamentally different from each other, as they are in Milton.[29]

Part of Milton's task in justifying the ways of God to men is to explain why these differences exist. One question we would ask now is whether they do, whether indeed men and women are dissimilar, but for Milton such separations are a necessary aspect of Creation itself. Creation is by contraries; things are defined only by their opposites; self requires other. As soon as there are opposites, there is the potentiality for conflict even though Creation's end is a higher unity. Milton's God, who contains all opposites, shows conflict within himself:[30] when these differences are externally realized, the possibility of problems is realized as well, and the problems themselves make possible growth and change. Everything in the epic portrays a universe in process: that is a large part of the explanation of God's ways. Even God, in Milton's view, could not make instant perfection. In addition, Milton is changing the terms of epic and the traditional ways of looking at reality. The extraordinary power of the poetry is its ability to celebrate simultaneously so many different ways of thought and being, both the God of Old Testament righteousness and the New Testament God of change, contraries and their dissolution, inequality and equality between men and women.

Eve reflects every female potentiality that could enter the mind of a Renaissance epic writer and Christian humanist. Placed in the chain of being in a position officially subordinate to Adam's, she combines the opposite epic functions of witch and inspiration, being both Adam's downfall and his means of recovery. As Northrop Frye shows, she contains and reflects all the values associated with the mother-goddess, as well as the demonic associations that the Renaissance made with that cult. And she is a strong, human woman. Since even—or especially—today, women are struggling with just this problem of the multiple roles and definitions that have been thrust upon them, and which, with varying attitudes and in varying combinations, they perceive in themselves, Milton's Eve does generate intense feelings of identification. The first acts of her life portray a familiar dilemma: she wants to reflect upon herself, to look at herself in a pool and gain self-knowledge, but in order to know herself she is required to turn her attention to Adam, an alien other. The whole relationship between Adam and Eve, in fact, is affected by this stress between self-sufficiency and mutual need. As I will show a little later on, either posture, overindulged, becomes destructive, and balance is hard to maintain.

Traditional epic poetry, like the Bible, is patriarchal. Superficially, at least, it has to do with battles, journeys, conquests, the founding of nations. Ordinarily no problem and no success in epic occurs independently of women. Yet despite the near equality of warrior women, as exemplified most outstandingly by Britomart in Spenser's *Faerie Queene, Paradise Lost* is the first epic in which the active heroic role is shared equally between the sexes. Despite Britomart's obvious worldly equality, her goal is to find Artegall and marry him. *Paradise Lost* is the first epic whose scene is, in effect, the home, woman's traditional sphere, rather than the world of warfare and quest outside. Adam is called "domestic Adam" (IX, 318); when he shows signs of interest in places far removed from home, Raphael chastises him. Eve, in turn, has no supernatural or witchlike powers with which to tempt Adam or initiate the subsequent process of restoration. Although their weaknesses and their strengths differ, they are equally fallible; their epic battle is in large part their struggle to recognize and support each other's humanity. Many critics have pointed out in contrast the satirical, mock-heroic tone of Milton's treatment of Satan's "heroic" journey to Eden and of the epic warfare between the angels. It is one of the most remarkable things about the poem that seemingly insignificant domestic quarreling, set side by side with traditional epic endeavor, achieves such obvious, overwhelming importance. Human relationships are at the center of cosmic loss and gain.

Thus, while in most epics marriage or some analogous union is a symbol of the fulfillment for which the hero strives, in *Paradise Lost* marriage is a main subject and theme of the poem. Although the setting of Eden seems far removed from ordinary life, much that happens there is commonplace. The poem traces the lives of a man and woman from their first courtship through their first great disillusionment to their acceptance of life in the world that their descendants and Milton's readers know. Contrary to Gilbert's idea that Eve is a "divine afterthought,"[31] she is from the beginning an essential part of the whole design of growth and change achieved through opposition, which involves risk. The first test laid upon both Adam and Eve, when they are created, is to recognize that they need each other as they exemplify that large pattern of opposites without which nothing in the world, or even the world itself, could exist. Definition is in relation to something or someone else: to recognize one's incompleteness is an essential sign of self-knowledge. So God was pleased with Adam when Adam expressed a longing for a companion, although not when Adam allowed himself to be dominated by desire and need.

Milton had an obvious dislike for the courtly tradition that reifies woman (and man too) by making her an object of adoration. Adam's disposition to do this falsifies both Adam's and Eve's positions, and prepares her for the false adulation of the serpent. Romanticized married love, relatively new in the Renaissance, was the preferred Puritan model:[32] recognition of the woman as helpmeet released her both from the decorative, idealized courtly role and from her more common treatment as household drudge, and gave her an everyday value and importance that she would not have again for a long time.[33]

Adam and Eve are often spoken of in language that implies absolute equality. Adam asks God for an equal, one who can share "all rational delight," and is granted "thy likeness, thy fit help, thy other self" (VIII, 450), whom Adam sees as "Bone of my Bone, Flesh of my Flesh, my Self / Before me" (VIII, 494). Eve, upon her creation, is less sure of Adam's importance to her, and shows preference for her own image reflected in a pool before she is persuaded that she is part of Adam's soul, and, as he tells her, "My other half" (IV, 488). Both Adam and Eve are majestic, made in the image of God, and free.

At the same time, in this many-faceted scheme of things, the sexes are different: men are suited to "contemplation and valor," women to "softness" and "sweet attractive grace." This is a summarizing of traditional epic virtues, as they are personified in Odysseus and Penelope, or Prince Arthur and Gloriana. "Sweet attractive grace" is the equivalent of the powers that enable Beatrice to bring Dante out of hell. Sweetness is a capacity for love which Adam said was lacking in him before Eve was created; grace is the capacity for salvation; and attractiveness is the quality that attracts or draws, making it possible for two to become one. We see frequent signs of Adam's or Eve's particular qualities turning up in the other: just as Adam acquires sweetness, Eve demonstrates the power of contemplation.

In addition to all these complex reformations of biblical and epic material, the reader is required to see Adam and Eve as symbolic reflections of the great contraries of the universe—sun and moon, earth and sky, reason and imagination. The act of Creation results in such contraries, which, however, are to be restored to wholeness in God by being raised to a fuller unity than they originally enjoyed. Creation is essentially divisive: heaven and earth were made by what Milton calls

God's "divorcing command"[34] that sorted out the warring but indistin-guishable elements of chaos. That is, Milton here thinks of the word "di-vorcing" as expressive of a positive act: only divorce could create coher-ence. Yet inherent in that word also is the recognition that Creation began with imperfection, that it consisted in separating rather than in uniting, and that the Creation therefore remains unfinished, caught up in a progress toward a higher unity.

Adam and Eve, two parts of a theoretically inseparable whole, were in this sense divorced at the moment of Eve's creation, and, god-like as they are, their harmony is possible only because of disjunction. Milton's justification of God is that Creation is good, that inherent in creation is this divorcing process, which is in itself some sort of fortu-nate fall. Milton is quite clear that divorce in our modern sense was not invented for Adam and Eve.[35] They are above, or prior to, that, but they feel the strain of their twoness. Even Eve's words, "unargued I obey," by calling attention to the possibility of argument, both demon-strate and deny the strain.

Thus, although Milton says that his divorce tracts are not intended for this couple, we cannot help seeing in their marriage an illustration of what he means by both the best and the worst of wedded bliss. Mar-riage for him is a covenant, like that between man and God, and the covenant can be broken by spiritual or intellectual disagreement and incompatibility. When adultery is the only permissible reason for di-vorce, and the risks of adultery are so much greater for women than for men, it is easy for the man to control the marriage and his own freedom. Milton argues that the physical bond is much less important than the spiritual one, and that as soon as spiritual attunement is denied, the marriage is ended. Although he did not conceive of marriage without a dominant partner, he did suppose that this role might be taken by the wife, if she should exceed her husband in wisdom, and that either wife or husband could initiate divorce.[36]

In the divorce tracts, Milton asks that marriage be removed from control of any ruling hierarchy, religious or civil, and placed in the power of the partners themselves. In theory, at least, this action would give the woman a legal means to remove herself from the power of paternal authorities and to negotiate equally in the matter of her own destiny. Milton's poem also makes it obvious that the reality of divorce affects day-to-day marital relations. Since marriage is based on mutual consent, unchangeable disagreement constitutes divorce. When Eve de-cides that the pair should work separately for a few hours, Adam cannot force her to change her mind. Since she is determined to go, a refusal of permission would constitute at the very least an opening of the way to divorce. Later, Adam could divorce Eve on any number of grounds, but he chooses to abandon himself to her.[37] In the recriminations which follow, they see that they have broken covenant with God, themselves, and each other, but as Eve took the first step away from the marriage, she now is first to try to repair the damage, and Adam, while pretending opposition, follows her all the way.

It is no mere lip service (Gilbert's term)[38] that Milton offers to matrimony. For him it is the basic, central figure of the way the world is, and of the way it could be—sometimes in a pattern of higher and lower status, sometimes in a balance of equals, sometimes stressing the separateness of the partners and sometimes their unity. For him the epic goal was the wholeness that marriage offers, figured also in every part of the universe that grows through its many opposites, and figured ultimately in the visionary time when "God shall be all in all." The challenge that confronts us now is whether it is possible to retain that ideal, perhaps the only remaining idea that makes poetry out of life, while reaching beyond the particular poetry that seems to promote male dominance. While accepting this dominance, Milton himself searched beyond it as much as anyone in his age.

Eve and Adam were meant to move upward through the chain of being, free of death, until they reached the status of angels, and, eventually, without suffering death, to become one with God. Their destiny as free agents required them to be educated, and for this purpose God sent Raphael to teach them. Among the many remarkable attributes of *Paradise Lost* is its pervasive didacticism. The four central books of the poem are devoted to the education of the first man and woman. Both Eve and Adam listen to and absorb all that Raphael has to tell them, understanding with equal aptitude, as Milton tells us.[39] When Eve leaves before Raphael does, her departure serves several purposes, the most important of which is probably that it leaves Adam free to discuss her with the angel, in the section where he is told, but does not really admit, that he is an excessively doting husband.[40]

Adam and Eve are both gardeners in this poem, a conception not without precedent, although Milton did choose to avoid the familiar division of labor according to which Adam delves and Eve spins. In her additional responsibilities for the household, Eve may be a prototype for the modern woman who fulfills her profession and is expected to do the dishes as well, or, more pleasingly, a forerunner of the Renaissance lady who presided over the great house and its surrounding villages. In any case, Adam is out of place here, nervously asking her to bring out

allegorize

her best stores for Raphael, and having no idea how food is preserved in Paradise. Since Eve's work is more comprehensive than his, it is understandable that she is the one who becomes preoccupied with the problem of their labor; Milton himself appears to agree that she has some reason for her concern.

Eve's cosmic association is with physical nature, which legitimately concerns the couple in their immediate day-to-day obligations, as well as in their thoughts about their descendants. Adam's association is with sky, which is supposed to make him more aware of God, but which also gives him a penchant for abstract speculation and generalization, and often makes him seem abstracted and ill at ease with ordinary life. Although both attend to lectures, Eve is more responsive to dreams: the work of reeducating her after the Fall thus is much less laborious than that of teaching Adam, who has to have everything explained to him. These are aspects of the traditional opposition between the minds of men and those of women. But both the way in which they are educated together by a tutor and the way in which they set forth together as travelers into an unknown world emphasize the opportunities which were at least sometimes available to both men and women in the Renaissance, and perhaps never again with quite the same balance of excitement and fear.

I have saved the problem of Satan for last, because it involves the most crucial issues for *Paradise Lost* and *Paradise Regained* in our time. Gilbert sees him romantically, commenting on his enormous attractiveness, especially to women, because he expresses their own need to rebel. But as most readers have noticed, Satan loses almost all his attractions after the opening two books of the poem, nor is there ever justification for describing him either as "a handsome devil" or as a "curly-haired Byronic hero."[41] Gilbert also sees him, more correctly, as a lover of incest and an artist of death. Here, more than anywhere else, it is important to recognize that for Milton God represents life. Because Satan has rebelled against life, he can love only himself and death (two objects which finally amount to the same thing). Gilbert does see women as being caught in a trap if they turn from God to Satan, but the attractiveness that she ascribes to Satan is more imaginary than she, and some of her authors, realize.

Satan is a perfect example of a patriarchal, domineering figure. His reason for rebellion is that he is totally threatened by God's decision to hand over the scepter to the Son. Abdiel's argument that the Son's new role will enable all Creation to be more closely united in God expresses exactly what Satan fears, that his own status must be lost or shared. He prefers hierarchy in hell to unity in heaven, and he tries to convince Eve of the rightness of his own distorted perspective. Satan is that odd kind of rebel who reacts against change: consequently, any reader who, like some of the romantics, wants to use him as a model has to misread and misinterpret Milton in order to do it.

Another point of importance: in all of Milton's poems there are patterns of resemblances, and in seeing affinities between Eve and Satan, Gilbert has merely selected one thread of this pattern in *Paradise Lost*. Satan also resembles the poet and God;[42] Eve resembles Sin, Satan, Adam, the earth, Mary, and God. Milton, like everyone else in the Renaissance, is concerned with correspondences; they are a way of ordering experience. He is characteristic of his time also in believing that sin easily disguises itself as virtue, that evil and good so greatly resemble one another that it is difficult to choose the right path. In emphasizing likenesses between Eve, Adam, himself, and Satan, the poet wants to show that they do exist, that they are a constant danger, and that they can be overcome. Awareness of the danger may help us to avoid being surprised by sin.

Roland M. Frye's recent book, *Milton's Imagery and the Visual Arts*, provides valuable information not only about the traditional nature of these parallels, but also about the choices Milton made. In deciding how to portray Satan at the moment of the temptation of Eve, Milton rejected the possibility of "a serpent with the torso and head of a man," by means of which he could easily have created a "curly-haired Byronic hero." He also chose not to portray a woman-headed serpent, possibly with Eve's own face, a device extremely popular in the iconographic tradition. Such a figure would stress Eve's self-love, and give credence to Gilbert's argument for an incestuous undertone in the connection between woman and serpent. But, as Frye notes at this point, Milton "was not an antifeminist and could scarcely have put a 'lady visage' on his Tempter without seeming to some readers to invite an identification of the devil with woman."[43]

Imagination, allied with darkness and the muse, seems to Milton particularly vulnerable to invasion by Satanic elements. There is darkness in God also—Milton makes that very clear: from a cave near the throne of God both darkness and light proceed, and Satan himself, after all, is of God's creation. Just because the faculty of imagination is not always subject to reason, it is more suspect than reason, but it is not therefore inferior. Milton suspects his own poetic gift: possibly it is something of his own invention and not of God. He will not therefore deny or suppress it, but it may be that he stresses imagination excessively because he works in an irrational medium.

The most important and interesting element in this train of

thought is the growth, in the Renaissance, of attention to subjectivity and to knowledge for its own sake. These are mirror images of each other: to be lost in oneself, Narcissus-like, may be to lose oneself; one may also become lost in the stars. Both activities are seen in the Renaissance as gifts which may be misused. Contemplation of self may lead to holiness or self-worship; contemplation of the stars may be a way of praising God's works or of trying to play God. As always, Adam's and Eve's vulnerabilities are opposite to one another. Eve's subjectivity makes her open to self-adulation; Adam's interest in the stars and his tendency toward idolatry make him forgetful of himself. Both lead to loss of accurate seeing of relationships. Satan exemplifies both extremes. The birth of Sin and his incest with her demonstrate his perverse self-love; his mastery of technology warns of the possible results of Adam's innocent speculations about outer space. Milton may have wished that these tendencies in human nature, both for good and for evil, could be shut off, but he knew better. They lead to alienation in our world, in any case.

Satan's alienation is absolute because he has carried to a perverse and absolute extreme the opposing tendencies manifested in Eve and Adam. Choosing self-love over love of life (an untenable paradox), his aim is to oppose God with himself, but God is the only standard to which he can apply. He argues that heaven and hell are both within, but has to choose God's standards (the norms of life) for definition. He wishes to make the world his empire, and does, by profaning it: everything is defined by its usefulness to him in his efforts to turn it against its true character in God's world. Thus he is unable to know either himself or the world, and becomes a totally alienated being.

The tendencies that destroy Satan are rejected by Eve and Adam as they choose each other and God (or life) over their own selfish and power-seeking propensities. Thus they have within them the possibility of paradise, even though it is apparent at the end of *Paradise Lost* that they must experience alienation henceforth as a way of life. Eve's unselfish recognition and acknowledgment of her need for Adam begins to save both of them from the negative tendencies in themselves. Previous scholars have observed the bold paralleling of Eve with the Son, at the end of Book X and the opening of Book XI, as both offer to accept all responsibility for human sin.[44] Frye too notes that Eve's compassionate and decisive role in the redemptive process has few precedents.[45] Yet sending Adam and Eve out alone, hand in hand (a detail apparently original in Milton) into the world,[46] Milton was not satisfied, and *Paradise Regained* is an attempt to deal with the central problem raised but not solved in *Paradise Lost:* what to do about subjectivity and alienation.

Subjectivity is seen in *Paradise Lost* as a female characteristic, and external knowing as a male one. Eve's first act is to contemplate herself, and Adam's to contemplate the heavens. Neither characteristic is in itself morally tarnished. In fact, both conventionally lead to knowledge of God. But they can also lead to individualism, another quality by which we now define the Renaissance and both praise and lament our own age. Modern readers often criticize the childlike natures of Adam and Eve. But Milton's first man and first woman are like that just because they have not yet fallen into self-consciousness and alienation, which are necessary to individualism as we know it. Renaissance thinkers clearly recognized that spiritual fragmentation and decay are allowed and even fostered by individualism. Milton had to consider this postlapsarian condition, which had become so evident in his time. The fear and fascination surrounding the problem are exemplified in Satan, who resembles numerous other Renaissance figures in the boundless energy with which he will address himself to any self-serving and ultimately self-destructive goal. He cannot be saved because he cannot submit himself to a larger whole.

If Sin is seen as female, so, obviously, is Mary in *Paradise Regained*, to whom Eve is often compared in *Paradise Lost*, and who traditionally is given the role of second Eve to Jesus' second Adam. She is the nurturing woman who helps Jesus to know himself, and helps to keep us from thinking of Jesus as either incomplete or aggressively masculine. In the poem he departs from and returns to his mother's house. His main activities in the poem (which, like *Paradise Lost*, rejects traditional epic action) are learning to know himself and rejecting the world that Satan has to offer. The poem says that he descended into himself (*PR* II, 111): it is the first epic in which subjectivity is made so explicit; and he names correctly the false worldly lures with which Satan would seduce him. Thus he repairs the damage done to self by Adam and Eve, and acknowledges the damage done to the world. Obviously, also, he combines the qualities of Adam and Eve which had been distinguished in their creation.

The sterility of both internal and external narcissism is well portrayed by Satan. Jesus' only recourse is to reject everything that Satan has to offer, as Satan had rejected everything of God. And one may read the poem as prophetic of the despair of the twentieth century, which has followed the Renaissance into a subjectivity now devoid both of God and of faith in anything. Satan and Jesus are two major aspects of modern consciousness, but one may conclude by feeling that there is nothing to choose between them. It is of course immensely important to recall that, as incarnation of the Son, Jesus is to represent and further the goal of reuniting all things in God. Satan has become devoted to holding in stasis the outward-moving, still hierarchical forms of Creation, turning them into grim parodies of themselves: thus an angel becomes a devil, and men and women become sex objects to one another. The Son's (and now Jesus') work is to carry all things beyond their separateness, into a fulfillment in perfect unity.

Jesus has rejected external things and power politics. Yet the "yes" that he says to life as symbolized by God, the "yes" that he says thereby to his own sense of wholeness, gives him the power to walk on water, stand on air, and be ministered to by angels. It also enables him to return to his mother's house instead of being dashed to pieces on the rocks. So a necessary conection between male and female may be restored here in a pattern of reciprocity that attempts to correct both the old patriarchal values and the medieval values of knight and lady. Standing on the pinnacle of his father's temple,[47] Jesus repeats the effort of *Paradise Lost* to reject patriarchal symbol and hierarchy. Learning from and in turn enlightening his mother, he restores the original pattern from which courtly love was derived.

Paradise Regained appears to be a poem of worldly rejection that prepares the way for romanticism by teaching descent into the self and admitting the total corruption of the world. Milton believed that humanity's only hope was in the subjective faith of the lonely man or woman. But it must also be remembered that Jesus, in appearing to reject everything the world offers, rejects only Satan's secular world. Under that tarnished surface, Milton believed, could still be found the perfect Eden of Eve and Adam, and human relationships based in natural love. In the atmosphere of doubt, fear, and greed in which the poem takes place, the role of Jesus must to a large extent appear negative. Mary's faith in the nature behind appearances, and her ability to make a link between the physical and the spiritual, are easy to miss in the context of the duel between Satan and her Son. But, as Michael has already insisted to Adam, the duel involves no exercise of power. Jesus rejects all of the so-called masculine values. His return to his mother's house is an affirmation of the new Adam, the new man.

NOTES

1. For documentation of this point, see Joan Webber, *Milton and His Epic Tradition* (Seattle, 1978).

2. If Homer's poems celebrate the prowess of Greece and detail the military cul-

ture, they also question (perhaps deny) the sanity of the Trojan War. The *Aeneid* describes both the founding of Rome and the huge price that had to be paid for it. Tasso tells of a city (Jerusalem) that had to be destroyed in order to be saved. Camoens describes the utter decadence that overwhelms new lands after they have been discovered and claimed for Portugal. Spenser, Milton's immediate predecessor, in his romance epic presents the profound inadequacies of courtly love. The epics do not describe a better way. In fact, they do not utterly reject the world that they have, but in seeing its limitations they prepare the way for advance.

3. By these words I mean to suggest the large-scale sculpturing and the spare story line that so totally distinguish Milton from most of his predecessors. This apparent clarity is deceiving, but its artistic provenance is quite legitimately Homeric.

4. It is commonplace to speak of the English Civil Wars as the watershed between the medieval and the modern world, and to recognize thinkers like Descartes as the fathers of modern consciousness. It obviously follows that a poet like Milton, who lived through the Civil Wars on the rebel side, might also be seen as having helped to shape our world. See Jackie Di Salvo, "Blake Encountering Milton: Politics and the Family in *Paradise Lost* and *The Four Zoas*," in *Milton and the Line of Vision*, ed. Joseph A. Wittreich, Jr. (Madison, Wis., 1975), pp. 143–84. On this point in general see also Christopher Hill, *Milton and the English Revolution* (New York, 1977).

5. Milton's genius for seeing the underlying issues in contemporary controversies, and for seeing issues of freedom where others had been unwilling to look, enabled him to pioneer the work of freedom on many different fronts. Rather than concern himself with the degree of liberty appropriate to Baptists, Levellers, or Quakers, as others were doing, he examined the validity (for him the necessity) of free expression. Rather than assume the divine sanctity of marriage, he examined it as a human institution entirely dependent for its success on the enduring compatibility of two fallible human beings. This almost unique ability to grasp the essentials of a problem makes us wonder why he could not trace out all the implications in the same way we ourselves would do it. Such an attitude not only shows a lack of appreciation for the magnitude of the achievement; it is also ahistorical.

6. "Patriarchal Poetry and Women Readers: Reflections on Milton's Bogey," *PMLA*, XCIII (1978), 368–82. Gilbert's focus is on the reactions to *Paradise Lost* of a number of (mostly nineteenth-century) women writers, but she indicates that they are reacting to a conservative, patriarchal, misogynistic poem. In other words, she is not just representing what she regards as their point of view: she believes them to be right. While her essay does summarize some very persistent complaints about Milton, it also badly misrepresents both Milton and many of her authors, and probably ought to be answered point by point on their behalf. However, such a direct attack would dilute concentration on the most essential issue of how to read Milton. In the present essay I have tried, in fairness to Milton's own style of argument, to speak to that underlying issue. In the course of this endeavor, I do not mean to argue that Milton was not in some sense a "patriarchal" poet: he lived in the seventeenth century, and it seems pointless to complain that he was of his age. It is much more worthwhile to celebrate the extent to which, by transcending his time, he enabled us to ask for freedoms that he himself could not yet imagine.

Some examples of Gilbert's misreadings of Milton are that in *Paradise Lost* a solitary Father-God is the only creator of all things, that Adam speaks for Milton (and for God), that the Fall is responsible for human generation, that Adam's fall is more fortunate than Eve's, that spirits are all masculine, that Satan is a handsome devil throughout much of *Paradise Lost*, that Satan "explores" his own secret depths, and that he is concerned with liberty and justice. Both in her reading of Milton, and in her analysis of women writers,

Gilbert makes the mistake of assuming that a character's viewpoint can be identified with the author's. For example, although Charlotte Brontë's Shirley has a low opinion of Milton's characterization of Eve, Milton is first on the list of authors whom Charlotte recommended to her sister Emily, ahead of Shakespeare, about whose morality she has reservations, and far ahead of Pope, whom she says she does not admire; see Elizabeth Gaskell, *The Life of Charlotte Brontë* (London, 1908), p. 85. For more accurate readings of these writers, one should look at the works themselves, as well as at those of other critics, as, to take one example, Stuart Curran, "The Siege of Hateful Contraries: Shelley, Mary Shelley, Byron, and *Paradise Lost*," in *Milton and the Line of Vision*, ed. Joseph A. Wittreich, Jr. (Madison, Wis., 1975), pp. 209–30.

7. Previous writing on this subject includes Marcia Landy, "Kinship and the Role of Women in *Paradise Lost*," *Milton Studies*, IV, ed. James D. Simmonds (Pittsburgh, 1972), pp. 3–18; Barbara K. Lewalski, "Milton on Women—Yet Once More," *Milton Studies*, VI, ed. James D. Simmonds (Pittsburgh, 1974), pp. 3–20; Di Salvo, "Blake Encountering Milton."

8. Gilbert, Abstract, p. 357. Lewalski's fine essay, referred to in my previous note, anticipates much that I have to say here and obviates some of Gilbert's arguments, such as the idea that Eve's creativity is only in motherhood, while Adam is the poet and intellectual.

9. Gilbert, "Patriarchal Poetry," p. 369.

10. Ibid., p. 381, n. 8.

11. On this point, see Northrop Frye, *Five Essays on Milton's Epics* (London, 1966), pp. 94 ff.

12. In "The Prose Works of Milton," *Papers on Literature and Art* (New York, 1846), pp. 38–39.

13. I am thinking especially of the mockery of the courtly codes in Ariosto's *Orlando Furioso* and, with more thoughtfully directed point, in Spenser's *Faerie Queene*, where the sexism of the Arthurian world is made apparent.

14. On the problem of censorship, see Hill, *Milton and the English Revolution*, chap. 29, "Paradise Lost."

15. For the most famous examples of Milton's practice, see his use of the biblical texts on divorce in the divorce tracts.

16. One might bear in mind this antithetical tradition in considering Sandra Gilbert's attack on Milton's "masculine" Latinity. The question of whether Milton was or was not a Latinate poet is still, oddly enough, very controversial; some of the scholarship is summarized in my book *The Eloquent "I": Style and Self in Seventeenth-Century Prose* (Madison, Wis., 1966), pp. 287–88. Northrop Frye argues that "simplicity of language is a deep moral principle to Milton," and that he was "the first great English writer to fight for semantic sanity" (*Five Essays on Milton's Epics*, pp. 122–24). In fact, heroic language is subverted in *Paradise Lost*, just as heroic ideas are, until what finally emerges is the stripped style of *Paradise Regained*.

17. William Haller, *Foxe's Book of Martyrs and the Elect Nation* (London, 1963).

18. IX, 31–32, in *The Works of John Milton*, II (New York, 1931), hereafter cited as CM. Future references will be to this edition and will be given in the text.

19. Abdiel is the obvious model of the fully formed heroic individual. The acceptance of the isolated person as heroic model occurs in Milton from necessity of his age, not from conviction. The concept of individualism is new in the Renaissance, not even fully articulated, yet the dangers of individualism inherited by our age are already apparent to Milton, as they were to a long line of subsequent antidemocratic English thinkers, and this problem will be a central issue in my discussion. For Milton, individualism is a means to a communal end.

20. On this see, for example, Rosalie Colie, *"My Ecchoing Song": Andrew Marvell's Poetry of Criticism* (Princeton, 1970), "Visual Traditions," pp. 192–218.

21. I am extending a suggestion made by Northrop Frye, who suggests that God's self-justifying speech in Book III is modeled on the speech of Zeus at the opening of the *Odyssey*; see *Five Essays on Milton's Epics*, p. 105.

22. Gilbert, "Patriarchal Poetry," pp. 368, 375.

23. For discussion and bibliography, see my "Milton's God," *ELH*, XL (1973), 514–31.

24. *Christian Doctrine*, in *Complete Prose Works of John Milton*, VI (New Haven, 1973), ed. Maurice Kelley, I, VI, "Of the Holy Spirit," pp. 281–98. This edition is hereafter cited as YP.

25. "Patriarchal Poetry," p. 373. As so often, here Gilbert accepts the word of a character, in this case disgruntled Adam, who after the Fall imagines that heaven contains male spirits only.

26. Northrop Frye, "The Revelation to Eve," in *Paradise Lost: A Tercentenary Tribute*, ed. B. Rajan (Toronto, 1969), p. 46.

27. For discussion and bibliography, see Robert Ornstein, *The Psychology of Consciousness* (New York, 1972), p. 67.

28. Webber, *Milton and His Epic Tradition*.

29. For women now the question of how to make use of this extensive literature is extremely perplexing. Women are not in agreement as to the validity of these sexual distinctions. Nor can one be sure to what extent the literature creates or merely reflects them. If the stereotypes ought not to be perpetuated, then how does one deal with the literature?

30. See Don Parry Norford, "'My other half': The Coincidence of Opposites in *Paradise Lost*," *MLQ*, XXXVI (1975), 21–53.

31. "Patriarchal Poetry," p. 371.

32. See William Haller, "Hail Wedded Love," *ELH*, XIII (1946), 79–97; William and Malleville Haller, "The Puritan Art of Love," *Huntington Library Quarterly*, V (1942), 235–72; C. S. Lewis, *The Allegory of Love: A Study in Medieval Tradition* (London, 1953).

33. Hill, *Milton and the English Revolution*, p. 119. Research on this subject has yielded controversial evidence. For a somewhat different interpretation, see Lawrence Stone, *The Family, Sex and Marriage in England, 1500–1800* (New York, 1977), p. 202.

34. John Milton, *The Doctrine and Discipline of Divorce*, YP, II, 273.

35. *Tetrachordon*, YP, II, 665. Christopher Hill speculates interestingly on Milton's possible influence, and lack of influence, on Charlotte Brontë, who compares blind Rochester to Milton's Samson. Like Milton, Rochester lives long enough to gain a happy marriage. The divorce that Milton could envisage "still seemed impossible two centuries later"; see *Milton and the English Revolution*, p. 140.

36. *Tetrachordon*, p. 589: "then a superior and more naturall law comes in, that the wiser should govern the lesse wise, whether male or female." It is apparent throughout the tracts that Milton addresses himself to both men and women; the title of his initial tract begins, *The Doctrine and Discipline of Divorce Restored to the good of both Sexes*.

37. Eve committed idolatry in worshiping the tree, and to Milton idolatry was a more serious offense than adultery. But Adam committed idolatry in worshiping Eve.

38. "Patriarchal Poetry," p. 374.

39. In allowing Eve an education equal to Adam's, Milton certainly departs very far from the usual practice of his day: only a few aristocratic women were ordinarily privileged to learn so much. Since this episode of the poem is central, it seems strange that critics continue to believe that Eve has been denied the benefit of Raphael's instruction. This is a

different kind of misreading from that which Gilbert claims women have had to exercise.

40. It also shows us, as Arnold Stein points out, that when Adam has other things on his mind, he is not so concerned about Eve's spending time alone in the Garden (*The Art of Presence: The Poet and "Paradise Lost"* [Berkeley, 1977]).

41. Gilbert, "Patriarchal Poetry," p. 375. Gilbert ascribes this unlikely epithet to T. S. Eliot, on the authority of Harold Bloom in *The Anxiety of Influence* (New York, 1973). I have not found the source in Eliot.

42. On these intentional parallels, see William Riggs, *The Christian Poet in "Paradise Lost"* (Berkeley, 1972).

43. *Milton's Imagery and the Visual Arts* (Princeton, 1978), p. 168.

44. Lewalski, "Milton on Women—Yet Once More," p. 19. Joseph Summers, *The Muse's Method* (Cambridge, Mass., 1962), pp. 176–85.

45. *Milton's Imagery*, p. 294.

46. Ibid., pp. 314–15.

47. The act of standing on the pinnacle of the temple, which concludes the series of temptations in Book IV of *Paradise Regained*, is meant to recall the opening of *Paradise Lost*, in which Milton says that the Spirit prefers "Before all Temples th' upright heart and pure" (*PL* I, 17–18).

ARCHETYPES IN MILTON'S
EARTHLY PARADISE

Joseph E. Duncan

THE IMAGINATIVE power and near universality of Milton's great
Mount of Paradise can be at least partly revealed and understood
through various kinds of archetypal approaches. Not only is paradise itself frequently regarded as an archetype, but it is associated with other
archetypal conceptions such as the *axis mundi* and the mother. As the
elemental forms of literature can be found in myth, in much the same
way the constituent elements of myth can be found in archetypes,
which are often, indeed, the genes of myth.

Maud Bodkin, apparently the first archetypal critic to discuss Milton's description of Paradise, sees the mountain with its underground
river as reflecting, along with Coleridge's "Kubla Khan," the archetype
of Paradise—Hades; she concludes that the sunlit, watered garden
shows "some persistent affinity with the desire and imaginative enjoyment of supreme well-being," while cavern depths appear as the objec-
tification of awe.[1] In his perceptive comment on the garden in *Paradise
Lost*, Arnold Stein observes that it is "an *image* of the archetype" that
the poet creates, "a symbolic image in a dramatic situation that helps
create the image and protect it at once—protect it by maintaining the
ultimate impossibility of the *image* of the real archetype."[2] In her valuable description of dominant mythic structures in *Paradise Lost*, Isabel
Gamble MacCaffrey refers to paradise as "the most intimate and universal of all archetypes."[3]

As Stein says, the ultimate image of the real archetype of paradise
eludes us. But we can discover more and more of the elements in the
symbolic image that Milton created. By employing different archetypal
approaches, one sees that Milton's Paradise and its life share in a large
number of patterns regarded as archetypal by different disciplines; Milton's Paradise can be seen as possessing several different levels of archetypal meaning or as belonging to several different systems of archetypal
relationships. I want to examine the description of Paradise and its life
in *Paradise Lost* through archetypal approaches of anthropology, psychology, and literary criticism. I shall focus chiefly on the studies of

25

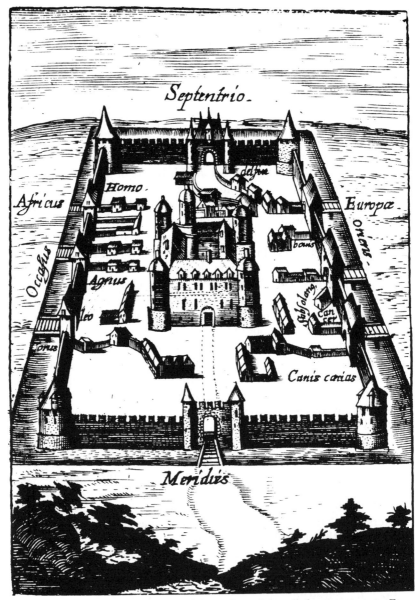

Figure 1. The symbolic city as center of the earth, its four walls forming a square. From Michael Maier, *Viatorium, hoc est, De montibus planetarum septem seu metallorum* (Rouen, 1651), p. 57. Courtesy of the University of Chicago Library.

occur where Milton could be most aware of them, in the Bible and in the Judeo-Christian tradition. In the Hebrew universe the world mountain, with the temple at its summit, reaches upward to the throne of God and downward to the waters of chaos. Jacob's dream, in which the angels are ascending and descending the stairs of heaven, places the center of the world in Israel. The psalmists find themselves closest to God at the center, marked by the temple on the holy mountain in Jerusalem. Ezekiel proclaims that Jerusalem is in the "center of the nations, with countries round about her" (Ezekiel v, 5).[18] In the sacred place on the holy mountain, heaven and earth truly meet, for God is simultaneously present in the temple and enthroned in heaven (Psalm xi, 4). According to Jewish tradition, the mount and the temple were also related to the underworld, for the temple-rock was thought to cover the abyss, source of the Great Flood.[19] In Christian tradition, the center was Golgotha, where Adam was created and buried and where Christ was crucified.

In Hebrew and Christian tradition, then, it was usually Jerusalem rather than paradise that was the center of the world. Those placing paradise and the Promised Land in the same location, at a single world center, were not generally the most respected commentators; they included Michael Servetus, Isaac de la Peyrère, and the credulous popularizer Eugène Roger.[20] Another, John Gregory, who was a contemporary of Milton's and an expert on occult lore, located paradise "toward the Equinoctiall East of the Holy Land" and directly beneath the throne of God.[21] The location of paradise and Jerusalem at the navel of the world also seems implied in the puzzling lines from John Donne's "Hymne to God my God, in my sicknesse":

> We thinke that *Paradise* and *Calvarie*,
> *Christs* Crosse, and *Adams* Tree, stood in one place.

The only biblical description of the Edenic garden as atop a high mountain occurs in Ezekiel xxviii, 11–19. This mountain, like Sinai and Zion, is associated with deity; here, though not in Genesis, it is described as "the garden of God," as it is in *Paradise Lost* (IV, 209). A work attributed to the fourth-century church father St. Basil pictured an Edenic mountain reflecting the archetypes described by Eliade and Campbell. This summit garden enjoyed the purest air and a perfectly temperate climate.[22] This mythic vision helped to crystallize in Christian literature the notion of a mountain paradise irrigated by a great river. Similar descriptions are found in the work of Lactantius, St. John of Damascus, St. Ephrem, and Moses Bar Cephas.[23] Also, at the summit

of Dante's Mount of Purgatory, at the highest point on the earth, is the
earthly paradise.

Partly because of the vast but clearly delineated cosmos of *Paradise
Lost*, Milton is more explicit than most poets and commentators in de-
picting paradise as a center and *axis mundi*. Milton regards the Mount
of Paradise as being a center long before Zion. Near the end of his long
flight from Hell, Satan sees stairs, like those of Jacob's dream, suspended from Heaven to the outer sphere of the universe:

> Direct against which op'n'd from beneath,
> Just o're the blissful seat of Paradise,
> A passage down to th' Earth, a passage wide,
> Wider by farr then that of after-times
> Over Mount *Sion*.   (III, 526–30)[24]

At the Creation, angels sing that the gates of Heaven will open
"Henceforth oft" so that angels can visit just men (VII, 565–73). In Paradise, Satan soliloquizes that Hell shall unfold "her widest Gates" to en-
tertain the first pair (IV, 281–82). Not only are these gates opened, but
the axis between Paradise, Heaven, and Hell is well traveled, especially
after Sin and Death construct the expressway from Hell to the entrance
to Paradise:

> and now in little space
> The confines met of Empyrean Heav'n
> And of this World, and on the left hand Hell
> With long reach interpos'd; three sev'ral wayes
> In sight, to each of these three places led.   (X, 320–24)

Even some of the paradisal sites of the pagan world which Milton compares to the true paradise are not just beautiful spots, but centers. The
fair field of Enna is an entrance to the underworld, and the temple of
Apollo in the grove of Daphne and the Castalian spring are points
where man is in close touch with the gods. Much of the drama in Milton's Paradise occurs as representatives of Heaven and Hell interact
with each other and with Adam and Eve, more so than in the works of
Milton's contemporaries dealing with the events of the "celestial cycle."
Satan initiates Eve's dream and then confronts the angelic guards. Raphael, the Son, Michael, and prevenient grace descend from God to
man; the prayers of Adam and Eve ascend. Sin and Death establish easy
access to earth over the causeway from Hell. Indeed, the passage from
Heaven down to "the blissful seat of Paradise" apparently disappears at
about the same time that the passage from Hell becomes a broad, secure
highway through Chaos.

Paradise as the center of the world is in the midst of the circling spheres and circling years. The earth, balanced on its own center (V, 242), is in the center of the World or universe. This in turn, like Paradise a protected place, is "enclos'd / From Chaos and th' inroad of Darkness old" (III, 420–21)—only Satan enters both. In Heaven the angels circle around God; the universe circles just beneath God and around the earth and Paradise. As the "garden of God," the prelapsarian Paradise is a still point, at the center not only of cosmic cycles but also of the "circling Hours" (VI, 3) and "circling years" (VII, 342.)

The description in Genesis, chapter ii, of the location of the garden in Eden does not mention a mountain; while some Renaissance commentators reasoned that rivers sometimes had their sources in mountains, most also did not mention a mountain. Milton's description differs from that of most of these commentators and from that of the other Renaissance poets of the "celestial cycle." His Mount of Paradise is in the same tradition with Mount Meru, Kuen-Lun, the mountaintop garden of Siduri in the Gilgamesh epic, and the "holy mountain of God" in Ezekiel. The Mount of Paradise towers toward heaven. Raphael in flight sees the mount "with Cedars crownd / Above all Hills" (V, 260–61), and from its highest point Adam and Michael see the "Hemisphere of Earth in cleerest Ken" (XI, 379). The Tree of Life, like various world trees, rises high above other trees in the center of the garden (IV, 195). The archetypal world center is thought to be the highest point in the world and the first created; in Hebraic tradition, creation began at Zion.[25] In Raphael's account of the Creation, God said

> let dry Land appeer.
> Immediately the Mountains huge appeer
> Emergent, and thir broad bare backs upheave
> Into the clouds, thir tops ascend the Skie.   (VII, 284–87)

George Yost has presented convincing evidence to show that Milton's description of the Paradise Mount (especially IV, 132–47) was derived from the description by Diodorus Siculus of the Hanging Garden of Babylon, complete with a mechanism for raising water, and from the description in Herodotus of the ziggurat Etemenanki-Babel. The description of the Tigris rushing beneath a mountain, as in *Paradise Lost* (IX, 69–73), is found in Pliny.[26] These descriptions, supported by authority and appropriate to the region, also contribute to the mythic or archetypal quality of the Paradise Mount. The Hanging Garden and the ziggurat Etemenanki-Babel were themselves probably seen as representations of the world mountain. Milton's Paradise Mount resembles other mythic creations; for example, the mountain plateau in Spenser's Garden of Adonis has also been cited as Milton's source.[27] The Paradise Mount rising above the river corresponds to both the earth and the universe, both "Built on circumfluous Waters" (VII, 270). And "The Lord sitteth upon the flood" (Psalm xxix, 10), whether enthroned in heaven or in the temple. Also, in his fanciful account of paradise, Moses Bar Cephas describes a mountain over a river from which water is mysteriously raised to water the garden.[28]

The center is sacred space and frequently the place of the sacred marriage or hierogamy. Campbell has included the sacred area or sanctuary among the archetypes which cut across cultural spheres and are "about coterminous with the human species."[29] Sacred space is bounded, often guarded, and contains a power of the other. Eliade has said that mountains are virtually universal symbols for representing the concentrated presence of God.[30] The higher the place, the greater is the intensity of the divine presence. Paradise as a sacred place corresponds to the temple as a sacred place. Ezekiel pictures the temple with four streams flowing from it (xlvii, 1–12). The temple with its three divisions corresponded to the composition of the universe (from waters to land to heaven) as well as to the nature of man.[31]

The garden in *Paradise Lost* is a sacred place, in close proximity with deity and out of ordinary time. It is the "Garden of God" (IV, 260) and was planted by God (IV, 215). It is "holiest place" (IV, 759) and "hallow'd ground" (XI, 106). It is directly oriented to the rising and setting of the sun. Adam and Eve hear celestial voices and have celestial visitors. Within the garden, as a holy of holies, is the nuptial bower, the place of the sacred marriage. The site of the "Blissful Bower" was chosen by God (IV, 690–91). The enclosure of this most sacred space is emphasized. It has "roof / Of thickest covert" (IV, 692–93) and "each odorous bushy shrub / Fenc'd up the verdant wall" (IV, 696–97). For awe of man, no other creature dares enter. No more sacred place, "though but feign'd," has ever existed (IV, 705–08).

Another sacred place in Paradise is that where Christ as judge and mediator appears to Adam and Eve. Heaven, Paradise, and Hell are brought into crucial relation as Christ reveals in "mysterious terms" the doom of Satan and the salvation of man through the grace of God (X, 163–81). Later, Adam and Eve feel that they must return to this place of judgment to express their repentance and seek forgiveness (X, 1086–104). It is here that they have their most direct relationship with deity.

Eliade explains that the sacred marriage, a recurrent element in ritual and myth, imitates the original hierogamy between heaven and

earth, and its prime purpose is creation or rejuvenation. It is a reenact-
ment of an event that occurred *in ille tempore*.[32] The marriage of the
King of the Wood with Diana or her double in the grove at Nemi is central in Frazer's *The Golden Bough*. Campbell has pointed out that the
marriage was frequently thought to occur in the topmost chamber of
the temple which represented the world mountain, and has cited a
fifteenth-century illustration for the *Divine Comedy* which depicts
Adam and Eve being married by God at the top of the Mount of Purgatory shown in the form of a ziggurat.[33] It is possible that the early Hebrews celebrated annually the sacred marriage of Jahweh and his bride
Anath, which probably took place in a sacred hut in a vineyard.[34] John
Broadbent has suggested that in this ceremony "we have an origin for
paradise; Adam and Eve are then actual god and goddess."[35] In any
case, in Scripture marriage is divinely instituted (Genesis ii, 21–24).

In *Paradise Lost* the marriage bed of Adam and Eve resembles that
of the deities of myth. In the *Iliad* Zeus and Hera lie together on the
"topmost peak of Ida of the many springs" on a bed of "dewy lotus and
crocuses, and a soft and crowded bed of hyacinths."[36] In the nuptial
bower Adam and Eve lay at the summit of the Paradise Mount, and
"the Violet, Crocus, and Hyacinth with rich inlay / Broiderd the
ground" (IV, 700–02). If Adam and Eve are not god and goddess, nevertheless their "mutual help / And mutual love" have been ordained by
God (IV, 727–28). God marries Adam and Eve, calls upon Eve to bear
children to Adam as "Mother of human Race" (IV, 473–75), and
"heav'nly Quires the Hymenaean sung" (IV, 711). Like the deities *in ille
tempore*, and also like the lovers in Donne's "The Canonization," the
first lovers leave posterity a pattern of their love. In their marital union
Adam and Eve represent the "Two great Sexes" that "animate the
world" (VIII, 151–52). It is they who checked "Fruitless embraces" and
"led the Vine / To wed her elm" (V, 215–17). Nature is sustained as long
as the perfection of their marriage is sustained, and earth feels the
wound at the Fall. If Milton had not hailed wedded sex or had found it
"unbefitting holiest place" (IV, 759), an important archetypal pattern
would be missing from *Paradise Lost*.

When Adam and Eve are at center, they live in the presence of God
at the highest point on the earth and breathe the purest air. They live in
a state of righteousness, potential immortality, and shameless nudity,
and in a world of cyclical time. If Paradise is a center, the true center of
Paradise is God's image planted in Adam and Eve. They understand
their relations only to those above them on the world axis, but God,
Satan, the epic poet, and the reader at the same time understand the re-

lations of the first parents to those below them. After the Fall, Adam and Eve enter an off-center existence in a world of sin, guilt, and death where they feel removed from the presence of God. They leave the world of cyclical time, but time is reversible in that "one greater Man" will "regain the blissful seat." The heavenly stair has been drawn up, the heavens altered by angels, and the broad passage from Heaven to Paradise has disappeared. In envisioning the Paradise Mount, rather than Zion, as the true center of the world, Milton has created a union of the place and the life which represents the archetypal ideal; but he has also given a historical reality to Paradise and to the freedom of Adam and Eve—Paradise could have remained as the center of the world and been indeed their capital seat (XI, 343).

II

In psychology, the seminal work of Jung has illuminated various archetypes closely associated with the earthly paradise. Jung distinguishes between the archetype as an irrepresentable model or potential inherited through the ongoing collective unconscious and its manifestation in conscious experience. Inherent in Jung's theory is not only recurrence, but depth of feeling and a dynamic sense of the archetype in time.[37] Though controversial, Jung's theory of the collective unconscious explains the origins, recurrence, and appeal of archetypes. Jung sees paradise as a symbol of the mother archetype and of individuation, the integration of the conscious and unconscious within the individual; paradise is also closely associated with the mandala and the archetype of quaternity.

As a symbol of the mother archetype, paradise is associated with fertility and with a longing for redemption. The mother archetype may be attached to a spring, well, garden, or forest, or particularly to a tree of life. In many creation stories, humans tumble from trees. Jung cites a legendary vision of paradise with the four rivers and a "mother" tree with a babe in its arms. The serpent often represents fear of incest. Paradise and fertility are associated with the archetype of quaternity. This archetype may be perceived as a square suggesting the womb or as a circle divided into four parts, as in a geometrical garden. Jung also notes that the mother archetype may appear as the mother of God.[38]

For Jung, the Garden of Eden, always a favorite pattern for a mandala in Christian iconography, is a symbol of the archetype of totality or of the self.[39] The mandala itself is also such a symbol. In interpreting a dream which Jung characterizes as "prodigal" in its meaning, he finds the keys to paradise to be the keys to individuation, to the discovery of the self; he also notes that this revelation comes through a union of opposites, including elements that are "half evil."[40] As a symbol, the mandala encloses in a magic circle the "sacred precinct" and "center" of the innermost personality.[41] Jung says, "The centering process is, in my experience, the never-to-be-surpassed climax of the whole development" of individuation. Indeed, Jung says that the center or goal is salvation.[42] Another aspect of integration is the inner hierophany, a union of the earthly and the spiritual, which can be symbolized by the marriage of Adam and Eve.[43] Patterns that are external for Eliade are inner patterns for Jung.

Four as a number represents order, totality, and the self; a circle or mandala divides naturally into four parts, as the human consciousness divides naturally into four functions. This archetype of quaternity is reflected in the conception of the four rivers of paradise and in representations of these; at the same time the four streams or radii in a mandala may make it a representation of paradise, a symbol of the totality of the self (see fig. 2). Adam was associated with quaternity: it was believed that he had been formed of dust taken from the four quarters of the earth and it was pointed out that the first letters of the words for the four points of the compass were included in the Greek version of Adam's name. The squaring of the circle, sometimes interpreted as the archetype of wholeness, can symbolize the union of the terrestrial and the celestial as in the combination of the four elements into a higher unity.[44]

One can find the mother archetype, quaternity, and the mandala in traditional Christian descriptions of the earthly paradise, including the one in *Paradise Lost*. However, for Jung the "paradise" of Genesis, chapter ii, and of Christian theology is a "paradise of unconscious childhood" or of "the fusion of all with all." From his own perspective, the paradise that is a symbol of totality and of the self is gained through individuation, the assimilating of the archetypes of the unconscious into the consciousness of the individual—and consciousness begins with the Fall, represented by the revolts of Satan and Prometheus and the disobedience of Adam and Eve. "And yet the attainment of consciousness," Jung writes, "was the most precious fruit of the tree of knowledge," but "consciousness is at once the highest good and the greatest evil."[45]

The archetypes that Jung associates with paradise are in *Paradise Lost*, but also occur repeatedly in earlier and contemporary cultures. The Bible refers to a Mother Jerusalem, though not to a Mother Nature. Lucretius provides an explicit description of the earth as a mother, which has womblike cavities and produces a milklike substance for the newly created.[46] The Hebrew temple is a paradise with four rivers flow-

Figure 2. Rectangular mandala with cross, the Lamb in the center, surrounded by the four rivers of paradise and the four evangelists. From Karl Löffler, *Schwäbische Buchmalerei in romanischer Zeit* (Augsburg, 1928), plate 20. Courtesy of the University of Chicago Library.

ing from it (Ezekiel xlvii, 1–12) and the New Jerusalem is a square city (Revelation xxi, 16). Myths and legends abound with the Jungian archetypes associated with paradise. Iranian myth tells of the ancestors of the human race growing from one "mother" tree.[47] In both pre-Christian and Christian literature square paradises, fairylands, and cosmic castles are familiar.[48] Philip Wheelwright has dealt with the "Archetype of the Vanishing Garden" as reflecting the individual's loss of the womb's security. This archetype appears in the expulsion in Genesis, in a Navaho legend of two boys, and "is a major idea underlying both *The Waste Land* and *Four Quartets*."[49] Proust's Combray, dominated by his mother, is a childhood paradise. And a recent study of the English country house as a "happy rural seat" relates it to Jung's mother archetype.[50]

For Mother Eve, in *Paradise Lost*, the earth is the "all-bearing Mother" who in Paradise yields "fruit of all kinds," though native to India, "*Pontus* or the *Punic* Coast" (V, 338–40). Adam wishes to return to earth as to his mother's lap (X, 775–78). Eve and various feminine figures associated with her—Juno, "*Ceres* in her Prime," and the Virgin— bring their maternal quality to the garden. Milton's earthly paradise is animated with images of fertility, sometimes combined with those of quaternity and the circle. In Book V, Adam and Eve pray:

> Air, and ye Elements the eldest birth
> Of Natures Womb, that in quaternion run
> Perpetual Circle, multiform; and mix
> And nourish all things. (V, 180–83)

Paradise itself with its "hairie sides" (IV, 135) and "veins of porous earth" is a womb enclosing the beginnings of the human race. Corresponding to Nature's womb and to Paradise as womb is the "fruitful Womb" of the "Mother of Mankind," which

> Shall fill the World more numerous with thy Sons
> Then with these various fruits the Trees of God
> Have heap'd this table. (V, 388–91)

Jung and others have dealt extensively with the seemingly universal desire to return to the womb, to regain the "vanishing garden," as this desire is revealed in dream and myth.[51] Not only does the garden symbolize the mother archetype, but our reentry into paradise as womb symbolizes the archetype of rebirth. MacCaffrey points out how the dreamlike quality of this reentry stirs the unconscious memory, and Stein speaks aptly of "a human groping toward a purely intuitive archetypal return."[52] The profusion and protection offered to Adam and Eve during their existence in the garden are most evident at the time of their repast with Raphael. Then the cycle continues with the expulsion of Adam and Eve. With poignant irony, Eve wonders how she will subsist "in other Air / Less pure" and without the "immortal fruits" of Paradise, but at the same time, as mother, worries about the young flowers which she has "bred up with tender hand" and named (XI, 273–85).

The archetype of quaternity is often inherent in the mythic vision of the world mountain. Jung refers to "four-faced Mount Meru," and Campbell cites the myth that a different race of men dwelt on each of its four sides.[53] Images of quaternity join with those of the mandala and circle in *Paradise Lost*. Heaven is referred to as a "Quadrature" (X, 381) and also as "undetermined square or round" (II, 1048). Similarly, Paradise is fundamentally circular, but has characteristics of the square and quaternity, so that it suggests both mandala and squared circle. The Paradise Mount is crowned by a "Circling row / Of goodliest trees" (IV, 146–47). The four points of the compass are mentioned frequently, and the relation of the circular garden to these points is usually clear. The two squadrons of angelic guards patrol to the north and the south and then meet in the west, completing another circle around the garden (IV, 782–83). Four sides of the great mountain itself are described at various times. In the north, the Tigris passes beneath the "shaggie hill," while on the south the waters that arose to irrigate the garden plunge down into the river emerging from its "darksom passage" (IV, 223–32). The eastern side is "craggie cliff" with one winding path and the single gate (IV, 543–50), and on the west is "steep wilderness" (IV, 135–37, 174–77). The gate is directly in the east, as its inner portal is struck "with right aspect" by the rays of the setting sun (IV, 540–43). The north-south line of the river and the east-west line of the rising and setting sun divide the mountain into quadrants. One is reminded of Jung's observation that "quaternity is an organizing schema *par excellence*, something like the crossed threads in a telescope," used for bringing order out of chaos.[54] Within the garden, as Adam, Eve, and Raphael dine together, man and angel, Heaven and Paradise, are linked in a new union, with a corresponding linkage between square and circle. The first couple with their first guest sit "round" the "ample Square" piled high with the fruits which Eve's "fruitful womb" (also related to quaternity) will yet excel (V, 388–95). Perhaps Paradise, uniting the craggy and the verdant, the wild and the cultivated, the waters below and the heavens above, is Milton's mandala.

For Jung, paradise is most important as a mandalalike symbol of individuation; encountering the mother archetype and its symbols, like a real or imagined physical paradise, is a part of this process. Though Milton's and Jung's terms and values are different, Adam and Eve through their self-discovery before, at the time of, and after the Fall experience the kind of development that Jung calls individuation. This is a development of consciousness, as through the mediation of symbols, material from the unconscious is accepted into the conscious mind. One way of viewing *Paradise Lost* is to see it as a narrative of the expansion of consciousness in Adam and Eve. We are used to thinking of action leading to the Fall or resulting from the Fall, but for Adam and Eve the Fall is only one event in the continuing process of the development of consciousness.

Several Jungian symbols of the development of consciousness are continually present in Milton's description of Paradise; the most important are the mountain, the tree, and light. The mountain may represent emergent consciousness, adult personality, wholeness, effort, or the goal of a pilgrimage.[55] Jung says that the widespread relation of mountain and tree, frequently the image of a tall tree on a summit, is not accidental, for both are symbols of personality and of the self. The tree, as a symbol of the mother, is associated with any life and growth. The tree of knowledge can be interpreted as "an earnest of the real life which waits the first parents when they emerge from their childlike (i.e., pleromatic) state."[56] The tree and light may appear together, as with the candelabrum or the Christmas tree. "Light symbols," in Jung's observation, "always refer psychologically to consciousness or to a content that is becoming conscious." The sun of consciousness may form the peak of the mountain of emergent consciousness.[57] (See fig. 3.) From the first, the mountain, trees, and light are controlling images in the description of Paradise. Uriel identifies for Satan Adam's light, the sun and moon, and "those lofty shades his Bowr" (III, 724–34). These images fuse in one familiar passage describing the Paradise Mount:

> And higher then that Wall a circling row
> Of goodliest Trees loaden with fairest Fruit,
> Blossoms and Fruit at once of golden hue
> Appeerd, with gay enameld colours mixt:
> On which the Sun more glad impress'd his beams
> Then in fair Evening cloud.   (IV, 146–51)

Imagery of this kind gives *Paradise Lost* its luminous green center.

In the process of individuation one encounters from the unconscious various tendencies and related psychic phenomena which are experienced as dream figures or as projections. They provide what is lack-

Figure 3. The mountain arises from the collective unconscious and symbolizes a new consciousness. The sun also symbolizes consciousness and the eagle, the animus. Picture by unidentified patient of Jung. From Jolande Jacobi, *The Psychology of C. G. Jung* (New Haven, 1968), plate 4. Courtesy of Yale University Press.

ing in the conscious mind. In the murky waters of the unconscious one perceives one's shadow, an unmasked image of oneself, an archetypal figure embodying characteristics which the conscious mind rejects. One also encounters the archetypes of the anima or animus, figures embodying contrasexual tendencies.[58] Before one reaches the center of the self, two other forms arise: for man, the wise old man, and for woman, the great mother.

Eve's first major confrontation with the unconscious occurs in her dream initiated by Satan (V, 28–92). Her consciousness has been expanded by experience "which my mind / Never knew till this irksom night" (V, 34–35). Eve's dream self, who wanders to the interdicted tree and thought she "Could not but taste" the fruit, may be seen as her shadow. The winged creature has several characteristics of the animus. The animus figure "possesses the magic power of words" and can both give feelings of inferiority and offer exaggerated praise; to the woman he appears to be superior, frequently represents knowledge, and issues commands. This archetype may be experienced as a pilot, aviator, chauffeur, lover, teacher, or even as the king of the underworld; he is often swift and light, traversing great distances.[59] The seemingly heavenly creature in Eve's dream both flatters and commands: "fair Angelic *Eve*, / Partake thou also" (V, 74–75); then he suddenly and swiftly guides her through the heavens. An experience with the shadow can lead to overconfidence, while the animus can make a woman opinionated and argumentative,[60] as in the first couple's first quarrel (IX, 205–374). Jung's associate Marie-Louise von Franz observes, "Animus and anima always tend to drag a conversation down to a very low level and to produce a disagreeable, irascible, emotional atmosphere."[61]

Adam also is discovering himself and expanding his consciousness, chiefly through Eve. As he tells Raphael, delight in all the beauties of nature "works in the mind no change," but in his sexual relations with Eve, "here passion first I felt / Commotion strange" (VIII, 524–31). Adam finds his anima, or feminine part, embodied in Eve, "Best Image of my self and dearer half" (V, 95). To the man, the anima figure is inferior, but irresistible. Eve is compared to other figures representing the anima, such as a goddess, wood nymph, or siren. Jung writes of the anima: "She is full of snares and traps, in order that man should fall, should reach the earth, entangle himself there, and stay caught, so that life should be lived. Eve in the garden of Eden could not rest content until she had convinced Adam of the goodness of the forbidden apple." Because she wants life, the anima wants both good and bad.[62]

Eve's impulsion by the animus and Adam's fascination with the anima lead to the Fall and to a further expansion in the range and depth of consciousness. By the end of Book X Adam and Eve have recognized within themselves the qualities represented by these archetypes. A man may see his shadow as Mephistopheles;[63] Adam finds himself "To Satan only like" (X, 841). Adam responds to Eve as an anima figure in her positive aspect when "his heart relented / Towards her, his life so late and sole delight" (X, 940–41). The anima can lead to marital harmony, put man in touch with the right inner values, and make him sensitive to his feelings.[64] Adam responds to Eve, but can distinguish among her ideas and is no longer dominated by her. In accepting her animus, the woman "must find the courage and inner broadmindedness to question the sacredness of her own convictions."[65] Eve admits to Adam that she has been "Unhappilie deceav'd" (X, 917) and that "by sad experiment I know / How little weight my words with thee can find" (X, 967–68). Integration of the anima and animus constellates the archetypes of the wise old man and the great mother.[66] Though Adam and Eve do not perceive embodiments of these figures, they approach the states of consciousness represented by them. Adam has witnessed the whole of human history and Eve in gentle dreams presaging good has understood that "By mee the Promis'd Seed shall all restore" (XII, 623).

By the end of *Paradise Lost* Adam and Eve have come far toward individuation and psychic wholeness, a reconciliation of complementary opposites within their personalities: the conscious and the unconscious, masculine and feminine, and thought and feeling. This corresponds to the reconciliation of opposites in the mandala and in the external paradise. For Jung, the inner paradise of psychic wholeness is the equivalent of the early Christian ideal of the kingdom of God within oneself.[67] Furthermore, for Jung the achievement of individuation is a fortunate fall, like that at the heart of the liturgy for Easter Eve.[68]

III

Frye is aware of the archetypal approaches of Eliade and Jung, but emphasizes the distinction between their methods and his own. In reviewing several books by Eliade, Frye writes that "such studies as Eliade's have an immediate relevance to literary criticism," but remarks that it is "the silliest kind of self-hypnosis to try to talk ourselves" into accepting again such psychological projections as the earth's navel and primordial time. Myth belongs to literature, rather than to anthropology or psychology.[69] The patterns dealt with by the literary critic should be the building blocks of literature itself. Criticism, Frye insists, "must be an examination of literature in terms of a conceptual framework derivable from an inductive survey of the literary field."[70] In his most comprehensive definition of literary archetypes, Frye refers to "certain structural elements in the literary tradition, such as conventions, genres, and the recurring use of images and image clusters, which I came to call archetypes."[71] As Frye has maintained an interest in the pervasive influence of the Christian tradition, many of his archetypes are derived directly from the vast literature in this tradition. He utilizes the categories of the great chain of being, of the four levels of existence, and of the apocalyptic and demonic realms. He has found a common quest myth in Judeo-Christian literature and joined archetypal and typological approaches.

Frye assigns a unique place in literature to the earthly paradise. Myth and hence literature began when man found an identity between himself and nature (e.g., a sun god). Man feels apart from nature, rather than a part of nature, and he longs to regain his imagined unity or identity with nature; similarly, he dreams of an upper world outside the cyclical world. Both this identity and the upper world of dream are symbolized by an earthly paradise. This paradise plays a role in three conceptions developed by Frye: the master myth which begins and ends in man's first home, the "point of epiphany," and "the analogy of innocence."

"The story of the loss and regaining of identity is, I think, the framework of all literature," Frye has said, and quoted from Blake, Wordsworth, Lawrence, and Yeats to prove it.[72] For Frye, this identity can mean, as it does in *Paradise Lost*, the union of the free intelligence with "the totality of freedom and intelligence which is God in the self."[73] In his essay on *The Faerie Queene*, Frye related man's "proper human home," "upper nature," and paradise, all representative of innocence and of one's identity with nature and with one's true self. Since the Fall, "upper nature" no longer exists as a place or physical reality, but is "the world of recovered human nature, as it once was and still can be when sin is removed." The Garden of Eden and the golden age, the happy gardens and golden cities, are symbols of this longed-for identification, the first home, the world of "upper nature." An important example of these symbols is the "natural society," a reflection of "upper nature," formed often at the end of romantic comedies.[74]

In romance and comedy this attainment of the first home is the triumph of fertility over death. The recovery of a lost Eden is presented in Book I of *The Faerie Queene*. But the archetypal pattern of romance, the quest, is best exemplified by Adam, who loses the Tree of Life, wanders in the wilderness of human history, and is restored to Eden by the

Messiah. Frye places the life of Adam and Eve before the Fall in the second phase of romance, which depicts the innocent youth of the hero. Since in Frye's great seasonal cycle of generic archetypes, romance is preceded by the spring of comedy and followed by the autumn of tragedy, the second phase or kind of romance corresponds to the second phase of tragedy ("the tragedy of innocence in the sense of inexperience") and probably to the fourth or fifth phases of comedy ("the ideal world of innocence and romance").[75] In the dialectic of comedy, especially romantic comedy like Shakespeare's, a young couple typically overcome an artificial society to restore a paradisal "natural society" in which characters identify with the miraculous reviving power of nature and discover their true selves. This "natural society" may be established in Shakespeare's regenerative "green world" (the Forest of Arden, Perdita's Bohemia) or in Portia's Belmont or on Prospero's isle.[76]

Paradise Lost provides one of the best examples of Frye's supermyth (it even contains within itself Campbell's monomyth) of the search for identity. Man's first home and "upper nature" have a particular relevance for Milton's Paradise, for it is indeed man's original home where nature as it was intended to be exists as a physical reality. Created in God's image and sharing in God's vision, man can identify with his surroundings. Adam shares in God's vision of nature when he answers Eve's questions about why the celestial bodies shine while they are sleeping and explains the cosmos in relation to unborn generations and to celestial as well as to terrestrial creatures (IV, 660–88). Adam and Eve are a part of a harmonious unity: God weds them and they wed vines to elms; they praise God in describing how everything else in the universe praises God. Eve's golden tresses "in wanton ringlets wav'd / As the Vine curls her tendrils" (IV, 306–07) and "compliant" boughs "yield" fruit to satisfy their "wholesome" appetite (IV, 330–34) until Eve "pluck'd" the fruit (IX, 781).

In Frye's scheme of generic archetypes, Books IV and V of *Paradise Lost* are chiefly second-phase romance moving away from romantic comedy toward the tragedy of the inexperienced. This kind of romance, which gives substance to the dream world of "upper nature," is set in a green and golden Arcadian landscape suffused with maternal imagery.[77] But the world of comedy, the mythos of spring, impinges on Paradise: "the *Hours* in dance / Led on th' Eternal Spring" (IV, 267–68). Birth (or creation) and marriage belong to the rising rhythm of comedy.[78] Frye finds three kinds of identity in comedy and comic romance: individual, amorous, and social.[79] Within Frye's perspective, Adam and Eve may be seen to resemble figures in Shakespeare's comedies, just as these participate in a "natural society" which symbolizes paradise and identity. In the prelapsarian Paradise, Adam and Eve possess their nature as it was intended by God—a nature possessed by Perdita and Florizel and perhaps recovered by Leontes and Polixenes at the end of *A Winter's Tale*. At the conclusion of *The Tempest*, all have found their true selves, "Where no man was his own" (V.i.211–12). The mutual love of Adam and Eve is "the Crown of all our bliss" (IV, 728); they dwell in the same world of "upper nature" with Lorenzo and Jessica of *The Merchant of Venice*, whose love is associated with the harmony of the spheres (V.i. 58–65). In comedy a fresh new "natural society" crystallizes around a young couple, like Marina and Lysimachus in *Pericles*, Perdita and Florizel, or Ferdinand and Miranda. In *Paradise Lost* Adam and Eve are the young couple about whom the natural society of the human race was to crystallize—if they had retained the nature intended for them.

At Frye's "point of epiphany" the "undisplaced apocalyptic world and the cyclical world of nature come into alignment." At this point, as at Eliade's "center," these worlds may be linked by a mountain, tree, or rope. Examples include Dante's earthly paradise, Spenser's Garden of Adonis, and Yeats's tower. It may be "the summit of experience in nature," as in sexual fulfillment. It is a point of union, but is not always related to a paradisal life.[80] In *Paradise Lost* the unchanging world of heaven and the changing world of earth meet. The sacred place and the sacred marriage are points of epiphany.

The "analogy of innocence" is the cluster of images characterizing the romantic mode, the dominant key of romance and romantic comedy. This imagery is the human counterpart of the apocalyptic world. It contributes to the expression of an idealized, animistic, usually pastoral world, filled with elemental spirits. To this realm belong images of childhood, chastity, magic, music, fire as a purifying flame, the moon, sheep, the ass, birds, butterflies, fountains, and streams. This imagery is characteristic of all of the medieval developments of the *locus amoenus* and of descriptions in which the body of the Virgin is the *hortus conclusus*. Frye finds the imagery of the "analogy of innocence" in *The Tempest*, *Comus*, *Songs of Innocence*, *Endymion*, and the rose garden of *Burnt Norton*.[81] Above the world of the "analogy of innocence" is the apocalyptic world, while directly below it is the realm of high mimetic imagery, which includes Venus and the gardens of courtly love. The lowest realm, the demonic, contains the siren's enchanted garden and the serpent.[82]

The cluster of images that Frye calls "the analogy of innocence" is an organic part of the description of the life of innocence in Milton's

Paradise. Frye mentions Raphael as an example of the friendly spiritual figures in this constellation of innocence.[83] Adam and Eve see the angelic guards and hear "celestial voices" and the "Heav'nly touch of instrumental sounds" (IV, 682–86). If not children, the newly created couple have the wonder and inexperience of children. The praise of marital chastity in *Paradise Lost* (IV, 758–70) corresponds to the praise of premarital chastity in *Comus* (418–75). If the marital chastity of Adam and Eve is not magical, as is the chastity of the Lady and Britomart, it is nevertheless mysterious and sacred. And if Paradise is not charmed by magic, it is nevertheless transformed by the miraculous: "Eternal Spring," "Blossoms and Fruit at once of golden hue" (IV, 148), the mysterious ascent of the waters from the Tigris, and the "immortal fruits" (III, 67; XI, 285). The flaming swords will appear to protect Paradise from corruption after the Fall. The moon, Frye says, "has a special importance for this world."[84] In Paradise the moon rises "in clouded Majestie" (IV, 606–07); Eve in her love lyric recalls "walk by Moon" with Adam (IV, 655) and the two pray beneath the "Moons resplendent Globe" (IV, 723). Adam and Eve are surrounded by animals in "their gentler aspects of fidelity and devotion."[85] The "happie rural seat" has "Flocks grazing the tender herb" (IV, 252–53), and the lion dandles the kid (IV, 343–44). The first parents are delighted by "charm of earliest Birds" (IV, 651), but it is the "wakeful Nightingale" (IV, 602) along with the "Celestial voices to the midnight air" (IV, 682) which provide the dominant harmony. And all is sustained by the "Saphire Fount" and "Crisped Brooks," life-giving waters "visiting each plant" (IV, 237–40).

This imagery of innocence is largely responsible for the serenity and sanctity of the first evening described in *Paradise Lost*. Eve in her love lyric speaks of "silent Night / With this her solemn Bird and this fair Moon" and "flowr / Glistring with dew" (IV, 647–54). Joined in the innocence of wedded love, Adam and Eve,

> lulled by Nightingales imbracing slept
> And on thir naked limbs the flowrie roof
> Showrd Roses, which the Morn repair'd.   (IV, 771–73)

It is when this mood of innocence is most dominant, the irony most wrenching, that Satan with "his Devilish art" inspires Eve's poisonous dream. Despite the presence of Satan and the allusions to Pandora and the "Serpent sly," finding true identity, "upper nature," and the "analogy of innocence" at the heart of Paradise shows how far the middle books of *Paradise Lost* partake of the world of romance and romantic comedy, a world which could have endured.

IV

The archetypal critic should be able to survey with "cleerest Ken" the world of mythical and literary gardens very much as Adam surveys the earth from the highest mount in Paradise. If we consider several archetypal approaches together, what essential patterns do we discover and what is the relation of Milton's Paradise to these? Archetypal criticism can reveal the most recurrent and fundamental elements in any group of related representations. Particularly applicable both in linking and in distinguishing between representations of the earthly paradise are Eliade's principle of the center and Frye's "natural society," bringing identity with an "upper nature." Eliade and Frye have affinities with each other and in some measure with Jung. In the work of all three, paradise is associated with fertility, and in Jung particularly with the mother. Jung finds paradise at an inner center, and for both Jung and Frye an external paradise is a symbol of an inner state. Both the center and "upper nature" are longed for, are timeless or both in and out of time, and are in close relation with deity and hence ethically superior. For Jung, the yearning for the mother who may be symbolized by paradise is ultimately a desire for rebirth and immortality.[86] Eliade's center and Frye's "point of epiphany" are similar. Besides Milton's Paradise, the pattern of the center would include the first age of the world in many myths, the earthly paradises of Genesis and Dante, the *hortus conclusus*, the Garden of Adonis, Marvell's "The Garden" (where the soul ascends and the "green thought" and "green shade" fuse), and Eliot's rose garden. The "natural society" would include these and the classical golden age, many pastoral episodes, Spenser's land of Faerie, and Shakespeare's "green world." The center and the "natural society" also bear a fundamental similarity to John Vernon's comprehensive archetype of the Garden,[87] yet are not as comprehensive as the Chinese literary garden examined by Andrew H. Plaks.[88]

An archetypal approach can also distinguish and illuminate special types of paradises. Within this kind of grouping the *hortus conclusus* and the enchanted garden, or false paradise, constitute a polarity, with many examples of the center and of the "natural society" in between. Specialized studies like those of Stanley Stewart and A. Bartlett Giamatti are indispensable in any comprehensive study of these gardens and the traditions lying behind them;[89] however, the studies of Eliade,

Jung, and Frye can elucidate the relations of these two gardens to major archetypal patterns and to *Paradise Lost*. Within this archetypal perspective, the enchanted garden appears as the direct inversion of the *hortus conclusus*. Both are enclosed: the *hortus conclusus*, identified with the Virgin at its center, is a garden of redemptive, fruitful chastity; the enchanted garden, identified with the siren at its center, is a garden of enslaving, sterile sensuality. The *hortus conclusus* offers absolute certainty beyond possible change; the enchanted garden brings deception, decay, and death. The Virgin symbolizes redemption, whereas the Jungian "terrible mother" poisons and devours. In Frye's view of the quest romance of Christianity, the first garden symbolizes the regained paradise, whereas the second symbolizes the wilderness in which the hero defends the world of innocence against the demonic.

While Milton's Paradise is in the center of the major patterns of the *axis mundi* and of "upper nature" and the "natural society," it also reaches up to the *hortus conclusus* and toward the celestial paradise and down to the enchanted garden. This is a part of the rich complexity of Eve, the garden, and *Paradise Lost*, a part of the paradox in the fortunate fall. Sometimes Eve reflects the garden, but more often the garden reflects Eve and the varying ways in which she is perceived. This relationship is primordial: Campbell points out that goddesses have presided over gardens of life for millennia, sometimes as "the serpent's bride," and that attributes of the Virgin belonged to mythical mother goddesses.[90] Jung would see the garden as a symbol of mother Eve. He is also aware of her ambiguity: the anima can change in a moment from a saint to a harlot, and it is not clear how much of the biblical Eve represents Sophia, how much Lilith.[91]

Sometimes Paradise almost simultaneously suggests the *hortus conclusus* and the enchanted garden. As the first parents greet Raphael, Eve is compared to Venus ("the fairest Goddess feign'd / Of Three"). Just after this, Raphael greets Eve with "*Hail*,"

> the holy salutation us'd
> Long after to blest *Marie*, second *Eve*.
> Hail! Mother of Mankind, whose fruitful Womb
> Shall fill the World.   (V, 385–89)

Mother Mary Christopher Pecheux has emphasized the relationship here between Eve and the Virgin. "Mother of Mankind" takes on the second meaning of redemption, and the "fruitful Womb" implies the divine fruit of Mary's womb.[92] However, Giamatti and S. A. Demetrakopoulos note that in Raphael's salutation Eve resembles a Venus

genetrix; they also show that the links between Eve and Venus suggest
the wantonness and sensuality of Adam's spouse.[93] The range of meaning between the "fruitful Womb" of Mary and that of Venus is a measure of the range of meaning within the garden.

The *hortus conclusus,* with the Virgin at the center, is an *axis mundi*
and a point of epiphany joining flesh and spirit at the center of the
Christian world. This mandalalike garden, often depicted with the four
rivers of paradise, is a sacred place with the Virgin as the protective
wall; it is also the setting of the sacred marriage of the Virgin with her
Lord. From a Jungian perspective, the Virgin is a symbol of the longing
for redemption and represents earth, spiritualized matter, and the
higher stages in the development of the anima and the mother archetype. As mother, she is associated with the garden, the fount, and the
protective mandala.[94] Also, the Virgin, symbolically identified with the
garden, finds identity with the "upper nature" of man's original home.
This garden, one image of the regained paradise, is filled with the imagery of the "analogy of innocence."

The links between Paradise and the *hortus conclusus,* though not
numerous, are a part of the structure of *Paradise Lost.* Just before the
Fall, the garden is compared to that of Solomon (IX, 442–43), described
in the Song of Solomon and interpreted as a prophecy of the Virgin as
the enclosed garden. From the time of Raphael's salutation, Eve is understood to foreshadow the Virgin. The sacred marriage of Adam and
Eve, which sustains nature in the womblike security of unfallen innocence, suggests the sacred marriage of the *hortus conclusus* which sustains spiritually and will lead man again to the realm of "upper nature."
The imagery of the "analogy of innocence," which Frye considers especially appropriate for the *hortus conclusus,*[95] is dominant in Books IV
and V. In Books X, XI, and XII, Eve is closely linked with the Virgin
and becomes the embodiment of the longing for redemption. Eve is
spiritualized matter, the redeemed earth which will nourish the "second root" (III, 288). In Book IX Eve is the instinctual Eve of the first
stage in the development of the anima, but she moves to resemble and
to represent the Virgin, a symbol of the third stage.[96] The first Eve, the
second Eve, and Christ are inseparably joined in the pronouncement of
the protevangelium, "Then verifi'd / When *Jesus* son of *Mary* second
Eve" witnessed Satan's fall (X, 182–84). It is through the two Eves that
Christ can offer his protective "Robe of righteousness" (X, 222). Eve
will never again violate the marriage by straying from Adam's side (XI,
176). Adam speaks "Hail" to Eve (as he later does to the Virgin, XII,
379–82) as "Mother of all things living" (XI, 158–60), all of those regain-

ing the realm of "upper nature." Both Eve and the Virgin are highly
favored by God (XI, 168–69; Luke i, 28, 30); both are "grac't / The
sourse of life" (XI, 169), including the meaning of a spring or fountain.
Briefly the garden shares in the felicity as the Morn with "rosie progress"
smiles on "pleasant Walks" (XI, 173–79). But the natural garden is being
supplanted by a spiritual garden in which Adam knows with Eve: "By
mee the Promis'd Seed shall all restore" (XII, 623) (see fig. 4).

The enchanted garden or false paradise has an illusory relationship
to the archetypal patterns of the true paradise. These enchanted gardens range from Cleopatra's Egypt to Renaissance bowers and from the
phantasmagoric paradises of E. T. A. Hoffmann (e.g., "The Mines of
Falun") to the bizarre Long Island estate that Gatsby built for the be-
witching Daisy. The enchanted garden is often an island, apparently an
omphalos offering a superior, unchanging, and desirable way of life.
But at the center of its concentric circles are not true reality and nature
at its most fertile, but the utmost in illusion, artificiality, and sterility.
The garden is dominated by the mother archetype, but by its negative
aspect, "anything secret, hidden, dark; the abyss, the world of the
dead, anything that devours, seduces, and poisons, that is terrifying
and inescapable like fate."[97] In their negative aspects the mother or the
anima may appear as a siren, mermaid, witch, lamia, bear, or even as a
serpent. The mother becomes "terrible" when the fear and guilt associated with incest are projected upon her.[98] In Scripture, Jung says, the
mother of the celestial city is contrasted with the mother of the terrestrial city (Galatians iv, 26–31), and the Lamb's bride (Revelation xxi, 9)
is contrasted with the "Mother of Harlots and the Abominations of the
Earth" (Revelation xvii, 5).[99]

Frye places the enchanted gardens of Circe, Tasso, and Spenser in
the realm of the demonic, along with Dante's *Inferno*, Eliot's *The
Waste Land*, Orwell's *1984*, and Sartre's *No Exit*. "One of the central
themes of demonic imagery," he says, "is parody." This world is ruled
by an "inscrutable fate," "remote" gods who "enforce obedience." It is a
world of "tragic dilemmas." The imagery of cannibalism or *sparagmos*,
with the "cannibal giant," is central. "The demonic erotic relation becomes a fierce destructive passion, which is symbolized by a harlot,
witch, siren, or other tantalizing female." The most common form of
the parody of marriage is incest. The world of demonic imagery is further characterized by beasts and birds of prey, the serpent, the dragon
like that in the Apocalypse, the tree of forbidden knowledge, "the labyrinth or maze, the image of lost direction," and "the sinister forest."[100]

Milton's Paradise can also veer from center, fall away from the

Figure 4. Workshop of Fra Angelico: *The Annunciation*. The garden is at once emblematic of Eden and the *hortus conclusus*. To the left, the Expulsion. Courtesy of Museo del Prado, Madrid.

positive aspect of the mother archetype, and reach down from "upper nature" and the "analogy of innocence" to participate in the patterns of the enchanted garden, part of the negative, demonic world of the false center. In Satan's flattery and in Adam's and Eve's minds, Eve becomes the universal cynosure (V, 43–47; VIII, 546–59; IX, 539–42). After the Fall, Sin and Death are the center of a fallen world. The sacred place is "now fenceless" and a part of Satan's "one Realm" (X, 303, 391–92). The sacred marriage is consumed in lust (IX, 1934–45). Despite their differing methods, Jung's analysis of the negative aspect of the mother and Frye's examination of demonic imagery reveal some impressive similarities. Both emphasize the siren, incest, beasts and monsters, cannibalism and other forms of devouring, and anything dark or frightening like the "sinister forest." All of these are found in the lower reaches of Paradise.

The siren, harlot, or witch, who for Jung embodies the negative side of the anima or mother, may symbolize both the destructive passions of the enchanted garden and also the parody of marriage, which is commonly incest. As a figure like the scarlet woman on the beast, drinking the blood of martyrs (Revelation xvii), she is associated with bestiality and cannibalism. The siren may be responsible for tragic dilemmas like Adam's conflict between God and Eve and may ultimately bring death. In *Paradise Lost* suspicion is cast on Eve as she is linked with such sirens as Pandora, Venus, Circe, and Delilah. Eve's roles as siren, courtly fatal woman, and even as witch have been carefully studied.[101]

The incest motif appears in two related forms. Plucking the forbidden fruit in itself is incestuous since a tree, particularly a sacred tree like the Tree of Knowledge, is in primitive religion, myth, and Jungian psychology a mother symbol.[102] Violation of the incest taboo constellates the "terrible mother"—who in *Paradise Lost* is Sin. Then, in a grotesque parody of the sacred marriage, the incestuous relations between Sin and her incestuously begotten son Death are brought into Paradise:

> Mean while in Paradise the hellish pair
> Too soon arriv'd, *Sin* there in power before,
> Once actual, now in body, and to dwell
> Habitual habitant; behind her *Death*
> Close following pace for pace.   (X, 585–89)

Sin, the "incestuous Mother" (X, 602), Milton's portrayal of the "terrible mother" who infects all (X, 608), dominates Paradise in the later books as maternal Nature presides over it in the earlier books. The "yelling Monsters . . . hourly conceiv'd / And hourly born" (II, 795–97) will follow their incestuous parents into Paradise and then down into the fallen world. Either the eating of the fruit from the "mother" tree or this continuing rape of Sin by Death would be enough to make the sun turn from its course "as from *Thyestean* Banquet" (X, 688).

In Books IX and X the world of bestiality, cannibalism, and darkness—all associated with Jung's "terrible mother"—inexorably threatens to destroy the new creation. This world is imaged vividly by Death's "Nostril wide into the murkie Air" (X, 280). Plucking the forbidden fruit, Eve "ingorg'd without restraint / And knew not eating Death" (IX, 791–92). "Sensual Appetite" holds sway over will, understanding, and reason (IX, 1127–31). Death himself is Frye's "cannibal giant" and his "Rav'nous Maw" is a controlling image. Death sniffs like a flock of "ravenous Fowl . . . lur'd / With scent of living Carcasses" (X, 273–77). God's "Hell-hounds" will be "cramm'd and gorg'd, nigh burst" until Christ seals the "ravenous Jaws" of Hell (X, 630–37). And it is to save the human race from the "Rav'nous Maw" of "so foul a Monster" that Eve suggests birth control and genocide (X, 980–91). The encroachment of Sin and Death pollutes the "pure now purer air" (IV, 153) of Paradise and darkens the minds and perceptions of Adam and Eve. Paradise becomes a "sinister forest." After the Fall the night, explicitly contrasted with the mild evening of the "analogy of innocence," comes "with black Air / Accompanied, with damps and dreadful gloom" (X, 846–48).[103] Adam becomes entwined in an inner maze corresponding to that through which the "surging Maze" of Satan led Eve through the garden. As he envisions Death's maw awaiting himself and his posterity, he is plunged into an "abyss of fears" (X, 842). The destructive passions of the enchanted garden lead to a wasteland. But from this wasteland we rise again to envision the *hortus conclusus* as the redemptive "Hail" is addressed to Eve.

Milton's Paradise possesses—or we may say *is*—an intensive concentration of patterns central to the life of religion, the life of the psyche, and the life of the Western literary tradition. In the thought of Eliade and Frye, paradise itself is central; for Jung, paradise can be a symbol of the mother and of the inner center of the self. Major patterns relating to paradise in the work of each of these are also in *Paradise Lost*: the *axis mundi* and world mountain, the sacred place and the sacred marriage, the maternal nature of paradise, the emergence and expansion of consciousness, the quest for "identity" and the "analogy of innocence." Milton's Paradise reflects these archetypes from the contexts of anthropology, psychology, and literary criticism; moreover, this intensive concentration of archetypes is evidenced also in the ways in which these patterns from different disciplines interrelate and correspond, revealing the parameters of Paradise and its relation to the most fundamental and recurrent patterns in the depiction of a paradise. Eliade and Jung are convinced that the patterns which they discuss possess great emotional power, that they continue to reverberate in the human psyche, and that they have a future as well as a past; Frye is convinced that the structures relating to paradise are among the great building blocks of Western literature. All three emphasize the great circle of the human imagination, the desire to return to the sacred time and the sacred place, the "identity," which can be called paradise.

University of Minnesota, Duluth

NOTES

1. *Archetypal Patterns in Poetry: Psychological Studies in the Imagination* (1934; rpt. London, 1963), pp. 90–99, 114–15.

2. *Answerable Style: Essays on "Paradise Lost"* (Minneapolis, 1953), p. 53.

3. *"Paradise Lost" as "Myth"* (Cambridge, Mass., 1959), p. 55. For a discussion of Milton's depiction of "a condition of life that is more nearly mythic than historic," see John R. Knott, Jr., "Symbolic Landscape in *Paradise Lost*," *Milton Studies*, II, ed. James D. Simmonds (Pittsburgh, 1970), pp. 37–58. For a discussion of Milton's use of generative imagery and symbolism in describing Paradise and the Creation, see Michael Lieb, *The Dialectics of Creation: Patterns of Birth and Regeneration in "Paradise Lost"* (Amherst, Mass., 1970), esp. pp. 56–78. Also see Lieb's "Holy Place: A Reading of *Paradise Lost*," *SEL*, XVII (1977), 129–47, for an illuminating discussion of the concept of the holy place in Hebraic and Christian thought and of the importance of this concept in the depiction of Heaven, Paradise, and Hell in *Paradise Lost*.

4. Although these recurrent patterns are different in important respects and range from motifs and *topoi* to controlling narrative structures and clusters of imagery, they are all used to help illuminate large bodies of literature by indicating important patterns and their variations and transformations in the literature under examination.

5. Robert O. Lagacé, *The Nature and Use of the Human Relations Area Files: A Research and Teaching Guide* (New Haven, 1974), esp. pp. 25, 43–44, 103; Thompson, *Motif-Index of Folk Literature*, rev. ed., 6 vols. (Bloomington, Ind., 1966).

6. *Man and Culture* (New York, 1923), esp. pp. 74–77.

7. *Images and Symbols: Studies in Religious Symbolism*, trans. Philip Mairet (New York, 1961), p. 16.

8. Ibid., p. 19; *The Myth of the Eternal Return*, trans. Willard R. Trask, Bollingen Series, 46 (New York, 1954), pp. 6–7, 91.

9. *Images and Symbols*, pp. 30–34.

10. *Myth of the Eternal Return*, pp. 12–16, 152–53; *The Sacred and the Profane: The Nature of Religion*, trans. Willard R. Trask (New York, 1957), pp. 36–37. See also Eli-

ade, "The Yearning for Paradise in Primitive Tradition," *Daedalus*, LXXXVIII (1959), 255–67.

11. *Myth of the Eternal Return*, p. 153.

12. *The Mythic Image*, Bollingen Series, 100 (Princeton, 1974), pp. 168, 186–88.

13. Ibid., pp. 77–83, 194.

14. Ibid., p. 165.

15. E. E. Evans-Pritchard, *Nuer Religion* (Oxford, 1956), p. 10.

16. Rafael Karsten, *The Head-Hunters of Western Amazonas: The Life and Culture of the Jibaro Indians of Eastern Ecuador and Peru* (Helsinki, 1935), pp. 502–03, 522.

17. M. B. Emeneau, *Kota Texts*, in *California Publications in Linguistics*, 2–3 (1944), p. 175.

18. See esp. Psalms ii and lxxxvii. The Bible is quoted from the Authorized Version.

19. Eric Burrows, "Some Cosmological Patterns in Babylonian Religion," in *The Labyrinth: Further Studies in the Relation Between Myth and Religion in the Ancient World*, ed. S. H. Hooke (New York, 1935), p. 56. This belief is probably alluded to in Psalms xxix and xciii.

20. See my *Milton's Earthly Paradise: A Historical Study of Eden* (Minneapolis, 1972), pp. 210–12.

21. *Gregorii Opuscula: Or Notes and Observations upon Some Passages of Scripture, with Other Learned Tracts* (London, 1650), pp. 72, 78.

22. Pseudo-Basil, *De Paradiso*, in *Patrologiae Graecae*, ed. J. P. Migne, 161 vols. (Paris, 1857–81), XXX, cols. 63–70.

23. Duncan, *Milton's Earthly Paradise*, pp. 49, 50, 60, 224.

24. Milton's poetry is quoted from *The Complete Poetry of John Milton*, ed. John T. Shawcross, rev. ed. (Garden City, N.Y., 1971).

25. Burrows, "Some Cosmological Patterns," pp. 54–55.

26. "A New Look at Milton's Paradise," *Milton Studies*, X, ed. James D. Simmonds (Pittsburgh, 1977), pp. 78–86.

27. Grant McColley, "Milton's Technique of Source Adaptation," *Studies in Philology*, XXXV (1938), 69–71.

28. "Commentarius de Paradise," *Patrologiae Graecae*, CXI, cols. 583–602.

29. "Bios and Mythos: Prolegomena to a Science of Mythology," in *Psychoanalysis and Culture*, ed. George N. Wilbur and W. Muensterberger (New York, 1951), p. 333.

30. *Patterns in Comparative Religion* (Cleveland, 1933), p. 100.

31. Irvin Friedman, "The Sacred Space of Judaism," *Parabola*, III, 1 (1978), 22.

32. *Myth of the Eternal Return*, pp. 24–27.

33. *Mythic Image*, p. 91.

34. Theodore H. Robinson, "Hebrew Myths," in *Myth and Ritual: Essays in the Myth and Ritual of the Hebrews in Relation to the Culture Pattern of the Ancient East*, ed. S. H. Hooke (London, 1933), pp. 188–89.

35. *"Paradise Lost": Introduction* (Cambridge, 1972), pp. 18–19.

36. *Iliad*, trans. E. V. Rieu (New York, 1950), xiv.292–353, p. 264. Frazer refers to this description of Zeus and Hera as a sacred marriage in *The Golden Bough*, 3rd ed., 12 vols. (New York, 1935), II, 142–43.

37. *Archetypes and the Collective Unconscious*, 2nd ed., vol. IX, pt. 1, in *Collected Works of C. G. Jung*, ed. Sir Herbert Read et al. and trans. R. F. C. Hull, Bollingen Series, 20 (New York, 1968), pp. 7, 19–25, 43–48, 58.

38. *Symbols of Transformation*, vol. V in *Collected Works* (New York, 1956), pp. 219, 248, 259; *Archetypes and the Collective Unconscious*, pp. 81, 368.

39. *Mysterium Coniunctionis*, 2nd ed., vol. XIV in *Collected Works* (Princeton, 1970), p. 210.

40. *Archetypes and the Collective Unconscious*, pp. 34–35.

41. *Alchemical Studies*, vol. XIII in *Collected Works* (Princeton, 1967), p. 24.

42. *The Structure and Dynamics of the Psyche*, vol. VIII in *Collected Works* (New York, 1960), p. 203; *Psychology and Alchemy*, vol. XII in *Collected Works* (London, 1953), p. 29.

43. *Mysterium Coniunctionis*, pp. 170, 384.

44. Ibid., p. 388; *Archetypes and the Collective Unconscious*, p. 388; *Civilization in Transition*, vol. X in *Collected Works* (New York, 1964), pp. 408–09, 424; *Psychology and Religion: West and East*, vol. XI in *Collected Works* (New York, 1958), pp. 51–54, 57–58; *Psychology and Alchemy*, pp. 31, 119, 124, 137–42, 204, 235.

45. *Civilization in Transition*, pp. 139–40; *Structure and Dynamics of the Psyche*, pp. 157, 388.

46. *On the Nature of Things*, trans. W. E. Leonard (London, 1916), pp. 219–21.

47. Albert J. Carnoy, *Iranian Mythology*, vol. VI in *Mythology of All Races* (Boston, 1917), pp. 295–97.

48. Arthur C. L. Brown, *The Origin of the Grail Legend* (Cambridge, Mass., 1943), 77, 367–70.

49. *The Burning Fountain: A Study in the Language of Symbolism* (Bloomington, Ind., 1954), pp. 349–50.

50. Richard Gill, *Happy Rural Seat: The English Country House and the Literary Imagination* (New Haven, 1972), esp. p. 66, n. 27, pp. 186–92.

51. *Symbols of Transformation*, pp. 268, 315, 405; Otto Rank, *The Trauma of Birth* (London, 1929), pp. 75, 103, 113; Joseph Campbell, *The Masks of God: Primitive Mythology* (New York, 1959), p. 65.

52. MacCaffrey, *"Paradise Lost" as "Myth,"* p. 145; Stein, *Answerable Style*, p. 56.

53. *Psychology and Religion*, p. 519; Campbell, *Masks of God: Primitive Mythology*, p. 148.

54. *Aion: Researches into the Phenomenology of the Self*, vol. IX, pt. 2, in *Collected Works* (New York, 1959), p. 242. See also *Civilization in Transition*, p. 423.

55. *Two Essays on Analytical Psychology*, vol. VII in *Collected Works* (New York, 1953), pp. 220–21; *Archetypes and the Collective Unconscious*, p. 219, incl. n. 14. See also Jolande Jacobi, *The Psychology of C. G. Jung: An Introduction with Illustrations*, trans. Ralph Manheim, 7th ed. (New Haven, 1968), p. 116 and plate 4 (see fig. 3).

56. *Alchemical Studies*, pp. 309, 272, 257, and fig. 11.

57. Ibid., p. 255 and fig. 3, p. 150, n. 77; Jacobi, *Psychology of Jung*, p. 116.

58. *Archetypes and the Collective Unconscious*, pp. 20–31.

59. *Two Essays on Analytical Psychology*, pp. 205–08; Emma Jung, *Animus and Anima*, trans. Cary E. Baynes and Hildegard Nagel (Zurich, 1974), pp. 19–20, 23, 28; Marie-Louise von Franz, "The Process of Individuation," in *Man and His Symbols*, ed. C. G. Jung et al. (Garden City, N.Y., 1964), pp. 189–90.

60. *Two Essays on Analytical Psychology*, pp. 136, 205–06.

61. "Process of Individuation," p. 194.

62. *Archetypes and the Collective Unconscious*, pp. 21, 26–28, 35–37.

63. Ibid., p. 284.

64. Von Franz, "Process of Individuation," pp. 183–84.

65. Ibid., p. 195.

66. *Two Essays on Analytical Psychology*, pp. 225–28.

67. Ibid., p. 224; *Archetypes and the Collective Unconscious*, p. 35.

68. *Civilization in Transition*, pp. 459–61.

69. "World Enough Without Time," *Hudson Review*, XII (1959), 423–31.

70. *Anatomy of Criticism: Four Essays* (1957; rpt. ed., Princeton, 1971), p. 7.

71. *The Critical Path: An Essay in the Social Context of Literary Criticism* (Bloomington, Ind., 1971), p. 23.

72. *The Educated Imagination* (1964; rpt. Bloomington, Ind., 1968), pp. 53–55.

73. *The Return of Eden: Five Essays on Milton's Epics* (Toronto, 1965), p. 31. In this work Frye discusses the four levels of existence, the four stages of redemption, and other large patterns, but he develops only a small part of the rich mine of critical observation in other works which may be related to Milton.

74. *Fables of Identity: Studies in Poetic Mythology* (New York, 1963), pp. 72–73, 78, 82; *Educated Imagination*, p. 152; *A Natural Perspective: The Development of Shakespearean Comedy and Romance* (New York, 1965), pp. 136–42.

75. *Anatomy of Criticism*, pp. 177, 181–95, 199–200, 220.

76. Ibid., pp. 163–71, 182–85; *A Natural Perspective*, pp. 140–49.

77. *Anatomy of Criticism*, p. 200.

78. Ibid., pp. 162–63.

79. *A Natural Perspective*, pp. 78–91; *Fools of Time: Studies in Shakespearean Tragedy* (Toronto, 1967), pp. 15–16.

80. *Anatomy of Criticism*, pp. 203–06.

81. Ibid., pp. 151–53.

82. Ibid., pp. 141–44, 147–50, 153–54.

83. Ibid., p. 151.

84. Ibid., p. 152.

85. Ibid.

86. *Symbols of Transformation*, pp. 223–24.

87. The Garden represents a unity of experience opposed to the schizophrenia of the Map. *The Garden and the Map: Schizophrenia in Twentieth-Century Literature and Culture* (Urbana, Ill., 1973). The Garden unites subject and object, space and time, fantasy and reality, madness and sanity, and all of these pairs with each other. Everywhere in the Garden there is a potential center. The Fall is from the Garden to the Map. Vernon includes Roethke's woods and greenhouses, Faulkner's wilderness, and even the jungle of Conrad's *Heart of Darkness*, which becomes evil only through exclusion.

88. Plaks says of the Chinese literary garden "that the enclosed landscape is intended to be apprehended as an entire world in miniature in both the spatial and temporal sense." *Archetype and Allegory in "The Dream of the Red Chamber"* (Princeton, 1976), p. 163. But Milton's Eden "is explicitly less than the sum of terrestrial existence" (pp. 141–42). Within the Chinese literary garden one finds the archetypes of "complementary bipolarity" and "multiple periodicity," which are "cultural preferences shaped by a given tradition" (pp. 13–14). This garden is characteristically related horizontally to the outside world, rather than vertically to heaven and the underworld.

89. See Stewart, *The Enclosed Garden: The Tradition and the Image in Seventeenth-Century Poetry* (Madison, Wis., 1966), and Giamatti, *The Earthly Paradise and the Renaissance Epic* (Princeton, 1966).

90. *The Masks of God: Occidental Mythology*, pp. 9–43.

91. *Archetypes and the Collective Unconscious*, p. 199; *Psychology and Religion*, p. 397.

92. "The Concept of the Second Eve in *Paradise Lost*," *PMLA*, LXXV (1960), 360–61.

93. Giamatti, *Earthly Paradise*, p. 322, n. 20, pp. 319–23; Demetrakopoulos, "Eve as a Circean and Courtly Fatal Woman," *Milton Quarterly*, IX (December 1975), 105. Similarly, Pecheux finds the comparison of Eve to Delia, Pomona, and Ceres (IX, 386–96) to be a part of "the spiritual virginity of Eve," part of the analogy between Eve and Mary, the Temptation and the Annunciation (p. 362), whereas Giamatti observes that the allusion to Pomona predicts the deception of Eve by Satan and that the allusion to Ceres reminds us that Eve, like Proserpina, is a flower among flowers (pp. 327–28).

94. *Archetypes and the Collective Unconscious*, p. 81; *Psychology and Religion*, pp. 60–64; *Mysterium Coniunctionis*, p. 167, n. 349, p. 170, incl. n. 354, pp. 464–68; von Franz, "Process of Individuation," p. 185.

95. *Anatomy of Criticism*, p. 152.

96. Von Franz, "Process of Individuation," p. 185.

97. *Archetypes and the Collective Unconscious*, p. 82.

98. Ibid., pp. 25, 183.

99. *Symbols of Transformation*, pp. 212–15.

100. *Anatomy of Criticism* pp. 147–50. Vernon, like Jung and Frye, considers devouring an important symbol; the perception of the body and of food as objects separate from the self characterizes the Fall and the world of the Map (pp. 8–9).

101. Besides Giamatti and Demetrakopoulos, see Davis Harding, *The Club of Hercules*, Illinois Studies in Language and Literature, vol. 50 (Urbana, 1962), and Linda Draper Henson, "The Witch in Eve: Milton's Use of Witchcraft in *Paradise Lost*," in *Studies in Honor of Arthur E. Barker*, ed. J. K. Franson, Salzburg Studies in English Literature (Salzburg, 1976). Demetrakopoulos describes Milton's Eve as "certainly the most imposing literary embodiment of The Fatal Woman" (p. 106).

102. *Symbols of Transformation*, pp. 247–48, incl. n. 83, pp. 269–70. In *The Christian Doctrine*, Milton includes sacrilege among the sins of Adam and Eve; he also recognizes the Tree of Knowledge as sacred and cites the practice of extending the punishment for the violation of the sacred to posterity (I, x, xi).

103. Adam sometimes sees the garden as a gloomy forest (IX, 910); he also sometimes sees the darkness as appropriate to his guilt (IX, 1080–90; X, 716).

CINYRAS, MYRRHA, AND ADONIS: FATHER-DAUGHTER INCEST FROM OVID TO MILTON

Noam Flinker

I N H I S *Metamorphoses*, Ovid has Orpheus relate the tale of Myrrha's passion for Cinyras, her father, which results in the incestuous birth of Adonis. This story attracted the attention of various authors from late antiquity through the seventeenth century. Some of the commentators nervously avoid the incest via rationalizing allegorical explanations, while others, like Dante, associate Myrrha with evil or her nurse with the devil. One medieval French source combines rational allegorizing with more explicitly Christian explanations to show that Myrrha signifies the Virgin Mary and Mary Magdalene, as well as the sinful soul of man. Although sixteenth-century England had little to say about Myrrha, the early seventeenth century had at least three separately published items devoted to her, and in 1667 Dryden pronounced that he had "a greater concernment" for Myrrha than for Virgil's Dido.[1] Milton's allegory of Satan's incest with his daughter Sin to beget Death in *Paradise Lost* can be seen as parallel to this Ovidian tradition.

Ovid's version of the story is his own interpretation of earlier accounts, some of which were available to Milton.[2] His primary interest is in Myrrha's character. Brooks Otis has suggested that the "emphasis is on the *horror* of Myrrha's *act* (after all Myrrha consummated her incestuous desire as Byblis did not) and on the special nuance which this gave to her metamorphosis."[3] She is aware of the nature of her passion from the first (unlike other women in the *Metamorphoses* such as Medea or Byblis) and struggles with herself about how to express it. Her opening soliloquy (X.321–55) portrays her resistance to libido, which she meets with a series of clever arguments. At the end of her speech, however, there is a sense of frustration that her father would never willingly consent to the incest she desires:

> pius ille memorque est
> Moris—et o vellem similis furor esset in illo!   (354–55)

                                   [and he is righteous,
                    Heedful of moral sanctions—and I wish
                    He had my kind of passion burning in him!]   (P. 245)[4]

Myrrha then decides upon suicide, but is balked by the interference of
her attentive nurse, who cuts the rope from the girl's neck just in time.
The nurse wheedles Myrrha's secret from her and offers aid if she promises to reject suicide as a solution. Ovid makes the nurse well meaning
and almost virtuous. The thought of incest repels her, and she tries to
dissuade Myrrha even though she finally agrees to help. Ovid does not
present their argument in any detail, but he does indicate that it took
place:

                    Multaque, ut excuteret diros, si posset, amores,
                    Addidit; at virgo scit se non falsa moneri,
                    Certa mori tamen est, si non potiatur amore.   (426–28)

                                   [She tried,
                    As best she could, to banish, if she might,
                    So mad a passion; Myrrha knew the warning
                    Was given in all truthfulness, but could not
                    Resign herself to living without having
                    The one she loved.]   (P. 248)

       The men in Ovid's story are less striking than the women. Cinyras
is somewhat indulgent and none too sensitive or quick-witted. When
Myrrha tells him that she wants a husband like him, he mistakes her
passion for piety. The nurse, finding him somewhat drunk during the
queen's absence, has no trouble acting as bawd, especially when she
states that the girl is "Just Myrrha's age" (p. 248). When she brings
Myrrha to her father, the nurse ambiguously half-reveals the girl's identity: "'accipe,' dixit / 'Ista tua est, Cinyra'" (463–64) ["'Take her, she is
your own'" (p. 249). No matter. Cinyras misses the subtlety.
       This kind of verbal wit is an important part of Ovid's story and
style. The Latin poet's suave sophistication presents Myrrha's plight
without moralizing or faultfinding. The reader is offered a series of
complicating factors which deepen the psychological insight into the
main focus, Myrrha. The moral outrage of the narrator at the outset of
the tale is thus that of Orpheus (and not Ovid himself), whose preaching tone of moral superiority is deliberately exaggerated:

                    Gentibus Ismariis et nostro gratulor orbi,
                    Gratulor huic terrae, quod abest regionibus illis,
                    Quae tantum genuere nefas.   (305–07)

[I would offer
Our land congratulations, that it lies
So far away from such abominations.]   (Pp. 243–44)

In his note on these lines William Anderson indicates that "Ovid may well be poking fun at his chosen narrator." Since Thracian lust was "a commonplace among the Romans . . . the self-congratulation of Orpheus and his people stirs a slight smile" (p. 503). Thus while Myrrha and her nurse are sympathetic characters with considerable dramatic power and appeal, the men in the story, Cinyras and Orpheus, are stuffy and even dull-witted, and as such are victims of Ovid's ironic wit.

Fulgentius provides an explanation of Ovid's story which found its way into many medieval and Renaissance works: "Let me explain what this story signifies. The myrrh is a kind of tree from which the sap oozes out; she is said to have fallen in love with her father. These same trees are found in India, glowing with the heat of the sun; and since they always said that a father is the sun of all things, by whose aid the growth of plant life develops, so she in this fashion is said to have fallen in love with her father."[5] This explanation was repeated almost verbatim by Arnulph of Orleans in the twelfth century, Thomas Walsingham in the thirteenth, and William Caxton in the fifteenth.[6]

Another rationalization to sidestep the issue of incest is that of Jean Le Clerc, late in the seventeenth century. Le Clerc relates the tale to the biblical account of Noah's nudity which had been observed by Canaan, his grandson (Genesis ix, 20–27). What really happened, this savant claims, was that Myrrha, the daughter-in-law of Noah (Cinyras), observed her father-in-law asleep and drunk in "an indecent posture." Instead of covering him she and her son Adonis called in Noah's sons to see the sight. When Noah awoke he cursed Myrrha and Adonis. Le Clerc assumes that Ovid's tale has a grain of truth and proceeds to find this in the correspondences between the biblical and the classical myths. In both stories the father figure is first drunk and later on extremely angry. Le Clerc explains the incest as a misunderstanding, by Greeks or Phoenicians, of an ambiguous Hebrew idiom (בילוי עריות [gilui 'arayot]) which he translates literally as *"voir ou découvrir la nudité de quelcun"* ("to see or uncover someone's nakedness") but which is more generally a euphemism for incest. Le Clerc asserts that "Les Phéniciens, ou les Grecs, trompez per cette maniere de parler équivoque, ont cru que Myrrha avoit couché avec son pere, au lieu qu'elle ne fit que voir sa nudité" ("The Phoenicians, or the Greeks, misled by this equivocal way of speaking, thought that Myrrha had slept with her father, whereas she did but see his nakedness").[7] Thus, rationalistic explanations of the tale of Myrrha were available to the seventeenth century in ancient and modern garb through the accounts of Fulgentius and Le Clerc.

Closer to the spirit of Milton's Sin and Death is the medieval tradition which saw Myrrha as evil. In his *De nugis curialium*, Walter Map warns that there are no chaste women anymore: "Friend, there is no Lucretia, no Penelope, no Sabine *left:* mistrust all. Against the Sabines Scylla, daughter of Nisus, and Myrrha, daughter of Cinaras, entered the fray, and there followed them many a band aided by the hosts of all the vices ready to give their captives groanings and sighs and in the end hell."[8]

Dante too treats Myrrha as a symbol of evil. She appears in the eighth circle of the *Inferno* as one of the falsifiers. The pilgrim is told

> Quell' è l'anima antica
> di Mirra scellerata, che divenne
> al padre fuor del dritto amore amica.
> Questa a peccar con esso così venne,
> falsificando sè in altrui forma.[9]

[That is the accursed Myrrha's dishonored soul; she became her father's lover with more than lawful love. She managed to sin with him by falsely taking another's form.]

A more intense indication of Dante's view of Myrrha occurs in one of his letters. In urging Henry VII to attack Florence in 1311, the exiled poet characterizes the city as, among other vile images, "the viper that darts at the bowels of its mother . . . the accursed and impious Myrrha, who becomes inflamed with passion in the embraces of her father, Cinyras."[10] Although the Latin text of this letter was not printed until the nineteenth century, an Italian translation was published by Antonio Francesco Doni in 1547 and again in 1551.[11] The original Latin was also available during the seventeenth century in three Italian manuscripts.

Pierre Bersuire's treatment of Myrrha in his *Ovidius moralizatus* continues to identify her with evil but balances this by association with the Virgin. His first explanation of the story is that the "evil and impudent daughter signifies ambition," especially the desire of an "ambitious person to be joined to Christ his father through an official position in the church."[12] The nurse signifies the aid of some malefactor in securing the position, and "he who so enters the church, ends up in bitterness and as a tree, that is, in hell."[13] Bersuire then provides another suggestion that "this daughter signifies the sinful soul."[14] His final reading of Myrrha's tale is that she "is the blessed virgin who conceived through the father and was changed into myrrh, that is bitterness and into the fragrance of scent." In support of this interpretation he juxtaposes scriptural passages traditionally associated with Mary: "Ecclesia. xxiii 'I gave a swete odour as the best myrrhe'.[15] She therefore conceived a son by her father: that is, Christ: & she contained him within the wood and bark, that is, within a pure and untouched womb without corruption, and afterwards she bore him, existing not as flesh but as wood, that is, not as a carnal being but as a perpetual virgin. Isaiah vii [, 14] 'Behold a virgin shall conceive and bear a son.'"[16]

In an even fuller account of the allegorical significance of Ovid's story, the medieval French poem *Ovide moralisé* also presents both positive and negative allegorizations of Myrrha. The author of this anonymous work suggests four different explanations of the tale. First he provides a versified account of the rationalization of Fulgentius,[17] but soon after he presents a "worthier explanation":

> —Autre sentence i puet avoir
> Mieudre et plus digne de savoir.
> La mirre amere signifie
> Nostre mere, sainte Marie.   (X.3748–51)

[It can have another meaning, better and more worthy of knowing. The bitter myrrh signifies our mother, holy Mary.]

The poet supports this interpretation by pointing to similarities. Like Myrrha, Mary is both daughter and maid servant ("ancele," 3753) of God. Beautiful, gracious, and lovable, she rejects her suitors for the love of God which "mist en refu / Toutes terriennes amours" ("rejects all earthly loves") (3765–66). Myrrha's pregnancy and the birth of Adonis are seen as emblematic of the incarnation and birth of Christ (3791–809). In addition, there are two other explanations. One interprets Myrrha's folly as an allegory of the sinful Christian soul, deceived by devils into approaching the communion altar without having confessed or repented. In this allegory Myrrha's incest is parallel to the sinful Christian's taking communion as a purely physical experience:

> O tenebreuse conscience,
> Vient a l'autier, c'est à la couche
> Où li cors Dieu repose et couche,
> Pour soi joindre à lui charnelment,
> Si le reçoit non dignement
> A Pasque, feste au Creatour.   (3821–26)

[Oh murky conscience, it comes to the altar, that is, to the couch where the body of God rests and lies down, to join itself to Him carnally, and receives Him unworthily on Easter, the Creator's festival.]

A final explanation is that the story concerns the rewards of repentance. Myrrha, like Mary Magdalene, has sinned greatly, but in the end she repents. After great suffering she is changed into a myrrh tree which, by arresting physical decomposition after death, is sweet satisfaction (3878–953).

The reading of Myrrha as Mary may at first seem shocking. Paule Demats feels called upon to point out that "l'auteur de l'*Ovide moralisé* est le plus pieux des hommes" ("the author of the *Ovide moralisé* is the most pious of men"), whose version of Ovid is different without being sacrilegious: "la fable telle qu'il l'entend ne ressemble guère à ce qu'elle était pour Dante et pour la plupart de ses contemporains" ("the story as he means it scarcely resembles that which it was for Dante and most of his contemporaries").[18] This positive attitude is, however, less surprising in the light of the church's attitude toward myrrh. The spice is mentioned in various places in the Bible, but its most important Christian associations are as a gift of the magi (Matthew ii, 11), a drink on the cross (Mark xv, 23), and a preservative for burial (John xix, 39–40). Fathers of the church interpret myrrh as signifying such qualities as mortification of the flesh, sweetness, incorruptibility, the bitterness of the Passion, faith, resurrection of the dead, and martyrs of the church.[19] Bersuire's *Reductorium morale* includes a chapter on myrrh which makes reference to the same verse from Ecclesiasticus that he quotes in his interpretation of Myrrha.[20] Doubtless the author of the *Ovide moralisé* was also aware of this tradition. A convenient indication of the availability of this material in England is *The Myroure of Oure Ladye* (1530): "Myrre is a tree that groweth fyue cubytes in lengthe and the gomme therof is bytter in taste. and swete in smelle. By the fyue cubytes. ys vnderstonded the fyue ioyes of oure lady that she had in erthe. By the bytter gomme. hyr bytter sorowes. but in this feaste. all was turned to endeles swetnesse that is vnderstonded by the swete smelle. And therefore she sayth as chosen myrre. I haue gyuen swetnesse of smelle [Ecclesiasticus xxiv, 20]."[21] It seems safe then to assume that the many Christian associations of myrrh played some role in determining the positive allegorical meanings suggested for Myrrha's tale by Bersuire and the *Ovide moralisé.*

During the Renaissance, some of these medieval traditions about Myrrha's tale were able to reach wider audiences through vernacular translation and humanist scholarship. Although the *Ovide moralisé* was not published until the twentieth century, its contents were readily available in the Renaissance through Colard Mansion's paraphrase of the *Metamorphoses* in French prose, *La Bible des poetes, metamorphoze*. Using both Bersuire and the *Ovide moralisé*, Mansion presents the allegorization of Myrrha as the Virgin:

> Sens moral dessus la cōcepcion de mirra par sō pere MIrra peut signiffier la glorieuse vierge marie laquele fut mueé en mirre, cest adire en amaritude de parfaicte odeur conuertie Comme il est escript. Quasi mirra electa dedi suauitatem odoris [Ecclesiasticus xxiv, 20]. Iay dist elle suauite de odeur donne: cōme mirre esleute. Cette vierge donques conceut de son pere un filz, cest assauoir jhesu christ, et le porta entre le bois et lescorce, cest adire dedens son chaste et non contamine ventre sans corrupcion lenfanta, & depuis demoura vierge sans charnel desir. comme dist isaye en son cinquiesme chappitre. Ecce virgo concipiet et pariet filium. Uecy la vierge dist il conceura et enfantera ung filz Ceste histoire fut figuree en la verge de aaron, laquel estant seche flourist [Numbers, chap. xvii].[22]

[Moral sense underlying (lit. over) conception by Myrrha and her father. Myrrha can signify the glorious virgin Mary who was changed into myrrh, that is converted into bitterness of perfect odor. As it is written: "I gave a swete odour as the best myrrhe" (Geneva Bible). I have, she says, given off a sweet odor: like choice myrrh. This virgin, then, conceived a son with her father, that is to say, Jesus Christ, and bore him between the wood and the bark. That is, from within her chaste and uncontaminated womb she gave birth to him without corruption, and henceforth remained a virgin without carnal desire. As Isaiah states in his fifth *(sic)* chapter: "Behold, a virgin shall conceive, and bear a son." Behold, he says, the virgin shall conceive and bear a son. This story is prefigured in the rod of Aaron, which bloomed even though it was quite dry.]

Mansion also presents the rational explanation of Fulgentius but only at the conclusion of Book X, whereas this allegory of the Virgin appears immediately after the story of Myrrha.

Although most humanist scholars avoid allegorical interpretations of Ovid, they are not averse to moral commentary, even when this is not clearly a central concern of the poetry. George Schuler's oft reprinted edition of the *Metamorphoses* explains that Myrrha's plight was inspired by the devil, not Cupid.[23] Then he asserts that nothing is more detestable than her crime and that the tale is meant to point out the "depravity of old women, the greater part of whom are assistants in crimes and shameful activities and who are especially ingenious at bringing such actions to fruition."[24] This now familiar treatment of Myrrha as evil thus changes the nurse, well meaning and almost virtuous in Ovid, into a depraved old woman.

Although Elizabethan England was not especially concerned with Myrrha's incest, numerous English versions of her tale were published in the seventeenth century, in addition to the more complete translations of Golding (1567) and Sandys (1626).[25] William Barksted, Henry Austin, James Gresham, and John Dryden published their own treatments of Myrrha. Of these, Gresham's *The Picture of Incest* (1626) is a fairly literal translation of Ovid, with little embellishment on the Latin text.[26] Dryden's "Cinyras and Myrrha: Out of the Tenth Book of Ovid's *Metamorphoses*"[27] is much finer poetry than Gresham's dull, plodding lines, but the former poet laureate was not interested in expanding his source. Barksted and Austin, however, published versions of the story which include a number of original additions to Ovid's tale.

William Barksted's *Mirrha The Mother of Adonis: Or Lustes Prodegies* (1607) expands upon Ovid's text in rather stiff English verse, presenting the poem as an introduction to Shakespeare's *Venus and Adonis*. He even concludes with instruction to his muse:

> But stay my Muse in thine owne confines keepe,
> & wage not warre with so deere lou'd a neighbor
>   . . . .
> His Song was worthie merrit (*Shakspeare* hee)
> Sung the faire blossome, thou the withered tree.[28]

Barksted changes some of Ovid's details and adds flourishes of his own. Thus he attributes Myrrha's passion to her earlier rebuff of the advances of Cupid, who appears in the slightly absurd guise of the god of love fated to see Myrrha's "face: / And seeing loue, and in that loue be slaine, / if beautie pittie not my wretched case" (p. 17). This highly self-conscious twisting of literary tradition is typical of Barksted's manner. Rather than present Ovid's dramatic monologue as such he has Myrrha speak to her father's picture and then "seeing no reply, / She answer'd for her father" (p. 24). Toward the end of the tale, Barksted has a satyr fall in love with the pregnant Myrrha as she flees her father's wrath.

Barksted associates Myrrha with evil to some extent, but makes her a victim of dark forces rather than a colleague of Satan. Just after the nurse agrees (with no argument) to help Myrrha seduce Cinyras, the narrator explains that

> Neuer did mortall with a vicious thought,
> wish to bring vices Embrion to a forme:

> But still the prince of darknesse to them brought
>   occasions fore-locke, which they off haue torne.
> Sin like a Cedar shadowes all our good:
>   Whilst vertues bounded like a narrow flood.   (P. 37)

Myrrha is not excused here, but neither is she reviled. Barksted's effect is quite close to Ovid's sympathetic portrayal as he avoids the intensity with which Dante makes Myrrha wholly evil.

The Scourge of Venus: or, the wanton Lady, with the Rare Birth of Adonis, first published in 1613 under the initials of H. A., is now generally attributed to Henry Austin.[29] This version of Ovid's tale is less independent of the Latin original than Barksted's but far from a literal translation. Austin's 966-line poem was evidently somewhat popular, since it went through three editions in seven years (1613, 1614, 1620). His ironic presentation of the incestuous pair makes Cinyras unconsciously eager to seduce his daughter, while the language is almost lascivious in its insistence upon wantonness, lust, and "filth."

Austin's treatment of Ovid's story is fairly standard. He expands some speeches and transposes others, but the basic elements are all present. Myrrha and her nurse are fuller than in Ovid, but they are not essentially different. Cinyras, however, is much more interesting than in other versions. He is no more discerning or sensitive, but his failures are constantly stressed as the nurse and Myrrha manipulate him. He first appears just after Myrrha has completed a long letter in which she confesses her love to him quite directly. As soon as he enters "she cast her letter quite aside"[30] while he urges her to choose a husband from among her many suitors. She cries, and he "thought it tender-hearted shame-fastnes" (186). Her desire for a husband "like to you" (192) wins her kisses which are so pleasing that she asks that he "Let me live still with you, let woers rest" (198). His response underlines both his failure to understand Myrrha's hints and his own naive crudity:

> Thou dost not know the pleasure it affoords,
>   Nor wanton motions that therein abound,
> It not consisteth all of pleasant words,
>   More gamesome tricks are there stil to be foūd
> A minde so chaste as thine cannot conceiue
>   What pleasing sports one shal thereby receiue.   (205–10)

Later, when the nurse comes to Cinyras as Myrrha's bawd, his unsuspecting trust has clear ironic import: "With *Bacchus* feasts do wanton sports agree, / I know thou wouldst no ill thing vnto mee" (515–16). The nurse gives him hints of the girl's true identity but he ignores them:

"there is a gallant Maide / Of Princely birth and Noble high degree" (517–18). How many such girls of Myrrha's age could there have been in the realm? Her conclusion actually insists upon the "resemblance" to Myrrha:

> If I do fable, put me vnto shame,
>   In saying she resembles *Myrha* much,
> For 'tis so much as if it were the same;
>   .   .   .   .
> And now you may, voide of suspected crime,
>   Dally with her in your lasciuious bed.   (565–67, 571–72)

She even gives him an ironic lesson in lovemaking, explaining that women "natures simple men abuse, / When what they loue they most of all refuse" (563–64). Of course, here it is she who is abusing the king, the archetypal "natures simple" man.

In bed with her father, Myrrha plays it coy while Cinyras is clearly fantasizing about incest. He calls her "love" and then corrects himself:

> And to hide all that idle heads may moue,
>   Hence-forth I call thee daughter and not loue.
>
> Come kisse thy father, gentle daughter then,
>   And learne to sport thee in a wanton bed.   (653–56)

Myrrha counters: "A daughters name, me thinkes, doth not agree, / Ist well with your owne child in loue to bee?" (659–60). After some colloquy, Cinyras concludes: "You must obey, I call you daughter still" and she responds: "Then talke no more, she said, I do agree / Thy daughter and thy subiect yeelds to thee" (682–84). Later, after Myrrha has fled from his wrath, Cinyras recalls these exchanges with shame, but at this point his conscious mind comprehends very little of what is happening. Unconsciously, his response to both daughter and nurse reflects a thinly disguised incestuous passion. Although Cinyras himself misapprehends everything at first, Austin must have expected his readers to savor the irony of the king's obtuseness.

Near the conclusion of the poem, as Cinyras begins to realize what has happened, he takes on some depth and possibly even admits to himself that he was not wholly unaware of the incest. He begins by cursing and condemning Myrrha, but some of his accusations apply equally to himself:

> How will thy mother thinke her selfe abus'd,
>   That hast made her a quot-queane shamefully.
> Of filthy incest I do thee accuse,

> That Lemmon-like didst with thy father lye,
> Then hye to hell, haste to the furies there,
>   When raging parents witnesse gainst thee beare.   (823–28)

Surely, however, Cinyras is more to blame than Myrrha for infidelity to the queen. Perhaps he realizes this as he relents in the following stanza:

> Oh but the fault thy owne was most of all,
>   Poore *Myrha* thou didst meane no hurt to me,
> It wot: thou saidst (my selfe, I witnesse call)
>   'Twas ill with your owne child in loue to be:
> And vrg'd againe, what if she *Myrha* were,
>   I basely said, there was no fault in her.   (829–34)

He leaves it less than clear whether "thy owne" (829) refers to Myrrha or himself, even though the context suggests the latter. In his final lines Cinyras sums up with an ambiguous admission of guilt: "Shee sin'd, and knew her father she abused, / I sin'd, vncertaine who it was I vsed" (845–46). Perhaps he merely means that his sin is infidelity to his wife with an unknown girl. Nevertheless his uncertainty about her identity suggests that he suspected something of the truth long before he knew for sure.

Austin's language ploddingly emphasizes the lascivious quality of the incest. From the very outset, the term "wanton" recurs again and again: "The wanton Lady" (title), "to descant wantonly" (4), "wanton bed" (190, 656), "wanton sports" (417, 515), and so on. "Filthy" too is repeated almost *ad nauseam*: "filthy shame" (10), "filthy lustfull fire" (22), "filthy staine" (171), "filthy blob and staine" (644), "filthy incest" (825). Austin is subtle enough to convince Grosart that "the story is told with all the realism of the original in Ovid; but nowise pruriently or offensively." In 1876 Grosart even guessed that "the Writer was probably a parson."[31] If so the preaching in the poem is remarkable in that it delights in the sin even while condemning it:

> O there they lie and glut themselues with sin,
>   A iocund sin that doth the flesh delight,
> A filthy flesh that can delight therein,
>   A silly ioy that gainst the soule doth fight,
> A fading sport, a pleasure soone forgot,
>   That bringeth shame with an eternall blot.   (715–20)

Although Milton did not treat the incestuous birth of Adonis directly, there are striking parallels between the infernal trinity in *Paradise Lost* and Ovid's account of Myrrha's passion for her father. Like Cinyras' daughter, Sin succeeds in winning sexual favors from her father:

                                but familiar grown,
        I pleas'd, and with attractive graces won
        The most averse, thee chiefly, who full oft
        Thy self in me thy perfect image viewing
        Becam'st enamour'd, and such joy thou took'st
        With me in secret, that my womb conceiv'd
        A growing burden.[32]   (II, 761–67)

Her "attractive graces" are not complicated with the guilt and inhibi-
tions of Ovid's women. Instead she must reestablish her claims over
Satan, who fails to recognize her in Hell: "I know thee not, nor ever saw
till now / Sight more detestable then . . . thee" (744–45). While Sin is
too depraved to suffer any of the conflicts of conscience that Myrrha experienced, her vanity seems hurt at Satan's lapse of memory:

        Hast thou forgot me then, and do I seem
        Now in thine eye so foul, once deemd so fair
        In Heav'n.   (747–49)

    The experience of birth is somewhat similar in Ovid's story and
Milton's allegory. Ovid's description of the birth of Adonis reflects the
normal strains of childbirth intensified by Myrrha's transformation into
a tree. The metamorphosis is bound up with suffering which is relieved
at the moment of birth:

        Nitenti tamen est similis curvataque crebros
        Dat gemitus arbor lacrimisque cadentibus umet.
                        .   .   .   .
        Arbor agit rimas et fissa cortice vivum
        Reddit onus, vagitque puer; quem mollibus herbis
        Naides inpositum lacrimis unxere parentis.
        Laudaret faciem Livor quoque.   (508–09, 512–15)

                            [like a woman in labor
        The tree, contorted, cried and wept.
                        .   .   .   .
                                and the tree cracked open,
        The bark was split, the burden loosed, a baby
        Gave his first cries, and naiads cradled him
        On the soft leaves, and used his mother's tears
        To wash him. Even Envy praised his beauty.]   (Pp. 250–51)

Sin's labor and delivery are much more hideous, but repeat some of the
same motifs. Instead of the Ovidian pattern of suffering relieved at
birth, Sin is subject to intense violence which causes painful metamorphosis without relief:

At last this odious offspring whom thou seest
Thine own begotten, breaking violent way
Tore through my entrails, that with fear and pain
Distorted, all my nether shape thus grew
Transform'd: but he my inbred enemie
Forth issu'd, brandishing his fatal Dart
Made to destroy: I fled, and cry'd out *Death;*
Hell trembl'd at the hideous Name, and sigh'd
From all her Caves, and back resounded *Death.* (781–89)

Thus, Myrrha's delivery, although characterized by contortion, cracking and splitting, is sweetened at last by the first cries and beauty of the child. Sin also progresses from the "prodigious motion . . . and rueful throes" (780) of labor to the painful lacerations of delivery, but instead of a beautiful baby she delivers the monster Death, whose first act is to rape his mother (790ff.).

Whereas Ovid's amoral interest in the "unnatural female libido"[33] concerns itself with an extreme case of basic human drives and passions, Milton's Sin is much less human than Myrrha. There is a superficial resemblance between her incest with Satan and Myrrha's with Cinyras, but this is overshadowed by the moral and emotional differences. Sin's lack of conscience is meant to present her as totally evil. Her recollection of how she was once "shining heav'nly fair" (757) recalls a time when she was physically different, yet even then her real nature was fully evil and thus morally hideous. Her transformations in Hell only add flesh to a being spiritually complete from the beginning. The superficial parallels between Sin and Myrrha point to the moral gap that separates them. Myrrha's act is the height of her folly, the final border of her moral degeneration. Incest for Sin is one of her most human accomplishments. She experiences "joy" (765), has "attractive graces" (762), and pleases Satan. Her memory of this condition sounds almost like a real woman's sorrow at having been forsaken and forgotten by a lover. But whereas Myrrha repents of her incest and seems to move closer to normal human experience, Sin, like Satan, moves in the opposite direction. She becomes hardened and hateful until her final words to Satan make her incestuous connection a parody of the Trinity and as such a blasphemous mockery of human love:

thou wilt bring me soon
To that new world of light and bliss, among
The Gods who live at ease, where I shall Reign
At thy right hand voluptuous, as beseems
Thy daughter and thy darling, without end. (866–70)

Milton would probably have been more sympathetic to the medieval traditions that view Myrrha as a symbol of evil than to those that
were less harsh with her. He read and referred to Dante's *Divine Comedy*[34] and in addition could have known the Italian poet's letter to Henry
VII either in one of the three manuscripts in Italy, or, more likely, in
the Italian translation published by Doni. C. H. Herford has compared
the relevant paragraph of Dante's letter with a section of the Second
Defense in which Milton "addressed to Cromwell, at the height of his
power, words of grave warning."[35] Although Herford's purpose is to
show the similarity in spirit between the two poets as they engaged in
politics, the thematic parallel could have been a direct influence. In
any case, whether or not he had read the letter, Milton's attitude toward Sin is similar to Dante on Myrrha. Perhaps "the viper that darts at
the bowels of its mother" associated with "the cursed and impious Myrrha" in Dante's letter helped to suggest the monsters begotten by Death
on Sin which "when they list into the womb / That bred them they
return, and howl and gnaw . . . [her] Bowels" (798–800). Other medieval and Renaissance treatments of Myrrha as evil, such as those of Walter Map and George Schuler, might also have appealed to him.

Roman Catholic sympathy for Myrrha, as reflected in Bersuire,
the *Ovide moralisé,* and Mansion, would have been rejected by the
Protestant Milton in favor of the spirit of Dante's references. The parallels between Myrrha and Sin, Satan's "voluptuous . . . daughter and
. . . darling" (869–70), suggest a mockery of the tradition which allego-
rized Ovid's heroine as the mother of Christ. Likewise, Austin's *Scourge
of Venus*, popular, lasciviously oriented, and fascinated with the incest
itself, provides a model for what Milton did not see in Myrrha. In *Paradise Lost* the incest of Satan and Sin provides parodic imitation of the
Trinity and is thus hierarchically anchored in a clear moral cosmos
which is very far indeed from Austin's view of Ovid's world.

Ben Gurion University of the Negev, Beersheva

NOTES

1. "Preface to *Annus Mirabilis*," *Essays of John Dryden*, ed. W. P. Ker (New York,
1961), I, 16. Quotation appears in L. P. Wilkinson, *Ovid Recalled* (Cambridge, 1955),
p. 227.

2. Ovid's sources are conveniently summarized in Wilson Brewer, *Ovid's "Metamorphoses" in European Culture*, II (Boston, 1941), pp. 346–49.

3. *Ovid as an Epic Poet*, 2nd ed. (Cambridge, 1970), p. 226.

4. All Latin citations of Ovid refer to *Ovid's "Metamorphoses" Books 6–10*, ed. William S. Anderson (Norman, Okla., 1972), pp. 136–41. The English translations are from *Ovid's "Metamorphoses,"* trans. Rolfe Humphries (Bloomington, Ind., 1955), pp. 243–51.

5. *Fulgentius the Mythographer*, trans. Leslie George Whitbread ([Columbus, Ohio], 1971), p. 92.

6. *Arnulphi Aurelianensis allegoriae super Ovidii Metamorphosin*, ed. Fausto Ghisalberti, *Memorie del Reale Instituto Lombardo di Scienze e Lettere*, 24, fasc. 4 (1932), 223 (Lib. X, 10–11); Thomae Walsingham, *De archana deorum*, ed. Robert A. van Kluyve (Durham, N.C., 1968), p. 155 (X, 10); William Caxton, *Ovyde Hys Booke of Metamorphose Books X–XV* (Oxford, 1924), p. 26. John of Garland provides no interpretation, content to pun on Myrrha's name in two lines of his *Integumenta Ovidii* (ed. Fausto Ghisalberti [Milan, 1933], p. 68 [11. 413–14]). Early in the fourteenth century Giovanni del Virgilio also quotes Fulgentius on Myrrha (cf. Fausto Ghisalberti's edition in "Giovanni del Virgilio espositore delle *Metamorfosi*," *Giornale Dantesca*, 34, n.s. 4 [1933], 91–92). D. C. Allen's *Mysteriously Meant: The Rediscovery of Pagan Symbolism and Allegorical Interpretation in the Renaissance* (Baltimore, 1970), pp. 163–99, provides an indispensable guide to all these sources.

7. *Bibliotheque universelle et historique de l'année 1686*, ed. Jean Le Clerc, 2nd ed. (Amsterdam, 1700), III, 21.

8. *De nugis curialium*, trans. Montague R. James, Cymmrodorion Record Series, 9 (London, 1923), p. 163.

9. Dante Alighieri, *Inferno: The Italian Text with Translation and Notes*, Allan Gilbert (Durham, N.C., 1969), pp. 252–53 (XXX, 37–41).

10. "Letter VII," *A Translation of Dante's Eleven Letters*, trans. Charles Sterrett Latham (London, 1892), pp. 156–57.

11. Dante's Latin is rendered: "questa é le uipera uolta nel uentre della madre . . . questa é Mirra scelerata & empia, la quale s'infiamma del fuoco degli abbracciamenti del padre," *Prose antiche di Dante, Petrarcha, et Boccaccio . . .* , comp. Antonio Francesco Doni (Florence, 1547), p. 11.

12. "Mala & impudẽs filia significat ambitiosum. . . . aliqua persona ambitiosa cupi patri suo Christo aliquo bñficio ecclesiastico iugari," *Metamorphosis Ouidiana moraliter . . .* (Paris, 1515), fol. 83ʳ. This was falsely attributed to Thomas Waleys.

13. "Qui sic intrat ecclesiam solet in amaritudinem terminari: & in arborem: id est in infernum transformari" (fol. 83ᵛ). The similarity in Latin between *myrrh* and *amarus* or bitter helped to support this reading. The correspondence is even closer in Hebrew. Bersuire's quotation from Ruth i, 20, shows that he knew this.

14. "Vel dic q̄ ista filia significat animam peccatricem" (fol. 83ᵛ).

15. Ecclesiasticus xxiv, 20. The translation provided is from *The Geneva Bible: A Facsimile of the 1560 Edition* (Madison, Wis., 1969), p. 433ᵛ, where it appears as xxiv, 17.

16. "Vel dic q̄ ista filia est beata virgo que de patre concepit: et in myrrham. i. amaritudinem est mutata: et in odoris fragrantiam cõuersa. Ecclesia. xxiii'. Quasi myrrha electa dedi suauitatẽ odoris. Ista igitur a patre suo filium concepit: id est xp̄m: & ipsum intra lignum & corticẽ. i. intra vterum castum & intactum sine corruptione continuit et postea eũ nõ caro: sed legnum existens. i. non carnalis: sed virgo permanens peperit. Esa. vii. Ecce virgo concipiet & pariet filium. Figuratur in virga Aaron que sicca floruit. Numeri. xvii" (fol. 83ᵛ).

17. *Ovide moralisé: Poème de commencement du quatorzième siècle*, ed. C. de Boer, IV (Amsterdam, 1936), 98–99 (X.3684–95). All citations of the *Ovide moralisé* refer to this edition.

18. *Fabula: Trois études de mythographie antique et médiévale*, Publications Romanes et Françaises, 122 (Geneva, 1973), pp. 110–11.

19. For mortification of the flesh, see *Patrologiae cursus completus . . .* Series Latina, ed. J.-P. Migne (Paris, 1844–1904), CXII, 999; CLXXIV, 986–87; CXCV, 1173; CCX, 86. Sweetness, CXCIII, 423. Incorruptibility, CLII, 829; LVII, 269, 283. Bitterness of the Passion, CLXXXIV, 646. Faith, CXCV, 1132. Resurrection of the dead, LVII, 259–60. Martyrs of the church, CXII, 999.

20. *Reductorivm, repertorivm, et dictionarivm morale vtrivsqve testamenti . . .* (Cologne, 1684), I, 830 (bk. 12, chap. 98).

21. *The Myroure of oure Ladye*, ed. John Henry Blunt, E.E.T.S. (London, 1873), pp. 285–86.

22. *Cy commence Ouide de Salmonēn son liure intitule Metamorphose. Contenāt. xv. liures particuliers moralisie par maistre Thomas vvaleys . . . translate & compile par Colard mansion* (Brussels, 1484), p. 261 (pagination in pencil in copy of first edition of this work in the Morgan Library).

23. "Deinde quò ostendat non libidinem, sed Diabolum eiusmodi amoris autorem esse, excusat Cupidinem, ac transfert culpam in ipsas furias" (*Fabvlarum Ovidii interpretatio, ethica, physica, et historia*, tradite in Academia Regiomontana a Georgio Sabino [Schuler] [Cambridge, 1584], p. 406). This same point is made by George Sandys in 1632: "*Cupid* (which is a desire of generation according to the order of Nature) denies to have kindled her unnaturall flames: imputed to infernall *Alecto*, or the Divell, who begets in the impious soule, deserted by Virtue, such hellish affections" (*Ovid's Metamorphoses Englished, Mythologized, and Represented in Figures*, ed. Karl K. Hulley and Stanley T. Vandersall [Lincoln, Nebr., 1970], p. 485).

24. "Alter de improbitate vetularum, quae plerunque sunt scelerum & flagitiorum administrẹ: ac inprimis ingeniosae in illis perficiendis" (p. 406).

25. In his expanded edition of 1632 (see n. 23), Sandys includes various comments about Myrrha, such as a suggestion of the similarity between her story and that of Lot (p. 487) and a summary of Fulgentius' rational explanation (p. 490).

26. *The Picture of Incest. Liuely Portraicted in the Historie of Cinyras and Myrrha* (London, 1626), ed. Alexander Balloch Grosart, in *Occasional Issues of Unique and Very Rare Books*, III, pt. 4 (Manchester, 1876).

27. Cf. *The Fables* (1700), in *The Poetical Works of Dryden*, ed. George R. Noyes (Boston, 1951), pp. 806–11.

28. *Mirrha The Mother of Adonis: Or Lustes Prodegies*, in *Occasional Issues,* III, pt. 1, p. 65.

29. Cf. Alexander Balloch Grosart, *Fly-leaves or Additional Notes and Illustrations on the Occasional Issues of Very Rare Books*, XVIII (Manchester, 1883), pp. 49–50.

30. *Occasional Issues*, III, pt. 3, p. 12 (1. 176). Grosart edited the 1614 text, which is twelve lines longer than those of 1613 and 1620. The line references in further citations from *The Scourge of Venus* are to my own numbering of Grosart's text.

31. *Occasional Issues*, III, pt. 3, pp. v–vi.

32. All citations from *Paradise Lost* refer to *The Complete English Poetry of John Milton*, ed. John T. Shawcross (New York, 1963).

33. Otis, *Ovid as an Epic Poet,* p. 226.

34. Cf. *The Complete Prose Works of John Milton*, Don M. Wolfe, Gen. Ed., I (New Haven, 1953), p. 366.

35. "Dante and Milton," *Bulletin of the John Rylands Library*, VIII (1924), 212.

"CHARACTER" IN *PARADISE LOST*: MILTON'S LITERARY FORMALISM

Edward Milowicki and Rawdon Wilson

THE PROBLEM of "character" in *Paradise Lost* defies the most concentrated efforts at formulation. Coldly reduced to theological postulates, Satan's glamor, Adam's nobility, and Eve's allure remain; hotly raised to naturalistic portraiture, their essential moral infirmities persist. Indeed, few aspects of the narrative structure of *Paradise Lost* are as elusive as "character" and few more deserving of continued critical attention.

If, as seems frustratingly the case, all questions about literary works are imprecise because of the shifting levels of reference and the multiplicity of formulations available, then those that pertain to character seem especially blurred. Questions about character point toward extrinsic evidence and, at the same time, centripetally toward evidence that inheres in the language of the text itself. On the one hand, readers may respond to characters as if they were actual persons and ask question of the type that one might otherwise put to friends or neighbors. On the other hand, readers may respond in terms of those formal questions that can be asked of all works of art. In every literary work there are implicit questions concerning the author's methods and the conventions that underlie specific instances of characterization.[1]

In this paper we shall examine a few questions of the second type. We propose to explore character in *Paradise Lost* as the embodiment of an intricate interplay of method and convention. We shall attempt to indicate certain formal approaches that Milton used in creating the major characterizations of *Paradise Lost*, what their provenances were, and the extent to which Milton modified, adapted, and combined them. Every literary convention stands between tradition and innovation and is both a reflection of prior literary practice and a promulgation of approaches not yet in use. Thus a literary work contains a great number of conventions which function, in Howard Felperin's phrase, like "archaic sign systems."[2] Such sign systems appear as vestigial remains of once thriving enterprises: all literature contains them; no analysis can successfully ignore them. In variable and unequal balance,

75

both archaic sign systems and fresh strategies coexist. Every major author renovates his inherited models. Furthermore, character, except in its most simplistic modes, cannot be accounted for fully by reference to conventions considered in isolation. The model of human nature that lies behind literary characterization, and which can always be inferred, resembles a network of superimposed tracings. The skeleton (and some of the flesh) of characterization is composed of partial, overlaid models that are inscribed in the text at different levels of cognition and availability. The phenomenon of character is never quite exhausted by the enumeration of these models, however; it is the interplay of conventions that determines characterization. In characterization, life studies are played off against literary allusion, precise descriptions against puns or other forms of embedded wit, and exterior appearances against interior mind processes.

Paradise Lost is a primary instance of this formal layering. Its multiple conventions in characterization operate on cognitive levels that range from the archaic to the most radical. In our analysis we shall consider the relationship between two of these independent conventions.

First, we shall discuss Milton's use of certain interconnected narrative strategies that date back, at the least, to Ovid. These strategies, which collectively may be called "split awareness," structure the experience of characters upon the basis of dilemmic contradictions between opposed, but equally felt, values. Characters that are created according to this fundamentally Ovidian convention derive their credibility—that is, their requisite illusion of psychic depth—from the awareness of more or less irreconcilable divisions in their minds. They are "split" between the call of antagonistic values or, it may be, duties. Second, we shall attempt to show how Milton makes use of a much later "Ovidian" convention (this one belonging essentially to the Renaissance Ovid, not the classical) according to which human beings are offered, at each moment of their existence, a choice between an upward and a downward path.

Milton's most striking innovation in the characterization of *Paradise Lost* is to compel the second convention to interact with the first, a move that shifts what had been a moral metaphor to the level of a structural function in the creation of character. The archaic Ovidian strategy in his narrative method is thus renovated by the remarkably original application of another convention (itself loosely Ovidian) that had not previously served this purpose. One consequence of this interplay is that *Paradise Lost* even now appears to be the most mind-conscious work in our literature.

In concentrating upon this interplay, we are not denying the presence of other partial models also inscribed in the text. Undoubtedly, the character of Satan owes much to the long series of literary Satans, many of whom can be rediscovered in *The Celestial Cycle.*[3] All literary characters cannibalize the substance of antecedent ones. Satan may be derived partly from different life studies, tyrants whom Milton may well have had in mind, such as, in particular, King Charles I.[4] And there are other extrinsic models, theological, historical, and literary, present in *Paradise Lost*, all of which are available for critical analysis.[5]

Whether in terms of theological postulates, biblical typology, rhetorical types, literary precedent, or historical life studies, the major characters of *Paradise Lost* have normally been treated as separate cases, each expressing a distinct problem in morality or a distinct schema of concepts drawn from the history of ideas. From the standpoint of the extrinsic conventions of characterization, all characters, illustrating different kinds of decisions and actions, will tend to appear as distinct. A significant aspect of our argument will be to show that the major characters of *Paradise Lost* have been shaped by intrinsic conventions that analogously determine the structure and range of their experience.

Only recently has the case been strongly argued that both Adam and Eve embody a single moral construct, and that in terms of centrally important issues, whether free will or responsibility, they are actually very much in the same condition.[6] If one of the multiple purposes of *Paradise Lost* is (as we believe) to provide an insight into the grounds of human experience through imagined forms, or prototypes, of that experience, then an exclusive emphasis upon the disparities among the characters must, in some sense, run counter to the poem's deep stress upon the original and universal structures of human cerebration. Significantly, a consideration of the characters of *Paradise Lost* from the standpoint of the intrinsic conventions of their creation restates their affinities, puts them into a common perspective and, hence, lends support to what is, it may be, the most important moral point of all: Milton makes a fundamental reflection upon the nature of *all* human experience and upon the possibilities of the mind itself.

Having assumed the possibility of a vertical paradigm of numerous inscribed models, we shall focus upon the interplay between the two Ovidian conventions (the archaic and the relatively modern, the traditional and the Renaissance) of characterization to which we have referred. In this discussion of Milton's literary formalism, we hope to cast some new light upon his remarkable capacity to employ the resources of tradition and upon his ability to experiment radically. However, we shall also seek to indicate how Milton's use of formal, intrinsic conventions of characterization reflects a concept of mind that, in its most lucid formulation, accounts for the scope, from ideal to perverse, of human thought. Milton uses these conventions, one Ovidian and classical, the other Ovidian in spirit at least, to articulate an underlying view of the human mind in its essential capacity as a maker of decisions.

Ovidian characterization is, for classical literature, exceptionally concerned with qualities of mind, with intellectual activity. This is most clearly seen in the creation of a small group of characters particularly distinguished by mental stages of sharply defined conflicts in values. This strategy of split awareness is of considerable importance in the development of Western literature,[7] so that Milton's characterization in *Paradise Lost* is not merely within a discernible literary tradition but marks one of its high points. The Ovidian convention is strikingly consonant with Milton's view that the human mind possesses a potential range of activity, invariably decision-making in its essence, that can be imagined in its original exercise.[8] The peak moment in this Ovidian tradition comes, then, when an organized view of mind coincides with established conventions for showing the anguish of decisiveness.

In discussing Ovid, we shall focus on the *Metamorphoses*, which so fascinated Milton. Repeatedly in the *Metamorphoses*, Ovidian heroines are torn between duty and desire, and seek to justify to themselves the pursuit of their passion through rationalization, a form of self-persuasion that has its basis in the rhetorical *suasoria* that were studied in the schools,[9] but which Ovid adapts to depict psychic division. In advancing what appear to her to be powerful justifications for following her desires, the Ovidian heroine reveals the depths of her passion and, almost inadvertently, also betrays her awareness of the enormity of the sin she contemplates. For example, Medea feels her passion is overwhelming: "In vain, Medea, do you fight. Some god or other is opposing you" (*Meta.* VII.11–12).[10] Byblis also uses the gods to justify her incestuous passion for her twin brother, Caunus, rationalizing that "in this we do but follow the example of the gods" (*Meta.* IX.555). Myrrha, another of Ovid's incestuously driven heroines (a student both of nature and of certain cultures with eccentric mores), does not ransack Olympus for her "reasons" but rather argues that incest is perfectly natural and that it strengthens family ties (*Meta.* X.324–33). Torn between duty and desire, Ovid's heroines are shown struggling in a decisive moment. In this moment, seized by deep passions that negate ingrained values, they engage in what appears to be genuine debate, but which, on closer scrutiny, must be seen as a series of rationalizations through which they justify themselves in the course of action they, inevitably, will choose.

Although it is extremely rhetorical, this rationalizing indicates a sharp awareness of conflicting values, a "split" according to which the heroine must choose either self or society, either desire or duty, so that the immediate sense is that of fierce struggle.

Since so many of the formal conventions of characterization in Western narrative have emerged from, though evolving further than, the basic strategy of split awareness in the *Metamorphoses*, it is unsurprising to find in *Paradise Lost* the Ovidian convention of showing characters, in a moment of decisive stress, engaging in self-serving rationalization. However, Milton extends this to indicate more than momentary self-division, an intensive yet truncated psychomachia. In *Paradise Lost* split awareness mirrors an inveterate potentiality of mind, always present in cognitive structure, that strains to reorder experience antithetically. Mind (since "Reason also is choice") must choose and, in so doing, struggles within its potentiality for self-division.

All choice—every exercise of rationality—tends ultimately toward either God or Chaos, mind or mindlessness. This is the most general formulation of structural division that *Paradise Lost* suggests. Yet for this antithesis to make sense it is necessary to recognize that, for Milton, mind is essentially uniform, varying in degree and application, but not in quality. Thus Adam recalls God remarking to him that the animals of Eden possess language and "also know, / And reason not contemptibly" (VIII, 373–74). Earlier in their conversation, Raphael had observed that reason, whether discursive or intuitive, was the soul's being and that, while the former was most often the mode of man's reasoning, the latter that of angels, they differed "but in degree, of kind the same" (V, 486–89). Milton indicates repeatedly that reason is "of kind the same": variations in degree, nuance, or subtle shift, not radical departure, mark the full, interlinked gradations of Creation. The problem of Satan's character reflects a conviction that his mind, though more powerful and capable of a greater degree of effect, is essentially, in structure and act, like that of men. Sin springs from his brow, in her original manifestation, just as she does, in some sense, in every later replicative birth from human minds. Similarly, Milton describes Satan, in profoundly human terms, as the first hypocrite, an "artificer of fraud" who "was the first / That practis'd falsehood under saintly show, / Deep malice to conceal" (IV, 121–23). When Adam remarks that evil "into the mind of God or man" may enter and yet, provided it is unapproved, depart without leaving "spot or blame behind" (V, 117–19), he clearly comments upon mind in some general definition, angelic and human. Satan, one should remember, approved Sin in an essentially human manner (II, 763–65). Too strong an emphasis upon the separation of one character from another in *Paradise Lost* must hit wide of the mark. *Paradise Lost* gazes steadily upon, as E. L. Marilla puts it, the "principles which condition the course of human affairs."[11] Rigorously to insist upon an explicit specification of principles—say, free will or responsibility—so as to separate and distinguish the minds of the characters leaves critical attention unstretched. Milton's concept of mind demands considerable synthesis in the act of reading.

Although obliquely evident in Book I (54–56), Satan's split awareness is most clearly seen in Book IV in the series of his soliloquies where, fully aware that his chosen values are distorted, he persists in self-rationalization, reasoning that (since "ease would recant / Vows made in pain") repentance is impossible (93–102). The formal posing of Satan's argument in this passage recalls the rhetorical balance of Ovidian heroines. Through this convention, Milton gives to Satan a recognizably human state of mind. Furthermore, Satan's need to persuade his reason indicates that even in Hell the concept of rational order established by God's mindfulness yet stands. When Satan's rationalizations shade off into defiance and he concludes that, all hope gone, evil shall be his "good" (IV, 103–10), he continues to follow, however poorly and obscurely, the formal lines of rationality. His repertoire is multiform.

The Ovidian conventions that shape the characterization of Eve are even more apparent. Nowhere else in *Paradise Lost* is Ovid's vast suggestiveness seen so acutely etched.[12] Eve's account of her initial experience upon awakening into life (IV, 450–90), with its description of the smooth lake that "seem'd another Sky" and the shape that appeared "within the wat'ry gleam," is an adaptation of the tale of Narcissus (*Meta*. III.402–510) and, what is more, works to reinforce the biblical suggestion that woman is the image of man as man is the image of God.[13] The Ovidian element in Eve's characterization goes far beyond the allusion to the Narcissus tale, important as this is; indeed, the allusion to Narcissus serves primarily to anticipate the nature of the psychic division that Eve will soon discover within herself.[14] In the exercise of her rationality, Eve will be compelled to choose, and the choice will be, as Cleanth Brooks puts it,[15] one of images, between herself in reflection (captured in Satan's rhetoric) or herself in Adam. Choice for Eve will lie, as it has for Satan, between a greater and a lesser alternative, an upward and a downward way.

Eve's character thus follows the lines of Ovid's heroines in the *Metamorphoses*. As they are shown in a moment of split awareness, torn between desire and duty, Eve is also presented as having two alternatives, either to pursue Beauty or to learn to go out of herself, to find (beauty "excell'd by manly grace") a better self in Adam (IV, 488–91). The Lord's voice "woos" her from contemplating her own image, and Adam also woos her from that image, all of which suggests that, in the necessity to be wooed, her image has made a deep impression.[16] Henceforth, the reader must keep in mind that Eve possesses a divided mind; the one side works on a conscious, rational level to seek fulfilment in an "other self," while the other side, suppressed (or diverted) by God and then Adam, tends toward love of self. Although Eve's characterization exceeds, in complexity and duration, the simpler figures of the *Metamorphoses* in whom split awareness is not sustained at length, it is essentially Ovidian.[17]

Although Eve does not continuously debate within herself to demonstrate extended psychic tension, her split awareness is foreshadowed from the moment of her introduction. The initial allusion to the myth of Narcissus points forward to the more developed division of consciousness in the later books;[18] equally significant, the account of Eve's dream in Book V suggests the inherent psychic division in her nature, the underlying basis of her split awareness in Book IX. Book V begins on a sensual note: the day opens with a "rosy dawn" (1), with "temperate vapors" (5) and with birdsong (8). Milton then states a theme that he will develop with increasing complexity and later interrelate with his characterization of Adam and Eve. When Adam looks upon the unawakened Eve, the narrative voice comments,

> with looks of cordial love
> Hung over her enamor'd, and beheld
> Beauty, which whether waking or asleep,
> Shot forth peculiar graces; then with voice
> Mild, as when *Zephyrus* on *Flora* breathes,
> Her hand soft touching, whisper'd thus.   (V, 12–17)

Adam, having touched Eve's hand, whispers to her. Here sight and sound, commonly regarded as the highest in the hierarchy of the senses, are interlinked with the lowest sense, touch. Indeed, in one line sound and touch join, so to speak, when Adam, "her hand soft touching, whisper'd." Since this occurs before the Fall, Milton does not imply at this point a "descent of the senses" (a *topos* of seduction since ancient times) wherein sight, sound, and smell lead to taste (the kiss) and touch (the embrace).[19] He *does* make an important comment upon the underlying patterns of the human mind. The downward paths of sense, toward pleasure and satisfaction (but, ultimately, toward chaos and blank

mindlessness), mark one of the alternatives of reasoning: it is implicit in
the mere concept of choice.

On awakening, Eve describes her dream to Adam, and her description is initially dominated by images of sight and sound (29, 36, 40, 41,
43–47, 53–55). Next, Milton introduces the sense of smell ("his dewy
locks distill'd / *Ambrosia*"; 56–57), so that the descent of the senses is
suggested. Milton then returns to sight and sound, and restates the descent theme with the sense of taste following sight and sound:

> on that Tree he also gaz'd;
> And O fair plant, said he, with fruit surcharg'd,
> Deigns none to ease thy load and taste thy sweet,
> Nor God, nor Man; is Knowledge so despis'd?
> Or envy, or what reserve forbids to taste?   (V, 57–61)

With "He pluckt, he tasted" (V, 65), the descent motif, initially presented neutrally when Adam awakens Eve, is restated with ominous
implications. The dream moves in a pattern that suggests a seduction—
and the sexual undertones of the climactic moment point ahead to the
actual seduction in Book IX, in which Eve is mastered by sensual appeal:

> he drew nigh, and to me held,
> Even to my mouth of that same fruit held part
> Which he had pluckt; the pleasant savory smell
> So quick'n'd appetite, that I, methought,
> Could not but taste. Forthwith up to the Clouds
> With him I flew.   (V, 82–87)

Traditionally, the descent-of-sense *topos* was a vehicle of seduction,
and it is not difficult to see here a kind of seduction. One must accord
this observation due caution, of course: sensuality has not yet corrupted
Eve's mind, not destroyed the Edenic condition, but its possibility, suggested variously and now by the implications of Eve's puzzling dream,
inheres in the structure of mind. Although the pattern of the descent of
the senses seems evident, it is presented with a significant variation.
The flight to the skies, with the subsequent looking back on earth in the
contemptus mundi tradition, appears in Cicero, Chaucer, and Dante,
among others, where it indicates the beginning of wisdom. In *Paradise
Lost* it is a climax following a sensual descent.[20]

Adam, too, is initially characterized in terms that anticipate a later
and more complex development of split awareness. The division of his
mind (not so much in act as in potentiality) is suggested as early as his
remark to Eve, "Best Image of myself and dearer half" (V, 95). This dis-

position in Adam, to love not wisely but too well (or to choose *his* image over Him of Whom he is the image), is restated in Book VIII, again in evident conjunction with the descent-of-sense *topos*. Adam tells Raphael that he

> must confess to find
> In all things else delight indeed, but such
> As us'd or not, works in the mind no change
> Nor vehement desire, these delicacies
> I mean of Taste, Sight, Smell, Herbs, Fruits, and Flow'rs,
> Walks, and the melody of Birds, but here
> Far otherwise, transported I behold,
> Transported touch; here passion first I felt,
> Commotion strange, in all enjoyments else
> Superior and unmov'd, here only weak
> Against the charm of Beauty's powerful glance.   (VIII, 523–33)

Although Adam acknowledges the delight of "Beauty's powerful glance" as he has experienced it through all the senses, he observes that he has stood "superior and unmov'd." Only the delight that touch engenders has actually "transported" him. This is the meaning that Raphael fixes on Adam's confession when he replies,

> But if the sense of touch whereby mankind
> Is propagated seem such dear delight
> Beyond all other, think the same voutsaf't
> To Cattle and each Beast.   (VIII, 579–82)

Trying to warn Adam against entering upon a descent of the senses, Raphael proposes an ascent instead:

> What higher in her society thou find'st
> Attractive, human, rational, love still;
> In loving thou dost well, in passion not,
> Wherein true Love consists not; Love refines
> The thoughts, and heart enlarges, hath his seat
> In Reason, and is judicious, is the scale
> By which to heav'nly Love thou mayst ascend,
> Not sunk in carnal pleasure, for which cause
> Among the Beasts no mate for thee was found. (VIII, 586–94)

Raphael's emphatic distinction between the human and the beastly commands attention. There are degrees, and distinct levels, of rationality, and these correspond to degrees, and levels, of sensuality in an inverse ratio. Adam's choice, made in complete awareness of the opposed values, will be between the directions adumbrated in Raphael's warning. This ultimate exercise in choice, between the paths of mind and mindlessness (between rationality and sense, God and Chaos) follows the opposition between ascent and descent.

The purposeful counterpoising of the descent of the senses and the ladder of love was a familiar literary strategy. As both were common *topoi*, the implications of opposing them seem always to have been clear. Parody, for instance, could be taken for granted: Faustus' words, "Her lips suck forth my soul. See where it flies" (*Dr. Faustus*, V.i), lose much of their impact without the recognition that they upend the ladder of love. The effect of Faustus' words depends upon holding in mind the *topos* of ascent from the senses to spiritual love. In its most famous version, Bembo's account in Castiglione's *Il Cortegione* of the spiritual kiss, physical love transcends itself and becomes its opposite. Moral judgments of all kinds assumed the meaningfulness of the opposition: the ethical fury of *The Faerie Queene*, II.12, where "comely man" and "beastly men" are contrasted, implicitly asserts the antagonism between ascent and descent.

It was also possible to make self-evident contrasts between the two *topoi*, as Jonson does in *The New Inn*, when Lovel attempts to win Lady Frampul with a "definition" of love that is nothing other than an elegant statement of the ladder of love. To this exercise of wit and idealism, Lord Beaufort juxtaposes the descent of sense:

> I relish not these philosophical feasts;
> Give me a banquet of sense, like that of Ovid:
> A form to take the eye; a voice mine ear;
> Pure aromatic to my scent: a soft,
> Smooth, dainty hand to touch; and for my taste,
> Ambrosiac kisses to melt down the palate.   (III.ii)

In Lord Beaufort's riposte, the descent of sense is called a "banquet of sense" and is compared to one in Ovid. The allusion illustrates the deep association that obtained between the traditional descent of sense and the literary understanding of Ovid. Chapman, to cite the obvious example, had written a narrative poem entitled *Ovids Banquet of Sence*. The image of the banquet to embody the concept of descent seems to have been normal. In Marvell's "A Dialogue between the Resolved Soul and Created Pleasure," Pleasure offers "Nature's banquet" but the Resolved Soul declines since he must hurry to "sup above." In *Comus*, Milton has the sorcerer argue the case for seduction in terms of feeding. The Lady responds that

swinish gluttony
Ne'er looks to Heaven amidst his gorgeous feast,
But with besotted base ingratitude
Crams, and blasphemes his feeder.　　　　(776–79)

The antagonism between the way down and the way up is sharp. It is also unexceptional: *Comus* uses, without extending, the traditional opposition.

In *Paradise Lost*, however, Milton's use of the descent-of-sense *topos* is revolutionary. His profound innovation lies in extending it to a strategy of characterization, combining the descent of sense with the Ovidian convention of split awareness. The effect is startlingly original. Milton's major characters take shape upon the tension between the antagonistic demands of the descent of sense and the ladder of love. Particular values place themselves along this tension: rational beings choose between alternatives that, formulated on an abstract level, conform to one or the other pole.

Milton's innovation within the Ovidian tradition of characterization is immense, but it is achieved by the adaptation of other Ovidian materials. In Book IX, the Narcissus myth with which Eve has been closely associated is projected upon Satan when he enters Eden by rising "up a Fountain by the Tree of Life" (IX, 73). (Ovid's word for Narcissus' stream is *fons*, fountain or spring.) There are, at least, two strong reasons for the Narcissistic function in Satan's characterization. In the first place, he is himself evidently Narcissistic, as the account of the birth of Sin demonstrates (II, 763–65) and the incestuous nature of his relations with Sin further corroborates. In the second place, Satan will force Eve's potential selfishness into actualization. In either sense, the clipped allusion to the Narcissus myth carries a complex significance. Satan is Narcissistic, as Eve can become; furthermore, he represents an upwelling of selfishness and irrationality in choice. Satan thus embodies the essence of the downward path: the sensual descent into irrationality and mindlessness. The movement away from God, from Form, is invariably one toward parodic inversion.

In the first two books the convention of split awareness helps to create a complex and dramatic Satan who, against all the obvious evidence and the warnings of the narrative voice, thrusts forward his appeal. As the convention of split awareness becomes less prominent, disappearing altogether in Book IX, Satan's characterization becomes melodramatic rather than dramatic, the psychic thickness that results from deep value conflicts greatly attenuated. Satan changes, and the mode of his change corresponds to Milton's decreasing use of the Ovidian strategy. Hence when Satan exclaims ("O foul descent!") that he who had aspired to deity must now be constrained into a beast, his essence incarnated and imbruted in bestial slime (IX, 163–69), he is, in terms of the structure of mental processes reflected, a different character. He is simplified and a more pure theological-literary type. However, the simplification follows the pattern already established: Satan now illustrates the descent of sense, the path taken and traversed. It is important to note that he uses both "descent" and "descend" in the passage cited. He understands the choice that he has made, and remembers just enough of love to regret the consequences of the choice (though not the choice itself), but he has become, through the process of simplification by which a formal convention for complex characterization is withheld, the type of that choice. No self-doubt now remains; he is single-minded.

When Satan continues his soliloquy, with its expression of the revenge motive, he calls attention to man's physical nature. Man, too, is an "essence" incarnated, though not yet imbruted:

> this new Favorite
> Of Heav'n, this Man of Clay, Son of despite,
> Whom us the more to spite his Maker rais'd
> From dust: spite then with spite is best repaid.   (IX, 175–78)

Milton's use of formal strategies is flawless: he wishes his readers to lose sympathy with Satan as the poem progresses, and this flattening of Satan's character, without abandoning the directions established by the original split awareness, is part of a careful process by which the reader is disentangled from the specious attractiveness of the initial Satan. This is a crucial moment in the poem, for Satan must be shown as diminished and, at the same time, the outline for Eve's eventual choice must be hinted. The latter glances from the language of Satan's soliloquy: "descent" (163) and "descend" (169) frame a context for the terms that suggest selfishness ("ambition," "revenge") and the final repetitions of "spite" convey both selfishness and illogicality, the misuse of rationality that (thought becoming chaotic) bad choice entails; moreover, there is the remarkably detailed narrowing of the Satanic psyche, as he imputes to God his own basic motivations. Finally, the emphasis upon man's physical nature provides an unmistakable symbol of the descent that Eve's wrong choice will take.

The foreshadowing of the formal structure of Eve's choice continues in the language that Satan uses to accomplish her seduction. Indeed, he appears to offer her, by implication, a complete sensual banquet. When Eve first encounters the serpent, the senses of sight and sound are focused in the foreground:

> His gentle dumb expression turn'd at length
> The Eye of Eve to mark his play; he glad
> Of her attention gain'd, with Serpent Tongue
> Organic, or impulse of vocal Air,
> His fraudulent temptation thus began.   (IX, 527–31)

Then, when Eve marvels at the serpent's ability to speak, he rejoins,

> on a day roving the field, I chanc'd
> A goodly Tree far distant to behold
> Loaden with fruit of fairest colors mixt,
> Ruddy and Gold: I nearer drew to gaze;
> When from the boughs a savory odor blown,
> Grateful to appetite, more pleas'd my sense
> Than smell of sweetest Fennel.   (IX, 575–81)

The middle sense, smell, has been introduced. Finally, Satan concludes the Banquet with touch and taste:

> Amid the Tree now got, where plenty hung
> Tempting so nigh, to pluck and eat my fill
> I spar'd not, for such pleasure til that hour
> At Feed or Fountain never had I found.   (IX, 594–97)

Eve then asks to be taken to the Tree, which request Satan greedily obliges, leading her to what might be described as an Ovidian Banquet of Sense:

> Beyond a row of Myrtles, on a Flat,
> Fast by a Fountain, one small Thicket past
> Of Blowing Myrrh and Balm.   (IX, 627–29)

Milton's imagery to describe Satan at the moment when Eve, too credulous and indefensive, says "lead then" (IX, 631) is magnificently infolded and implicative:

> Hee leading swiftly roll'd
> In tangles, and made intricate seem straight,
> To mischief swift. Hope elevates, and joy
> Bright'ns his Crest.   (IX, 631–34)

Not only do Satan's serpentine movements anticipate the properties of his seduction argument, in which fallacy seems sound, but his actual physical appearance, with his "crest" brightened by joy, suggests an erect phallus.[21] Satan is preparing to seduce Eve and, although his method is speciously that of logical argumentation, the structure of the imagery demonstrates the manner in which the descent-of-sense *topos* permeates the language of seduction.[22] It is appropriate that a passage working on the levels of both moral reference and sensual implication should culminate in an image that, at once, serves emblematically for the nature of the argument and for the nature of the feeling engendered. The subsequent epic simile, ending "So glister'd the dire Snake" (IX, 643), stresses both the delusive quality of Satan's argument (Eve is like a "night-wanderer" who falls into a bog or mire) *and* his erect, glowing appearance. The "unctuous vapor" to which he is compared is, after all, "Kindl'd through agitation to a Flame" (IX, 637). Yet this kind of compact ambiguity would lose much of its significance if it were not seen in terms of the seduction argument, structured along the lines of the descent-of-sense *topos*, that precedes it.

Once at the Tree, Satan, as "some Orator renown'd" (IX, 670), delivers an encomium on the powers of the Tree that, actually making "intricate seem straight," seems to reason away all objections to eating the fruit. Then, Eve being seduced, or nearly so, Milton's narrative voice restates with economy and force the Banquet of Sense:

> He ended, and his words replete with guile
> Into her heart too easy entrance won:
> Fixt on the Fruit she gaz'd, which to behold
> Might tempt alone, and in her ears the sound
> Yet rung of his persuasive words, impregn'd
> With Reason, to her seeming, and with Truth:
> Meanwhile the hour of Noon drew on, and wak'd
> An eager appetite, rais'd by the smell
> So savory of that Fruit, which with desire,
> Inclinable now grown to touch or taste,
> Solicited her longing eye.   (IX, 733–43)

"Solicited her longing eye" suggests that Milton has reversed the process of descent—sight, sound, smell, touch, and taste—with a return to sight. Actually, in bringing the *topos* full circle, the passage implies the total debasement of the highest sense by the lower. Reason, traditionally associated with sight, the highest sense (and with hearing, the second sense), now serves sensual desire in Eve's consciousness.[23] Eve's speech to the Tree indicates precisely this inversion. Like Ovid's heroines, she is gripped by desire and, rationalizing why she ought to eat the fruit, she uses her reason to serve that desire (IX, 753–59). The prohibition to taste becomes, in her mind, a prohibition to be wise. Eve's language in this passage, posing a series of alternatives and forcing a rhetorical conclusion rather than a rigorously logical one, reflects the state of her mind, now replicating the sinuous folds of Satan's serpentine mazes. Her split awareness, present before only in varying degrees of potential, is actively drawn. As she continues, it seems almost possible to hear Ovid's Myrrha lamenting that animals enjoy what is denied to humans (*Meta.* X.324–31).

Eve, her rational powers perverted, then confuses the Banquet of Sense with the ladder of love:

> Here grows the Cure of all, this Fruit Divine,
> Fair to the Eye, inviting to the Taste,
> Of Virtue to make wise; what hinders then
> To reach, and feed at once both Body and Mind?   (IX, 776–79)

After plucking and eating, Eve becomes "Intent now wholly on her taste" (IX, 786). One might think that the descent is now complete, and in a way it is. Yet Milton works out Eve's debasement to its inevitable end, demonstrating step by step the excesses of corrupted reason. Eve worships the Tree for endowing Sapience when she is furthest from having it. In Frye's phrase, the Tree has become a "demonic emblematic vision"[24] that focuses Eve's idolatrous condition of mind, itself evidence of the perversion of the natural internal hierarchy of reason, will, and appetite. Her paganlike idolatry is further underscored when she speaks of the "Gods." Having disobeyed God's authority, she creates a pantheon of her own, and worships Experience as well as the Tree. Eve's characterization is drawn with consistency: she begins life with sharp perceptions of the attractive elements in sensual experience and continues closer to the sensual side of the original dualistic experience. Her consciousness is always delineated in radically extreme terms, with the descent of sense clearly latent from her creation. It is worth observing that in their first post-Edenic lovemaking, Adam praises her for her skills in sensuality:

> Eve, now I see thou art exact of taste,
> And elegant, of Sapience no small part,
> Since to each meaning savor we apply,
> And Palate call judicious.   (IX, 1017–20)

Obviously, it would be a massive error to see Eve as sensual before her sin—or perverted before the act that corrupts her reason—but it would also be a misreading to fail to note the deeply implicit structure of appetite and sensuality that provides the negative pole of her characteristic split awareness.

Eve's subsequent decision to include Adam in her sin stems from selfish rationalization and follows inevitably upon the ascendancy of sensuality, the inversion by which appetite has mastered will and reason. In her reflections upon Adam's possible union with "another Eve," she projects her feelings beyond death, steeped in sense as she is. Later, a righting of the balance between the values of the spirit and those of the senses occurs, when both Eve and Adam learn that, even in their fallen condition, the way of ascent remains open; but in the dark, immediately post-Edenic moments, Eve, "defac't, deflour, . . . to Death devote" (IX, 901), acts in terms of the structure of descent, aware only of the demands of appetite. Milton's point seems both lucid and biting: the original split awareness of Eve's character anticipates the latent pattern of all human minds; the mastering force gained by the appetite (and the values of sense) points ahead to the authentically challenging imbalance between contrasting values in all subsequent human minds.

Adam's decision to follow Eve in sin also reflects an actualization of a latent structure of divided awareness, already foreshadowed in Milton's treatment of his strong inclination toward the physical side of Eve's nature. Like Eve, Adam acts irrationally, corrupting his reason and inverting the natural hierarchy of functions, yet doing so in terms of clearly articulated "reasons." Speaking to Eve of the "foretasted fruit" (IX, 929), he observes that the serpent lives, that he and Eve may hope to attain "proportional ascent," and that God will not "in earnest" destroy them (IX, 932–40). Adam continues this mode of rationalization until he arrives at his actual "reason" for joining Eve: "However I with thee have fixt my Lot, / Certain to undergo like doom" (IX, 952–53). At this moment of wrong choice, Adam's mind replicates the structure of split awareness that Eve has already exemplified. Ironically, he speaks, in the process of rationalization, of attaining "ascent" (936) when his choice leads him to descent. Thus Eve and Adam's separate sins imply an analogous structure of mind.[25]

In this discussion our chief aim has been to make clear certain formal conventions in the major characterizations of *Paradise Lost*. We have argued that "character" can best be understood as the interplay of conventions, some extrinsic and referential, some intrinsic and formal; following this proposition, we have tried to show Milton's remarkable originality in his approaches to characterization. A secondary aspect of our discussion has been to indicate the bearing of Ovid's formal narrative methods upon Milton and, hence, to clarify Milton's position in the Ovidian tradition. Milton's use of Ovidian conventions is more far-ranging, especially in characterization, than scholars have perceived, even when they were committed to discerning Ovid's influence.[26] There is no doubt that Milton knew the classical heritage, both roots and branches, but the synthesis seems, even today, overwhelming. A large part of this synthesis is demonstrably Ovidian. And, in certain aspects of their vision of the human condition, both epic poets hold similar ideas: men do not always reason well, or thread their ways through the tangles of dilemmic passions with objectivity. Rather, they rationalize in favor of one alternative because a dark level of their minds, not reason, would have it so. In this both poets see a structure of mental processes, an inherent aspect of human cerebration, that underlies all reasoning and all decisiveness. Both, through their formal conventions of characterization, the vertical paradigm of strategies implicit in their work, indicate that division, in passion and mind, is fundamentally transindividual, a problem of our race and not uniquely of oneself. The intricate, deep-reaching relation between Ovid and Milton would be instructive to follow out, but it is, at least in its full ramifications, beyond this essay's scope. In any case, since critical interpretation is an ideal activity in which, out of the densely infolded complexity of the work, much must needs be neglected, Milton will remain more fundamentally provocative than his critics' responses.

Mills College
University of Alberta

NOTES

1. On approaches to "character," see Rawdon Wilson, "The Bright Chimera: 'Character' as a Literary Term," *Critical Inquiry*, V (1979), 725–49, and "Drawing New Lessons from Old Masters: The Concept of 'Character' in the *Quijote*," *Modern Philology* (in press).

2. *Shakespearean Representation: Mimesis and Modernity in Elizabethan Tragedy* (Princeton, 1977), p. 8.

3. Watson Kirkconnell, *The Celestial Cycle* (Toronto, 1952).

4. That case has been put thoroughly by Joan S. Bennett, "God, Satan, and King Charles: Milton's Royal Portraits," *PMLA*, XLII (1977), 441–57.

5. For example, John Steadman, *Milton's Epic Characters: Image and Idol* (Chapel Hill, N.C., 1959), brilliantly expounds the theological commentaries on moral causation and derives from them a complex model to explain the disobedience of Adam and Eve. However, in *Milton and the Renaissance Hero* (Oxford, 1967), Steadman analyzes literary conventions of characterization. His practice thus corroborates our main point: character results from many conventions, some extrinsic, some intrinsic.

6. Diane Kelsey McColley, "Free Will and Obedience in the Separation Scene of *Paradise Lost*," *SEL*, XII (1972), 103–20; Stella P. Revard, "Eve and the Doctrine of Responsibility in *Paradise Lost*," *PMLA*, LXXXVIII (1973), 69–78. In particular, Revard argues the similarities of the characters: "Passion is not a peculiarly female disability . . . [it] is the very essence of all sin, be it Satan's, Eve's or Adam's" (p. 73).

7. Similar conventions occur elsewhere in classical literature, particularly in Virgil and Apollonius of Rhodes. See Robert Scholes and Robert Kellogg, *The Nature of Narrative* (New York, 1966). Nonetheless, we believe that Ovid presents the most extensive and varied use of the convention. Further, his influence was pervasive in the Renaissance and perhaps greater (though this is immeasurable) than that of Virgil.

8. The term *mind*, along with such related words as *reason*, echoes persistently through Milton's writings. William Ingram and Kathleen Swaim, in *A Concordance to Milton's English Poetry* (Oxford, 1972), list 102 references to "mind," "minded," "mindless," and "minds," some of which are, no doubt, perfunctory. But most are not. Fifty-five of these are in *Paradise Lost*.

9. See, for example, Hermann Frankel, *Ovid: A Poet Between Two Worlds* (Berkeley, 1945), p. 6, where Frankel discusses Ovid's interest in the *suasoria* and *controversia ethica*.

10. All citations of the *Metamorphoses* will refer to the parallel text edition of the Loeb Classical Library, translated in two volumes by Frank J. Miller (Cambridge, Mass., 1968), and will be given parenthetically in the text. *Paradise Lost* is quoted from *The Poetical Works of John Milton*, ed. Helen Darbishire (Oxford, 1958).

11. *The Central Problem of "Paradise Lost": The Fall of Man*, Essays and Studies on English Language and Literature, ed. S. B. Liljegren (Upsala, 1953), p. 19.

12. On Ovid's influence upon Milton, see Mary C. Brill, "Milton and Ovid" (Ph.D. dissertation, Cornell University, 1935), Davis P. Harding, *Milton and The Renaissance Ovid*, Illinois Studies in Language and Literature, 30 (Urbana, 1946), and Albert C. Labriola, "The Titans and the Giants: *Paradise Lost* and the Tradition of the Renaissance Ovid," *Milton Quarterly*, XII (1978), 9–16. However, Ovid's strategies of characterization, transmuted in *Paradise Lost*, have not been previously studied. The importance of mythological allusion to characterization has been commented upon, but we take that to be only one of the several elements of "character."

13. One of the most provocative of the many analyses of Eve's experience is Arnold Stein's in *Answerable Style: Essays on "Paradise Lost"* (Minneapolis, 1953), pp. 75–118.

14. In the Middle Ages, Narcissus was often seen as a symbol of vanity, vainglory, and arrogance. See Louise Vinge, *The Narcissus Theme in Western European Literature up to the Early Nineteenth Century*, trans. Robert Dewsnap et al. (Lund, 1967), p. 76. Narcissus could also be a symbol of beauty, as in Chaucer's *Knight's Tale* (1941–50). For an analysis of a highly sophisticated adaptation of the Narcissus myth, wherein the myth symbolizes the love of an idealized self, see Frederick Goldin, *The Mirror of Narcissus in the Courtly Love Lyric* (Ithaca, 1967), pp. 37, 45, et passim.

15. "Eve's Awakening," reprinted in *Milton: Modern Judgments*, ed. Alan Rudrum (London, 1968), p. 175.

16. Adam's "wooing" seems to hint at another aspect of the Narcissus myth in Ovid: the story of Echo (*Meta.* III.379–84).

17. We are speaking here in relative terms: the split awareness of Byblis, for instance, is rather extended, in that so much of the story is taken up with her psychomachia. Note, too, that she examines her incestuous longings only after explicitly dreaming of a sexual union with her brother (*Meta.* IX.468 ff.). Eve's dream in Book IV may be thought to

have some similarity to Byblis' dream. Northrop Frye remarks that it is not only a wish fulfilment but, since it involves flying, a "sexual dream as well." *Five Essays on Milton's Epics* (London, 1966), p. 79.

18. Eve is virtually personified as Beauty, reinforcing the contention that Milton must have been aware of the tradition that made Narcissus (with whom Eve has been very obviously linked) a symbol of beauty (see also VIII, 533). Furthermore, the physical descriptions of Eve inescapably recall the Petrarchan language of Tudor and Jacobean love poets. No doubt there are several reasons for this—we shall argue the central importance of one reason in this essay—but one deserves more consideration than it ordinarily receives: Milton was writing a poem about the archetypal expression of human love and not simply a theological epic.

19. Aristotle (*De Anima* II.vi–xii) gives the hierarchy as Vision, Hearing, Smell, Taste, and Touch. St. Augustine (*Confessions* X.6) retains this order but introduces the concept of the inner senses in which the external order is replicated. One descent *topos*, probably derived from or suggested by the hierarchy of the senses, usually omits smell, with sex becoming the "fifth sense." Thus from classical times—but not in Xenophon, where smell does occur in Hercules' temptation—through the Middles Ages the usual order appears to have been sight, sound, touch (the embrace, doubtless), the kiss (taste), and then sex. With but a slight variation, Ovid appears to be using this version, called the "*quinque lineae*," in the *Metamorphoses* (X.343–44). For obvious reasons, Milton used a version that put taste lowest. In *The Faerie Queene* Spenser uses the Aristotelian order to provide structure for Malaeger's assault upon Alma's Castle/Body. The scholarly comment in the *Variorum* (II.339–41) is instructive. For discussions of the "*quinque lineae*" *topos* see Ernst Curtius, *European Literature and the Latin Middle Ages*, trans. W. Trask (New York, 1953), pp. 512–14; Peter Dronke, "The Text of *Carmina Burana* 116," *Classica et Mediaevalia*, XX (1959), 167–69, and the more general discussion by J. F. Kermode, "The Banquet of Sense," *Bulletin of the John Rylands Library*, XLIV (1961), 68–99. In noting that taste and touch are the lowest of the senses (p. 69), and that they are "sometimes reversed" in the literature (p. 78, n. 1), Kermode allows us to see the "*quinque lineae*" as one version of the descent theme.

20. For an exhaustive treatment of the flight to the Heavens, see John Steadman, *Disembodied Laughter: Troilus and the Apotheosis Tradition* (Berkeley, 1972). In Eve's dream, Milton uses the apotheosis tradition as a visual pun, a negative analogue to the Neoplatonic ladder of love. Nor is this flight to a heaven of sensuality unforeshadowed: Eve has told Adam that her image in the lake had been framed by what "seem'd another sky" (IV, 459). The "heavenly bliss" to which the descent of the senses leads is an illusion: an ironic copy of the true case.

21. Stanley Fish analyzes the first half of this proposition fruitfully in *Surprised by Sin: The Reader in Paradise* (Berkeley, 1971). The second half of the proposition has been less remarked.

22. The sexual undertones of Satan's seduction of Eve are quite explicit. Even earlier than the phallic imagery of lines 631–34, Satan is described as moving "on his rear, / Circular base of rising folds, that tower'd / Fold above fold a surging Maze, his Head / Crested aloft" (497–500). Besides the phallicism of the description, there is also a suggestion that Satan acts like a courting animal, performing what might be called a mating dance to attract Eve's attention: "and of his tortuous Train / Curl'd many a wanton wreath in sight of Eve, / To lure her Eye" (516–18). (*O.E.D.* gives "lascivious, lewd," as the second sense for "wanton.")

23. In this light, Adam's talk on the passions engendered by touch becomes clear

(VIII, 526–33), for there also a circular pattern is followed when he moves from touch to "Beauty's powerful glance" (533).

24. *Five Essays*, p. 79.

25. Our discussion of the formal aspects of characterization in *Paradise Lost* supports Stella P. Revard's argument ("Eve and the Doctrine of Responsibility") that Milton does not make Eve either less or more responsible than Adam. Eve, she observes justly, is "female by subclassification: her primary classification is human" (p. 74).

26. Bearing in mind that there were two Ovids, the classical and the Renaissance figure, his influence upon Milton appears to have been on three levels: a large number of specific allusions; the incest imagery generally; and the formal convention of characterization that we have called split awareness which, in *Paradise Lost* at least, is renovated through interpenetration by another Ovidian convention, the descent of the senses seen as the opposite of the ladder of love.

STYLING THE STRIFE OF GLORY:
THE WAR IN HEAVEN

James G. Mengert

I. ANALOGUES AND THE NARRATIVE FRAME

WHEN ABDIEL, returning from Satan's proud towers in the north, arrives at the camp of the faithful angels, he finds preparations already under way for war. The lengthy periods of the first eighteen lines of Book VI are changed for an emphatic announcement: "Warr he perceav'd, warr in procinct."[1] The sweep and assurance of the opening lines, describing the changeless changes of eternity, its grateful vicissitudes, give way to the announcement of an anomalous change in heaven. The language, no less than the syntax, negotiates this shift from eternity to time. The phrase "in procinct" is a direct borrowing from the Latin *in procinctu*, prepared or girded for battle.[2] We know not only that there is to be war in heaven, but what kind of war—one out of the classics, from Hesiod, Homer, Virgil, Statius, with contributions from more recent history and literature.

One might well ask where else Milton would have gone for the language and incidents of a mighty war if not to the heroic tradition; such, after all, was his source for no small part of hell and even for some of Eden. And yet there is a crucial distinction to be made, a distinction best approached from the dramatic proprieties of the war's narration. Raphael, as well as Adam and Eve, can know nothing of the great military encounters of myth and human history. Furthermore, although Raphael might have been inspired (as Michael is later) with knowledge of these encounters, any reference to them by the angel might signal to the human couple that they or at least their descendants would indeed fall, a signal that would undercut the admonitory function of the narrative.[3] Consequently these encounters cannot be explicitly and directly invoked in simile and allusion. Addison and Newton, for example, praised the dramatic propriety of the simile of the birds (VI, 73–76) since it was an example that would be familiar to Adam. This simile was also, as commentators have noted, found in both Homer and Virgil.[4] Milton thus indirectly suggests the great classical epics while still suiting dramatic propriety. But there could not be many such felicities,

since there could not be many points of contact between the experience
of unfallen Adam and the tumultuous history of fallen man as embodied in his myths and histories.

It is through language and narrative incident, then, that Milton
must suggest the tradition to his readers; and any well-annotated edition of the poem provides ample testimony to the range and number of
Milton's implicit evocations of the heroic tradition. Even the overall
shape of the war may have been suggested, if we credit Newton's observation, by the method of the classical epic: "It is remarked by the crit-
icks in praise of Homer's battles, that they rise in horrour one above another to the end of the Iliad. The same may be said of Milton's battles."
And this observation as well:

And indeed within the compass of this one book we have all the variety of battles
that can well be conceived. We have a single combat, and a general engagement.
The first day's fight is with darts and swords, in imitation of the ancients; the second day's fight is with artillery, in imitation of the moderns. . . . And, when the
poet has briefly comprised all that has any foundation in fact and reality, he has
recourse to the fiction of the poets in their descriptions of the giants' war with the
Gods.[5]

The language contributes as well to the evocation of classical epic
and history. In addition to the initial and strategically placed "procinct," there are words such as "impediment," "interval," and "quadrate," all of which, in the senses and contexts in which Milton uses them,
echo the warfare of epic. The word "impediment" meant, in Latin, the
baggage of an army—the baggage was often placed in the center of the
"quadrate" formation.[6] And "interval," as used by Milton at line 105,
suggests its origin in Latin as the space between the ramparts of an army.
Nor are any of these words, including "procinct," used elsewhere in
Paradise Lost.

The main function of these "literalisms" in Book VI is to suggest the
classical contexts in which such words appear. Sometimes a particular
choice of meaning may be explained by these contexts. We may take
"circumfused" as an example. The Messiah has appeared in his chariot,

> Under whose Conduct Michael soon reduc'd
> His Armie, circumfus'd on either Wing,
> Under thir Head imbodied all in one.   (VI, 777–79)

Here "circumfused" means basically "surrounded with"; yet its appearance here is a bit unusual since the word (from *circumfundere*) literally
means a flowing around and so was associated with liquids or clouds or

often light. Milton so uses the word with reference to the ocean at VII, 624. The reason for its use here in Book VI lies in part, I think, in the word's frequent appearance in the Latin histories, especially in Caesar, where *circumfundere* means "to press upon, crowd upon." (The word also provides here a suggestion of the lightness of the angelic substance, especially now that it is no longer encumbered with the armor.)

We need not insist, however, on the peculiarly classical or even literary character of the terminology here; we are dealing rather with a continuous tradition. Much of the military terminology and many of the strategies in this book are both classical and modern, for seventeenth-century military theory and practice were very much indebted to and familiar with the ancient accounts of wars, historical and fabulous. The language and incidents of Book VI, then, would have suggested to Milton's readers a wide range of parallels to and analogues for the heavenly war. J. H. Hanford documented long ago the connection between the Renaissance and the ancient world in warfare:

The study of the military classics of antiquity, however superfluous it may be in the training of an officer at present, was then of the utmost practical importance. The application of the principles set forth in them had revolutionized the art of war in the early Renaissance and upon them the actual practice of Milton's time was based. They were therefore indispensable text-books for the soldier and as such they were edited and re-edited throughout the sixteenth and seventeenth centuries, with more or less adaptation to contemporary conditions but with little thought of their being superseded.[7]

So Milton evokes a tradition at once ancient and modern, literary and practical, fabulous and historical.

Thus the incidents, shape, and even language of this book evoke a tradition and history that the dramatic decorum must exclude. We may feel that Milton has successfully coped with a considerable handicap. And yet our experience of Book VI is necessarily affected by the particular mode of presentation (a mode itself sanctioned, to be sure, by epic precedent). If we recall the function and effect of the similes and allusions in the opening books of the poem, as well as in the descriptions of Eden and its inhabitants, we begin to appreciate what is different about Book VI. It is not merely a question of richness or display of learning; it involves the very claim to significance of the subject matter. Since the heavenly battle cannot be put in precise relation to earthly events and fables, it cannot exert fully its claim to be the archetypal battle: to be first, in relation to the battles of human history, and to be truer, in relation to the claims of myth and fable. The narrative method thus produces an almost paradoxical effect, for even while the range and shape of the battle invite maximum imaginative association with numerous military events, the lack of explicit reference to those events has the effect of limiting the significance of the War in Heaven. It is just another battle, albeit spectacular, in the long tradition of warfare. This peculiar effect of limitation I shall consider as a form of literalization.

Todd records a controversy relevant to my point here about literalization. At VII, 605, the angels celebrate the creative activity of the Son as being even greater than his destructive activity in the defeat of the "Giant Angels." Bentley emended this phrase to "rebel Angels" on the ground that the word "giant" suggests that the episode of the War in Heaven was as fabulous as the giant war of Hesiod. Pearce countered, unconvincingly, that Milton used the word "giant" not to suggest any mythical analogue, but rather to describe "that disposition of mind, which is always ascribed to giants, namely, a proud, fierce, and aspiring, temper." Then Thyer, rejecting Pearce's saving of appearances as a "little forced," met Bentley head on:

Milton, I doubt not, intended to allude to Hesiod's giant war; but I do not see with Dr. Bentley, that therefore he must insinuate that this relation is as fabulous as that. He probably designed, by this expression, to hint his opinion, that the fictions of the Greek poets owed their rise to some uncertain clouded tradition of this real event, and their giants were, if they had understood the story right, his fallen Angels.[8]

Thyer might have remembered the "giants on the earth in those days" of Genesis who had long been associated with the fallen angels. Hence Milton may have been evoking not a "false" and "pagan" tradition but a true biblical one. But then the rebel Titans had also been associated with the rebel angels. The point is that, even while Milton's account invites such associations, the method ensures some uncertainty as to the exact relationship between the War in Heaven and its many analogues. Bentley, typically, responds to the uncertainty by determining to clear it up; he wishes for a clear dissociation such as occurs in the narrator's description of the fall of Mulciber (I, 738–50), wherein the narrator declares authoritatively, once the parallel with the fall of Pandemonium's architect has been established, that the classical tradition was in error. This is not, however, Milton's characteristic procedure in Book VI.

This peculiar character of the method of the war's narration—at once suggesting the broadest possible relevance and yet limiting the significance of that relevance—enabled Milton to affirm the fact of such an encounter and yet avoid an explicit, comprehensive affirmation of the prophetic and spiritual significance of the events he describes in the book. It is a question perhaps of degree only, since the explicit affirmations elsewhere in the epic inevitably tend to support the claims of the war narrative; and any approach to this narrative must begin with the realization that Milton believed in the *fact* of some such encounter. But surely degree is important in the light of presenting a battle of spirits and in the light of the aversion to martial encounters that Milton evidences elsewhere in *Paradise Lost*. Exalting the claims of such encounters seems rather to be Satan's technique, in which the poet would prefer not to be too much implicated. It is Satan, we remember, who in the book tells Michael that the rebel angels "style" the battle as the "strife of Glorie." Elsewhere in the poem this collocation of "style" and military encounter occurs again, only to be rejected by another angelic narrator:

> Such were these Giants, men of high renown;
> For in those dayes Might onely shall be admir'd,
> And Valour and Heroic Vertu call'd;
> To overcome in Battel, and subdue
> Nations, and bring home spoils with infinite
> Man-slaughter, shall be held the highest pitch
> Of human Glorie, and for Glorie done
> Of triumph, to be styl'd great Conquerours,
> Patrons of Mankind, Gods, and Sons of Gods,
> Destroyers rightlier call'd and Plagues of men.   (XI, 688–97)

Michael describes the rise of Nimrod thus: he

> Will arrogate Dominion undeserv'd
> Over his brethren, and quite dispossess
> Concord and law of Nature from the Earth;
> Hunting (and Men not Beasts shall be his game)
> With Warr and hostile snare such as refuse
> Subjection to his Empire tyrannous:
> A mighty Hunter thence he shall be styl'd.   (XII, 27–33)

Such passages remind us of the progeny of Satan and of later reenactments of the heavenly battle. Nimrod and the great conquerors of history might well have been significantly related to the battle in heaven but for the dramatic mode of presentation. The ultimate heroism for Milton was spiritual; and, as he tells us in his invocation to Book IX, it is displayed in moral rather than in military encounters.[9] Allegorizing the battle—or turning it into a metaphor, as Arnold Stein would do[10]—can be an acceptable description of Milton's procedure here only if we recognize the peculiar mode of translation he employs—that is, only if we realize the peculiar, indeed, unique, way in which action relates to meaning in this book. To understand Milton's mode of translation into "allegory" or "metaphor" we must consider briefly the implications of the conventional mode of allegorizing martial combat.

There is an obvious but significant implication in an allegorical treatment of martial encounter. It is that such a treatment inevitably affirms that physical combat can be a vehicle of significant meaning. The form can express value. This implication is present here by definition: Milton is using a battle to say something and to say something about spiritual reality since this battle is given as one of spiritual beings. But this implication is precisely the one unwanted by Milton, at least in its suggestion of the most obvious points of correspondence between literal combat and spiritual value. For the relation of this battle to spiritual value seems clear: good against evil, virtue against vice, truth against falsehood. The implications of this correspondence for the Milton of *Paradise Lost* are awesome. Here is a real battle with clear political dimensions, one in which moral stature is rigorously determined and apparent. And in this battle the good side wins and the state is restored to ideal order. Everything about this battle, on the face of it, contradicts Milton's own painful experience of political reality; everything, on the face of it, celebrates the very values Milton had found to be false to the experience of human life in a fallen world.

In order to minimize what would seem to be the obvious spiritual significance of the battle, Milton's procedure must be quite the opposite of allegory.[11] The basic mode of translating action into meaning in this book can be characterized as a refusal to accept the obvious allegorical implications of the material. Here Milton depreciates the *spiritual* level by putting greater pressure on the *literal*. In this way he at once insists on the literal truth of the event he records and yet avoids what would be, in effect, an affirmation of the capacity of that event to convey spiritual significance directly. We have already seen one major way in which Milton emphasized the literal—the dramatic mode of presentation that tends to limit this celestial combat to the same plane as the combats of human history and story. He thus claims kinship with the epic tradition while implying that this celestial encounter has the same degree of reality as the siege at Troy or the campaigns of Caesar. True and real, yes; but hardly the archetypal encounter of good and evil, hardly a model for human spiritual life.

Raphael's own description of the mode of his narration—"lik'ning spiritual to corporal forms"—suggests at least a reversal of direction in developing correspondences between levels. Earlier, in Book V, the correspondence was viewed as a working *up* to more spiritual being; things "up to him return" and the "grosser feeds the purer." (It should be pointed out that even the word *correspondence* is not accurate in this context since it suggests that the levels are more discrete than Milton considered them to be; *continuity* is a better term. Because of the common "first matter" of all created things, there is an essential continuity in the chain of being.) Rather than a working up, the narration of the heavenly battle proposes to approach the same continuity from the other end. If the ladder of creation is a means by which things ascend to God, it can also be a means of descent from God. Since a descent is precisely what Satan's rebellion entails, physically and morally ("gross by sinning grown"), the method of narration that Raphael proposes is particularly apposite to his subject.

Two words that figure prominently in Raphael's dissertation in Book V reappear in significantly altered contexts in Book VI. Satan describes the potential for transformation that inheres in the materials underground: they are "of spiritous and fierie spume"

> till toucht
> With Heav'ns ray, and temperd they shoot forth
> So beauteous, op'ning to the ambient light.   (VI, 479–81)

The puns on "toucht" and "shoot" emphasize that the "spiritualization" of which Satan speaks is a physical process; what is inherent in matter is not spirit but chemical power. Raphael, on the other hand, makes the natural process gesture upward to the spiritual, rather than downward to the material:

> one first matter all,
> Indu'd with various forms, various degrees
> Of substance, and in things that live, of life;
> But more refin'd, more spiritous, and pure,
> As neerer to him plac't or neerer tending
> Each in thir several active Sphears assignd,
> Till body up to spirit work.   (V, 472–78)

Similarly, "concocted" describes part of the process involved in the making of artillery in Book VI; but it is as well a word used twice in Book V to describe a process of progressive spiritualization. Raphael eats "with keen dispatch / Of real hunger, and concoctive heate / To transubstantiate" (436–38). The weight of significance on a word like "transubstantiate" underlines the spiritual content of the natural process. By contrast, "concocted" in Book VI shares with words like "pregnant," "entrails," and "conception" the reduction of meaning from a physiological process that generates higher forms of life to a physiological process the end of which seems to be merely defecation: the belching and disgorging cannons, behind which are the rebel angels, whose "posture to displode" has decidedly obscene connotations. This is indeed "lik'ning spiritual to corporal forms." Raphael's narrative technique can thus be seen as a part of Milton's own literalizing design for Book VI.

We can observe Milton's employment of other devices as well that illustrate a similar determination to depreciate the obvious spiritual significance of the battle. Critics such as Fish and Stein have observed how frequently Milton disappoints conventional expectations for heroic encounter, how little real *effect* heroic physical action seems to have. This is another way in which Milton denies direct spiritual significance to epic values. If we start, not with the literal action as these critics do, but instead with the apparently "given" spiritual meaning, we discover the same balked connection between meaning and physical action. It has struck almost every reader—Dr. Johnson not the least among them— how little effect spiritual condition seems to have on performance in the battle. Milton must accord some degree of superiority to the unfallen angels, but in no instance is the moral difference decisive. The good angels cannot feel pain and are not fatigued; yet they are not thereby rendered the superior warriors. Conversely, the fallen angels suffer pain and fatigue; but these liabilities seem to incite them to greater resourcefulness in the battle. Indeed, the good angels seem every bit as destructive to the heavenly landscape as are the Satanic forces, although they are less methodical about it. Milton in fact seems deliberately to echo, in a purely physical and neutral context, St. Paul's "fiery darts." But whereas in St. Paul the fiery darts are the weapons of the wicked host to be quenched by the shield of faith, in Milton's battle both sides employ them, so that the darts "vaulted either host with fire." Milton could not ignore moral distinctions between the two forces; but he does not permit these distinctions to issue in decisive physical distinctions.

Here we can appreciate the uniquely definitive nature of Milton's treatment of physical combat; for by minimizing the obvious spiritual values that the literal level would seem to have, Milton might be said to create a value vacuum for the literal level. Whatever "meaning" is to emerge from his battle would then have to be negative, developed out of the very gap between action and meaning. This is exactly the kind of meaning some of the best critics of Book VI have offered. Joseph Summers derives this meaning from Milton's treatment of martial combat:

Physical heroism is not enough. Knowledge and intelligence are not enough. Abandonment to action, patriotism, or even self-sacrifice is not enough. . . . To claim that we can change the course of history, even when fighting on the side of God, is also absurd—although, without any claims, we must act as if our actions could do so, for we do not know their ultimate effects.[12]

Likewise, Stanley Fish sees Milton manipulating the reader with a view toward forcing him "to separate the drama from the heroism." Such critics say, in effect, that the particular literal context is not significant and that this is precisely the significance of Milton's treatment. Whereas the allegorical treatment implies that a particular action or configuration of physical forces is especially appropriate for figuring forth spiritual realities, Milton's treatment implies that *any* action is appropriate because no one is necessarily so. Love of God or trust in him can be displayed, as Fish observes, in any circumstances and roles in life. However valid such a statement may be theologically, in terms of literary representation Milton's procedure signals the end of both the heroic and the allegorical traditions. For the former is predicated on the physical as itself a value, while the latter is predicated on the ability of physical activity and things to adumbrate "corresponding" spiritual and psychological values. What is at stake, fundamentally, is the analogical universe. (What is at stake in terms of literary theory is the whole notion of genre and "styles.") Milton is part of the tradition because he does, after all, use a battle to convey a spiritual meaning. He is the last of that tradition because his meaning is that spiritual meaning has no necessary correspondence to the vehicle used to convey it. Thomas Greene has some comments about Milton's epic as a whole that seem especially relevant to Book VI: "It is important to see how the last of the great poems in conventional epic dress contained within itself, not accidentally but essentially, the seeds of the genre's destruction."[13]

II. The Metamorphosing Language

We have seen that the tendency for analogues of the heavenly battle to become identifications with it is one of the means that Milton employs to depreciate the spiritual significance of his battle, to thicken, as it were, his literal context without at the same time claiming more meaning for that context. In this way Milton subverts the obvious significance of such an encounter.

But there were available other sources from which to provide himself with means for representing this war. The biblical references to and uses of beasts, especially in Revelation, had contributed to a tradition of representing a spiritual combat as an assault of beasts or monsters. Further, once the revolt of the angels had been associated with the classical myth of the Titans' war on Zeus, the various representations and interpretations of this latter encounter became obvious sources for the Christian poet. Certainly some aspects of meaning traditionally derived from the Titans' revolt—such as materialism and atheism—are present in Milton's version of the revolt in heaven. According to Merritt Hughes, "The Titans had become a symbol of moral degeneracy—hence the half-human, half-serpentine form often attributed to them; and they had also become a symbol of the free-thinkers who despise or deny the gods."[14] The Dutch poet Vondel's *Lucifer*, Hughes points out, represents the final defeat of Satan by his transformation into a multiform beast symbolizing the seven deadly sins. Hughes sees traces of this bestial allegorical tradition in the various imbrutings of Satan throughout *Paradise Lost*. Yet he finds no evidence of this tradition in the one book of the poem that would seem most to warrant it: "More remarkable is Milton's deliberate intention to keep away from allegory in the main scene of his celestial battle."[15] Once again, in his avoidance of explicitly feral representations, we see Milton refusing to provide spiritually significant physical details.

Yet Davis P. Harding has discerned parallels between Milton's Satan and Spenser's monstrous dragon of Book I of *The Faerie Queene*. Apparently some "traces" of the allegorical representation are to be found in the battle. Harding compares the passage in Spenser wherein the dragon receives its death blow from the Red Cross Knight (I.11.54) with Satan's reaction to Abdiel's sword stroke. The verbal parallels are very strong indeed.[16] The effect of Michael's sword stroke offers another, more subtle echo of Spenser. Satan, lying wounded in his chariot, is "Gnashing for anguish and despite and shame." In Spenser the word "gnash" is associated with moral depravity and bestiality. Those who "gnash" in *The Faerie Queene* are Furor, Pain and Strife, the beast Envy, Hatred, a Pagan, the monster-tyrant Gerioneo, the covetous fiend, the wicked forester, a baby-snatching bear, and the Savage Man, this last being the only morally acceptable character, although his gnashing—when attacking Timias—is decidedly an aspect of his savage nature. (And behind Spenser and Milton lies the familiar passage from Matthew viii, 12: "But the children of the kingdom shall be cast out into utter darkness: there shall be weeping and gnashing of teeth.") Thus Satan here in Book VI is the last (or the first) in a long line of moral monsters, one not so explicitly monstrous as those in Spenser, but subtly revealing his lineage nevertheless.

There are, then, some distinctive traces of an allegorical tradition of associating physical bestiality with moral depravity in Book VI. We should be sensitive, however, to the differences, to the considerable indirection with which Milton utilizes the tradition. Satan is clearly not a dragon or a half-serpent or a multiform monster. Here again the narrative frame Milton chose for the war becomes relevant. Wild beasts, to say nothing of monsters, would hardly be comprehensible to Raphael's unfallen auditors. Again Milton must limit himself to a form of indirection, but again this limitation serves his design of limiting the significance and stature of the battle. Perhaps the best way to pursue this point is through an examination of the "animalizing" language of Book VI. Let us begin with a description of the fierce encounter as rendered by Raphael:

> now storming furie rose,
> And clamour such as heard in Heav'n till now
> Was never, Arms on Armour clashing bray'd
> Horrible discord, and the madding Wheeles
> Of brazen Chariots rag'd; dire was the noise
> Of conflict; over head the dismal hiss
> Of fiery Darts in flaming volies flew. (VI, 207–13)

(The very contortions of the syntax in the first lines of this quotation anticipate the horrible transformations.) Three implements of war are mentioned in this passage: armor, chariots, and darts. Each implement derives part of its furious energy from association with animals. Armor "brayed"; that is, it made a loud, jarring sound. But another, perhaps more common, meaning was the sound made by animals, especially asses. Likewise the madding wheels of a raging chariot suggest a rabid dog—"mad" had such a meaning, and "rage" derives from the Latin *rabies* (whence our word for the disease), which was used in Latin first of all to designate the madness and frenzy of dogs and other animals. Finally, the "hiss / Of fiery Darts" suggests the sounds made by serpents, geese, and so on. (We recall the "hiss" of the devils' wings in Book I that led us into the bee simile.)

The Father characterizes the battle in these animal terms: "Warr wearied hath perform'd what Warr can do, / And to disorder'd rage let loose the reines" (695–96). So also Michael was sent forth "to tame / These disobedient."[17]

The real force of this animalizing tendency is reserved for the rebel angels. Let us look at a rather quiet example. Gabriel has bested

> Moloc furious King, who him defi'd,
> And at his Chariot wheeles to drag him bound
> Threatn'd, nor from the Holie One of Heav'n
> Refrein'd his tongue blasphemous. (VI, 357–60)

The spelling of "refreined" in the first edition gives a clear indication of its etymology and puns on the English "rein." The word "refrain" is derived from the Latin *refrenare*, to bridle. In the context of this passage where Moloch threatens to drag Gabriel at his chariot wheels, we cannot resist the quiet implication that Moloch's tongue—and by synecdoche Moloch himself—is something like a runaway horse. His chariot is not running away with Gabriel; instead his tongue is running away with him. Appropriately, Moloch flees from the victorious Gabriel "bellowing."

In Book IV, when Ithuriel's spear, heaven-tempered, touched Satan "Squat like a Toad," he immediately returned to his proper shape. The touches of such heaven-tempered weapons in Book VI have precisely the opposite effect. They metamorphose Satan and his crew from their proper shapes into the brutes they will become: "then Satan first knew pain, / And writh'd him to and fro convolv'd" (327–28). The word "writhed" appears only once more in the poem, at X, 569, where it describes the contortions of the devils transformed into serpents. Likewise, "convolved," meaning coiling or twisting, very much suggests a serpentine motion.

Thus the striking animal simile at lines 856–58, where the fleeing angels are described as "a Heard / Of Goats or timerous flock" is a culminating description, making explicit the previous animal implications of the language. And yet a goat simile is hardly Vondel's literal transformation of Lucifer into a multiform monster. Indeed, if we review the animal suggestions in Book VI, we discover that, with the appropriate exception of the serpent, all the animals are domestic: asses, dogs, horses, geese, goats, sheep. In part this language serves quietly to denigrate the threat represented by the rebels. We are witnessing a kind of barnyard uproar with the boundaries of disorder set—supervised by the farmer or shepherd from an all-powerful perspective. Wild beasts carry a threat and an imaginative dimension that are not accorded to the domestic rebel angels, for all their posturing and power. In its aspect of denigration, this domestic animal language contributes to Milton's purpose of limiting the significance of the battle as a confrontation of cosmic, spiritual forces. While the tendency to identify the battle with its historical analogues makes the angels seem less like angels and more like men, this suggestion of domestic animals associates the angels with still lower levels of the scale of being.

Milton is certainly unobtrusive in suggesting animal characteristics for the combatants; any explicit representation would have defeated his purpose by inviting allegorical interpretation and consequently by enhancing the claim of the battle's significance. These suggestions are more of an atmosphere than anything else; and, although they attach principally to the rebels—anticipating later bestial transformations within the poem and as the brute-idols of human history—so pervasive is their operation that the whole atmosphere of the battle is affected.

So Milton took a physical combat with apparently obvious spiritual significance and refused to accept the correspondences. Similarly, he utilized an aspect of physical representation—animal imagery—that came complete with well-established allegorical significance; but he drastically attenuated that significance—first of all by turning explicit representation into verbal suggestion or simile, and then by altering the *type* of animal from wild to domestic. A multiform monster obviously requires interpretation; even a dragon, with its inevitable biblical affiliations, trails an extensive history of significance. Half-human, half-serpentine figures invite speculation. But an ass is an ass and a goat a goat. In his attenuation of the significance usually accorded this type of representation, Milton seems to be saying that, just as the true Christian virtues can be practiced in any calling or context, so a moral monster may come in many familiar forms, like the wolf in sheep's clothing.

III. DEMONIC CORRESPONDENCES

What Milton seems to be about in his representation of this battle is a depreciation of signs or vehicles of significance. In effect, his treatment is a refusal to treat his literal material as a sign of something else. This attitude has its converse in Satan's, for Satan is engaged in quite the opposite enterprise in this book. We recall that it is Satan who affirms the significance of the encounter as a "strife of glory." It is also Satan who realizes that this affirmation is very much a product of "style." He is the symbolist or allegorist par excellence for whom all things and words are implements for use. In Satan's perspective all things are viewed in terms of their utility, of their becoming rather than being. Let us consider Satan's speech to his disconcerted crew after the first day of battle:

> Which of us who beholds the bright surface
> Of this Ethereous mould whereon we stand,
> This continent of spacious Heav'n
> · · · · · · · ·
> Whose Eye so superficially surveyes
> These things, as not to mind from whence they grow.
>
> (VI, 472–77)

Satan offers a new way of looking at the world. Isabel MacCaffrey has interpreted this new way:

In a world without sin, "bright surfaces" reflect the essences of archetypal beings; they are sharp, simple, unmistakable, instantly visible. This is the first time that a survey of them has been called superficial; there is no such thing as superficiality in a world of Platonic essences, but Satan invents it by distinguishing between the surfaces and the elements "from whence they grow." Surface and implied depth are complementary aspects of single beings whose source is God, properly regarded, but Satan's dark imagination insists on tearing the two apart and exploring the depths alone.[18]

The language in the Milton passage rewards closer scrutiny. Milton underlines the novelty of this way of observing the world by the use of "ethereous," unique in Milton and new to English. The word "ethereal" is so common in *Paradise Lost*, and in the very phrase "ethereal mould" (II, 139; VII, 356), that the new word seems all the more deliberate and striking—a new word for a new way of looking at matter as instinct not with heavenly spirit but with chemical power. The word "superficially" also occurs only here in all Milton's poetry; the words "superficially surveys" have a decided literal resonance of method and measurement. So *superficies* in Latin often meant a measurement of length and breadth, without depth, and "superficial" had had this meaning in English since 1571. Similarly, "survey" can denote a quite precise act of determining the measurements of a portion of land surface. Further, the word "continent" contributes to this new view as well. Its oldest and still current meaning in Milton's time—from the Latin—was "that which contains." The land continent, the ethereous mould, is thus implicitly seen as a container, as a means and a medium and not as "itself." The act of separating the world into divisions of surface and depth, which MacCaffrey describes, is simultaneously an act of exploitation of the world. Divided into classifications, the world can be manipulated by the mind. Sight itself is an instrument of the mind here—the eye as surveyor's theodolite. Although MacCaffrey is quite correct about the initial separation of surface and depth here, nevertheless Satan's point is that one can discover, can "read" the depth from the surface. With the proper instruments and methods, all things become signs. What Satan offers is his own mechanical version of the process that elsewhere produces, through the touching and tempering of heaven's ray, the higher products of the surface. His process transforms the crude materials of the depth, not into higher forms such as fruits and flowers, but into "implements of mischief." The very word "implements"—also peculiar to this book—underlines the functional character even of the *products*. The crude materials are read in terms of how they can be used, but so also the "finished products" of these materials are perceived in a similarly functional context. What Satan postulates is actually an endless process of reading everything as gesturing beyond itself to some further thing. For the unfallen, the plants and gems of the surface "adorn" heaven; they are adornments, not implements. Their function is not to be distinguished from their being.

Raphael as much as acknowledges this new application of the mind to things when he speaks of men in later times as being perhaps "inspir'd / With dev'lish machination." At least three meanings of "machination" current in Milton's time are suggested here: plotting, intrigue; the construction of a machine; the machine itself, sometimes used of a weapon. The activity of mind becomes itself mechanical; like the machine it devises, the mind is for use. Everything is in motion here—the mind, the body in constructing, and even the machine constructed. If we could contrast the proper and improper function of things by the terms "adornment" and "implement," then perhaps the corresponding contrast for mental activity would be "contemplation" and "machination." Adam declares that "In contemplation of created things / By steps we may ascend to God" (V, 511–12). The activity of ascent is contemplation, and here in Book VI the activity of descent is machination.

It is appropriate that the language of this book is constantly suggesting methodologies or systems, all instruments of power for developing or interpreting the meaning of "things." Both in its tendency to call attention to itself and in the meanings it uses or implies, the language of this book reminds us very much of processes chemical, physical, medical, mathematical, technical, even legal. Milton was the first to use the word "discontinuous" in English; but related, as it is here, to a wound, it has a clearly marked medical ancestry. Verity informs us that "Bacon uses *discontinuation* in the medical sense, 'solution of continuity,' in a list of diseases. . . . Cf. also his Essay *Of Unity in Religion:* 'as in the natural body a wound or solution of continuity is worse than a corrupt humour, so in the spiritual.'"[19] Likewise, "displode" appears in English for the first time here in Book VI and is a literal adaptation of the Latin. But however new "displode," "displosion" had been current at least since 1656; and, significantly, the two occurrences of the word cited in the *OED* (before the publication of *Paradise Lost* in 1667) are either technical or medical: Thomas Blount's *Glossographia* (1656) and Gideon Harvey's *Morbus Anglicus: or, the anatomy of consumptions* (1666). Blount wrote books on legal subjects; Harvey, on medical ones.

Such words as "divisible," "dissipation," "contraction," "composition," "indissolubly," "precipitate," and "combustion," although not always used in an explicitly scientific or technical sense, nevertheless create a scientific atmosphere for the battle. Even the use of "assessor" to describe the Son beside the Father—a literal signification new in English—strikes us as curiously technical. The word meant an advisor expert in technical matters. In all these literalisms the narrator, like the new philosophers and the fallen angels, is going back to the "originals of nature," but the movement seems designed to suggest the process itself. We must observe here, however, that Milton's own technique of putting pressure on the literal in Book VI relates to Satan's functionalism in a complex way. The sheer abundance of terminology and the literal, physical meanings of much of the language serve to thicken Satan's media until these implements and methods take on weight and substance. Thus Milton is at once able to represent the Satanic preoccupation with making things into signs or vehicles of significance while demonstrating the ultimate psychological and spiritual truth of such a preoccupation: that its real effect is to make ends out of means, to transform putative instruments of liberation into vast encumbrances. Surely this is the meaning of the armor that so bothered Dr. Johnson—an instrument of power producing only impotence. So the language turns itself into a thing that restricts; its literal meanings lie heavy as physical objects. The angels thought to turn the features of landscape into implements of warfare, but in the end those very implements—the hills—that seemed so light and usable, lie with an enormous weight of "thingness" on them. So also the language thickens "obvious hill"—something clear and evidently significant—into an obstruction literally thrust in their way.

Of course, verbal communication itself is the most obvious methodology or system of signs. Book VI also examines the forms of communication among men in society; and, characteristically, in this book using words as links between levels of signification is a Satanic occupation. We can appreciate the point most readily by contrasting Abdiel's unfulfilled expectations with the rebels' punning exhibition.

Abdiel initially assumes a relationship between physical and verbal contact when he expresses his conviction that "he who in debate of Truth hath won, / Should win in Arms" (122–23). From the Old French *débatre*, "debate" meant literally "to fight." The word functions here on the physical as well as the verbal level. Abdiel postulates a kind of correspondence between two levels of activity, a correspondence expressed and validated by the ability of "debate" to operate on two levels simultaneously. As the event proves, however, that correspondence is anything but clear. Abdiel's encounter with Satan is not decisive. The implication is that one may win in one kind of debate but lose in another.

In the notorious punning exhibition put on by Satan and Belial, the various aspects and characteristics of verbal debate have direct relation to physical debate. The capacity of language itself to combine literal and figurative significations determines its utility as a vehicle, as an instrument. It is Satan who sees the "meanings" of things in this book and it is Satan for whom the medium of language seems to work.

There are other examples of such correspondences between physical and verbal encounters. Satan, with his scorn somewhat strangled by his syntax, defies Michael thus:

> Hast thou turnd the least of these
> To flight, or if to fall, but that they rise
> Unvanquisht, easier to transact with mee
> That thou shouldst hope, imperious, & with threats
> To chase me hence? (VI, 284–88)

A "transaction," usually commercial and implying a set form, seems at first an odd word to use here for physical encounter and aptly communicates Satan's scorn for Michael. Perhaps it was more than scorn that motivated the choice of this particular word: *transigere* meant literally to thrust or stick a weapon through, to stab; it could also mean to settle any business. So martial and commercial contact merge neatly in the word "transact."

Raphael describes the degeneration of the battle into chaos: "So Hills amid the Air encounterd Hills / Hurl'd to and fro with jaculation dire" (664–65). The word "jaculation" obviously and rather obtrusively means a literal throwing; yet we cannot exclude the impression of a physical hurling accompanied by a dreadful verbal (e)jaculation. (The submerged contrast between the verbal ejaculation that was often a short prayer and the physical jaculation of hills is quiet but telling.) Physical and verbal seem inextricable.

When the second day of battle dawns, the two armies approach each other for the encounter: "At interview both stood" (555). Milton's use of "interview" here to mean a mutual view was rare in his own time; in fact, this instance in Book VI is the last recorded use of the word in this sense. Its usual meaning was the modern one of a meeting face to face for a formal conference.

The council of war is itself a verbal debate that parallels the physical debate of arms; and words take on the aspect of weapons: the debate of truth is often "far worse to beare /. Then violence." Stanley Fish has observed this parallel and notes, "Forensic wars are not unlike real ones."[20] And the language, in its simultaneous applicability to the physical and mental, enforces the parallel. Satan holds out to his dispirited followers the hope for "perhaps more valid Armes"; "valid" is used here in the literal sense, of things, strong and powerful. This recovery of a Latin literalism was rather new to English (1656)—as was the particular "arm" that Satan devises. Other and older meanings in English may apply as well: "Of arguments . . . : well-founded and applicable; sound and to the point" (*OED*). We are back to Abdiel's double debate and the "terms of weight" of the punning exhibition. Satan wants something that will clinch the argument as well as win the war. And the rebels' shields "with boastful Argument portraid" not only present images or themes of glory; they associate physical and forensic prowess. Rather than means for arriving at truth, logic and the rational process become means of conquest.

In Satan's lexicon, then, physical martial encounter does have significance, and the encounter corresponds to encounters on the intellectual and social levels. In Book VI it seems to be Satan who exploits extended meanings, of things and of words. Here Satan participates in Milton's own usual operation of utilizing the multisignificance of words. The effect, however, is actually to reduce the utility of language as a vehicle of genuine communication. The exaggerated, self-conscious nature of the punning display undercuts the genuine associative capacity of language by making the process so patent and mechanical. And notice how the association with physical combat reduces the corresponding types of verbal encounter to formalized, aggressive modes of contact: debates, transactions, arguments, interviews. Communication becomes merely another form of attack, like "subtlety" as a form of conquest.[21]

So we have on the one hand Milton, depreciating the significance of his vehicle, and on the other Satan, extending the claims of his. Perhaps the armor is, after all, one of the best metaphors for the complex relation of Milton to Satan in Book VI. Milton himself accepts the armor as the appropriate limitation—it constrains him to the physical, literal level. (It is like the narrative frame, the restrictions of which have directed the shaping of the war's significance. It was a barrier chosen by the poet, one he could have breached at any time but did not.) The armor is an "exclusive bar" that properly reduces the pretensions of this martial combat to figure forth spiritual truths directly. Satan, on the other hand, accepts the armor as an instrument of power, as a vehicle. To him it is an instrument for imposing his will and his meaning on things. Milton's literalizing technique thus refuses to participate in Satan's pretensions, while at the same time representing the effect of those pretensions: a world of means become ends, vast encumbrances that do not liberate the self but, because they are merely extensions of the self, imprison it. The poet represents the Satanic preoccupation with utility by an appropriately exaggerated focus on Satan's various media until they are thickened into a resistant "thingness." In this way the poet makes Satan's competing strategy a part of his own.

Indeed, in a certain sense the real issue of the significance of the battle is joined right here in Milton's unique kind of collaboration with Satan. For Milton is himself *using* Satan as a vehicle; he uses Satan as part of his own solution to the problem of establishing significance for the battle. But he allows that vehicle to yield its significance precisely by letting the vehicle "be" itself—by letting the logic of Satan's own nature limit his creative pretensions by the very means he employs to express them. In this way Milton founds his own claim to creative power not on the violations of things but on his sensitivity to their "proper motion," to the logic of their own natures. He therefore never actually offers a claim of his own for the significance of the physical events, but rather focuses on Satan's perverse method for claiming significance and incorporates this perversion into a model for the proper method by which one claims significance for anything. Milton's self-confinement within the restrictions of the narrative frame is a part of this model also: he insists on letting the logic of this frame shape the presentation of the battle, in terms of both military analogues and imagery. Hence it is not so much a merely "negative meaning" that emerges from the war as Milton constructs it; he is not so much implying that the particular vehicle does not matter as he is demonstrating that what does matter is the *way* that vehicle is used to yield meaning.

Finally, one of the purposes of Book VI is to expose and overcome the demonic side of Milton's own vocation: the temptation for a man who is master of his medium to "create" his own significance, to use his ability as an instrument of power rather than as a servant of truth. According to Joseph Mazzeo's reading of St. Augustine's *Christian Doctrine*, only God has the power "to confer on realities their significance as signs." It is impossible for man—or Satan—to create such signs. "They can be discovered, in Scripture or in life, and they can be used, but they cannot be invented."[22] What Milton explores and exposes in Book VI is the diabolic ambition to do exactly that, to invent signs, to confer one's own significance on things. What Milton does is consistently to treat his own and Satan's signs as things, and by his refusal to endorse Satan's creative ambitions in Book VI, the poet authenticates his own claim to recreate, in collaboration with the Son, the true creation of Book VII.

Atlanta, Georgia

NOTES

1. All quotations from *Paradise Lost* are taken from *The Student's Milton*, ed. Frank Allen Patterson (New York, 1933).

2. The phrase, as a direct borrowing from the Latin, had been current in English since 1611. We are not, then, necessarily dealing with a direct, Miltonic Latinism, though the point—*pace* Alastair Fowler—is hardly important, since Milton's readers would have recognized the word's source and its characteristic context. (The entire phrase—"Warr he perceav'd, warr in procinct"—becomes even more emphatic when we recall Aubrey's report that Milton pronounced the letter *r* very hard.)

3. I owe this observation to Professor J. Max Patrick, in a letter to me.

4. Newton is quoted in *The Poetical Works of John Milton*, ed. Rev. Henry J. Todd, 2nd ed. (London, 1809), III, 266n.; Anne Davidson Ferry has discussed the propriety of the similes in Raphael's narration in *Milton's Epic Voice: The Narrator in "Paradise Lost"* (Cambridge, Mass., 1963), pp. 70–73.

5. Todd, *Poetical Works*, III, 321n., 323n.

6. Keightley glossed "quadrate" at line 62 as "the *agmen quadratum* of the Romans, in which the baggage was placed in the centre"; he cited Sallust and Tacitus as examples. *The Poems of Milton* (London, 1859), I, 420n.

7. "Milton and the Art of War," reprinted in *John Milton: Poet and Humanist* (Cleveland, 1966), p. 188. The essay originally appeared in *Studies in Philology*, XVIII (1921), 232–66.

8. Todd, *Poetical Works*, III, 411n. Along these same lines we may call attention to the title "Divine Hystorian" that Adam gives Raphael in Book VIII (6–7). This is Milton's only use of the word "historian," and its meaning combines the sense of a storyteller (as the epic poets were, or as Aeneas and Odysseus were within the epics) with the sense of a writer of history (as Tacitus, Sallust, Caesar, and others were). Raphael seems only a *divine* historian in a hyperbolic or complimentary sense; that is, we are left more with an impression of similarity than of difference.

9. Stanley Fish has developed his fine interpretation of the strategies and meanings of this book on this aversion of Milton to military heroics. According to Fish, the battle is constructed to undercut and expose to ridicule its own epic values. See *Surprised by Sin: The Reader in "Paradise Lost"* (London, 1967), chap. 4.

10. *Answerable Style* (Minneapolis, 1953), pp. 17–37. Stein's discussion of this book of the poem is a very perceptive and seminal study, though I draw back, as will be evident from the rest of my discussion, from Stein's characterization of the book as an "epic farce." Fish notes, for example, that his own interpretation begins with an acceptance of the validity of Stein's interpretation (p. 179). George deForest Lord has explored the tradition of farce in the epic with illuminating results for Milton's treatment of the War in Heaven in *Heroic Mockery* (Newark, Delaware, 1977).

11. The same point has been made about *Paradise Lost* generally by John M. Steadman in chapter 8 of his *Milton and the Renaissance Hero* (Oxford, 1967); but Steadman does not address Milton's treatment of the War in Heaven in these terms. Such statements as this one, however, seem to invite us to ask about the war: "Basing his argument on spiritual conflict rather than physical warfare, he prefers to present moral ideas immediately through direct imitation rather than mediately through allegory" (pp. 183–84).

12. *The Muse's Method: An Introduction to "Paradise Lost"* (London, 1962), p. 137.

13. *The Descent from Heaven: A Study in Epic Continuity* (New Haven, 1963), p. 407.

14. *Ten Perspectives on Milton* (New Haven, 1965), p. 214.

15. Ibid., p. 216.

16. *The Club of Hercules: Studies in the Classical Background of "Paradise Lost,"* Illinois Studies in Language and Literature, 50 (Urbana, 1962), pp. 55–57.

17. The only other use of "tame" in the poem occurs at XII, 191, where the hardened Pharaoh is tamed by the plagues—a clear analogy to the Son's activity and effect here in Book VI. Significantly, in the passage in Book XII, the Pharaoh is referred to merely as the "River-dragon."

18. *"Paradise Lost" as "Myth"* (Cambridge, Mass., 1959), p. 163.

19. A. W. Verity, ed., *Paradise Lost* (Cambridge, 1929), II, 515.

20. Fish, *Surprised by Sin*, p. 170.

21. This same point about Satan's language, especially the punning exhibition, has been made by Stephen Wigler, "Outrageous Noise and the Sovereign Voice: Satan, Sin, and Syntax in 'Sonnet XIX' and Book VI of *Paradise Lost*," *Milton Studies*, X, ed. James D. Simmonds (Pittsburgh, 1977), esp. p. 159: "Satan's language ceases to be a tool of communication and regresses to the level of primitive aggression."

22. *Renaissance and Seventeenth-Century Studies* (New York, 1964), p. 6.

"BOUNDS PRESCRIB'D": MILTON'S SATAN AND THE POLITICS OF DEVIANCE

Marcia Landy

MILTON'S USE of Satan and Satanic figures affirms the continuing importance in the seventeenth century of traditional Christian images and the continuing appeal of the Satanic as a central factor in an ideology of death. Like other medieval and Renaissance writers, Milton was challenged by the traditional Christian use of the devil as a means of visualizing death and signifying resistance to it.[1] But the relationship between death and the devil in Milton's work reveals more than the traditional religious equation of sin and death; it reveals Milton's attitudes toward historical change, revolution, law, politics, domestic relations, and community. Milton's representations of death are not primarily concerned with biological death. They are concerned with and dramatize his struggle to comprehend, if not control, history and historical change.[2]

Milton's portraits of the Satanic, most particularly of Satan in *Paradise Lost*, have long been thought to constitute a critique of temporal kingship with its dependence on external, ritualized, and coercive forms of power. The notion that Satan also dramatizes the threat of rampant individualism, "the anarchy of individual interpretation"[3]— coercive and extreme, too, in its flouting of the collective good—has not been so well analyzed. In this latter respect, Milton's historical insights can be most appreciated. His Satan is not an anticipatory and submerged image of the true revolutionary individual born before his time. He is more properly the result of Milton's political and personal assessment of the dangers of individualism masked in revolutionary zeal and the rhetoric of liberty.

Christopher Hill reminds us that while Milton shared many affinities with the radical thinkers of his time, he could not accept Ranter antinomianism "nor the early Quaker doctrine of the self-sufficiency of the inner light."[4] Milton's mistrust of self-sufficiency and false notions of individual autonomy are nowhere more evident than in his insistence on "merit," which restricts absolute and spontaneous ideas of egalitarianism. His emphasis on the importance of the Fall of Man, with its attendant ravages of reason and will, functions in a similar critical manner. Satan's rejection of the rule of conscience, of history, of education, of the internalizing of God's will, his unabashed individualism, his refusal to find a balance between liberty and discipline—all document his absolute disregard for external restraints, which becomes one, where extremes meet, with the absolutism of sovereign power.

The character of Satan can be read as anticipating a new historical conception of the power of deviancy as a form of social constraint. The delinquent, the criminal, the madman, the antisocial individual assume increasing historical and literary importance as the old theatrical displays of political power—with their scenarios of public torture, punishment, and exposure—give way to a more psychological, abstract, secular, hidden, and internalized drama of social control, where conceptions of normality and abnormality rather than good and evil govern acceptable and unacceptable behavior.

Through Satan, Milton evokes the fear of death as an instrument for controlling individual and group behavior;[5] deviance becomes the connecting link between the threat of death and the inculcation of proper social and political attitudes. Satan's power derives from traditional associations with the scapegoat, but, more significantly, from Milton's association of Satan with historical conditions peculiar to the seventeenth century. Rather than diminishing with the rise of rationalism, the threat of deviance became an integral mode of social control by substituting criminal and madman for demon and witch, a result of the emphasis in bourgeois ideology on individualism and self-determination rather than on collectively determined modes of action.

Satan, while sharing certain archetypal qualities of the scapegoat, actually has more in common with notions of the delinquent as they emerge in the seventeenth century. He takes on a historical shape determined by a society which is in the long process of transforming itself from an older moral economy to the economy of a free market. This change becomes even more evident in the eighteenth century, as the works of E. P. Thompson and Michel Foucault demonstrate.[6] Increasingly the deviant and the fear of deviance come to define the social codes, the boundaries of acceptable behavior. Already in Milton one can see how Satan is the signifier of the negative dimensions of power, force, and subversion of the community. By presenting the consequences of Satan's actions as stigmatization, isolation, surveillance, and imprisonment, Milton puts Satan in the company of the criminally delinquent.

Satan's association with the threat of death and ostracism provides a powerful psychological means for internalizing negative behavior. Paul Rock has described how "the expensive drama and rituals which surround the apprehension and denunciation of the deviant are directed at maintaining the daemonic and isolated character of deviancy. Without these demonstrations, typification would be weakened and social control would be weakened accordingly."[7] Such typification is not characteristic of the modes of formal penance representative of a Catholic society, but rather of the role of social ostracism or outcasting representative of a Protestant society. The deviant is regarded "as a wicked outsider who has lost his right to claim membership in the normal community."[8] Milton's contribution to the aesthetics of demonism lies in his portrayal of sin in social terms and in his psychological application of the threat of deviance through the image of the socially delinquent individual.

I. Satan and the Critics

A reading of the Satanic in Milton is crucial to decoding the role of ideology in Milton's art. Milton critics have had to tackle the "Satan question," and Milton criticism reveals an intricate history of attitudes toward Milton's identification with the Satanic. From the seventeenth to the twentieth century, a respectable number of critics have adhered to the idea that Milton was himself a Satanist. If not all of these critics have specifically labeled Satan the hero of *Paradise Lost*, they have certainly affirmed the portrait of Satan as representing the highest point of Milton's creativity, often seeing the portraits of God, of the Son, of Jesus in *Paradise Regained* as suffering, in comparison to Satan, a loss of vitality and concreteness.[9]

Furthermore, these critics have asserted that Milton as a rebel could not help but identify with a figure like Satan, who opposed rules and conventions. The problematic aspect of the pro-Satanist faction is a disregard for history, Milton's history and seventeenth-century social history. They disregard Milton's conscious polemic and artistic design in their willingness to sacrifice the total context of *Paradise Lost* to the individual portrait of Satan and to Milton's unconscious. They underestimate Milton's self-conscious use of the Satanic as an overall strategy to develop important distinctions between rebellion and revolution. Milton's own position as narrator is closer to the revolutionary (as we would define it for a seventeenth-century Puritan) than that of his Satan, a conservative who engages in the outward motions of constant change but is actually committed to no change at all. Milton's liberal values, derived from the Renaissance and modified by Puritan ideas of individual struggle, political responsibility, and political change, are dramatized in *Paradise Lost* in conscious ways. These ideas were progressive for Milton; he had little need to conceal them in the figure of Satan.

The contributions of the Satanists cannot, however, be disregarded. In their struggle to articulate conscious and unconscious motives in the epic, they reminded other Milton critics that the text should be examined beyond Milton's statements of narrative intent and religious piety.

Satanists have been widely attacked and mostly silenced for their error of regarding Satan as attractive, a positive symbol of rebellion, and a manifestation of Milton's attraction to the demonic. The anti-Satanist critics have situated Milton's work more soundly in literary history. Past decades have witnessed numerous studies of Milton's ties to the past, to tradition, to Christian doctrine, to Plato, Dante, and Shakespeare, to church history, Protestantism, and rhetorical traditions. These critics have insisted, for example, that the characters, events, and language of *Paradise Lost* be viewed primarily in relation to the total design of the epic, in relation to "this great argument."[10]

Other critics, most notably Stanley Fish, in recent years have posited an active and Christian reader, one who is either "surpris'd by sin," entranced by it wrongly, or properly attentive to its reality and the necessity of grace.[11] Recent Milton criticism advances the idea of an active rather than a passive role for the reader as a means of demonstrating Milton's rhetorical skill and the fact that the text is still alive. I believe there is more to be said about Satan's role and the modern reader.

The Satan of *Paradise Lost* is no mere traditional figure, derived from past representations of the devil. He takes on new dimensions which reflect Milton's contemporary situation. Milton's devil is not so grotesque that his qualities are beyond human comprehension. In a way this makes him more frightening. He is not relegated to the demonic depths but moves freely. He does not consort with witches, does not engage in the Black Mass, and he is not insane. Milton's portrait of Satan has great power precisely because it does not emanate from pathology, the irrational, or nightmare. The psychological qualities with which Milton endows Satan are familiar. He makes Satan's suffering and sense of difference from others accessible to our understanding. Also understandable, if frightening, are his rage, his tendency to provoke aggression in others, and his psychic sensitivity, acute to the point of obsession. The reader is familiar with Milton's description of Satan's desire to be recognized and his inability to cooperate with others.

There is weighty critical evidence for accepting Milton's portrait of

Satan as negative, and for reading the conflict in *Paradise Lost* between God, the Son, and Satan for the soul of man as a conflict between positive and negative moral positions and between utopian and dystopian worlds; but Milton's portrait of Satan has more to teach us about the role of the deviant in literature and history than about sin and evil.[12] Beyond the particular qualities typified by the deviant is the process of typification itself. Milton's does not demystify deviant reality but exploits its existence and uses it to consolidate values and behavior. The use of the devil as an instrument for control and exemplification is commonplace. The power and originality of Milton's portrait of Satan lies in its power to capture and capitalize on the terror of deviant reality: ridicule, ostracism, and death.

Accordingly, this essay does not argue whether Satan is hero or villain, revolutionary or reactionary, or a pure reflection of the poet's unconscious desires. Examining Satan in relation to conceptions of deviance shortcuts a moral or purely subjective interpretation and identifies his function and form in social as well as aesthetic terms. Satan may, of course, embody Milton's anger toward the defeat of the "good old cause," but predominantly Satan is a strategy for containing the threatening imperatives of individualism, coercive power, and undeserved privilege. Milton's Satan is contained within a religious context of providential views of history and the Bible, the source for Milton of objective definitions of good in human society. Thus Milton's typification of Satan's "criminality," his "deviance," does not assume the awesome role deviancy was to play later, in eighteenth-century literature and society, as the indicator of good and evil measured in relation to conceptions of normality and abnormality.

II. SATAN AS DEVIANT

One of the best-known and most straightforward presentations of the creation and early uses of deviance can be found in Book II of the *Iliad*, where Homer uses Thersites to dramatize discontent about the Trojan War. Thersites voices reasons why the war is a failure and why the men should return to the ships. He succeeds for a moment and persuades others to leave, but Homer then shows how cleverly Odysseus, by ridiculing and castigating Thersites, brings the group closer together with a renewed resolve to remain and to fight. Unity is bought at the expense of the scapegoat.[13]

The phenomenon of deviance dramatized in Homer is not unique. It is evident also in drama, especially in tragedy. The deviant plays a role in mythology, and deviance and its consequences can even be observed among nonhuman animals.[14] What varies from age to age and from culture to culture is the character of the deviant, his or her changing representations in literature, and the role and extent of typifications in different societies.[15]

The epic artist constructs a world for the reader, a world partially conforming to the world he knows and partially evoking a more ideal world. Milton, most particularly, integrates myth with social reality, real with utopian constructions. In the encyclopedic manner of the epic poet, he presents the evolution of moral systems as parallel to the creation of the world and also to the process of artistic creation. He distinguishes positive from negative, acceptable from unacceptable, and destructive from vital forms of behavior, so as to convince the reader of the rightness of his constructions. Although considerations of good and evil are relevant to the portrait of Satan, another process accounts even more for Milton's (and Satan's) continuing attraction for readers. Milton transcends the moral categories he explores by creating an artistic totality which is not contained in simple designations of good and evil. He forces the reader's attention beyond the mere existence of his characters and situations onto the processes and motives of social reality and of creativity itself. And as with so many other world constructions, the world of *Paradise Lost* depends on the misfit to help define the rules.[16]

Thus it is not Satan's sins and vices which engage the reader primarily, but the *process* whereby Milton distinguishes, labels, and isolates certain forms of behavior as negative. Satan's role in *Paradise Lost* reflects a common social phenomenon of creating outcasts, scapegoats, and exiles who dramatize the boundaries between conformity and nonconformity. Negative qualities are defined against positive ones, because deviance implies straying from certain recognizable and agreed-upon attitudes. The typification of deviant reality reminds others, not yet implicated, of the consequences of straying. It allows the writer to express, if not to accept, divergent views of behavior.

Milton's portrait of Satan, through contrast with examples of fit discourse, reciprocity, and cooperation embodied in Heaven and Earth, becomes progressively not only an example of deviance from the collectivity, but a concrete demonstration of the terrors of deviant reality. The dominant threatening characteristics of deviant reality from both the group's and the deviant's perspectives are exclusion and isolation. Moreover, the process of stigmatizing, objectifying, and dehumanizing the deviant serves as a powerful force for separating the deviant from others. The threat of exclusion is a useful instrument in regulating or resisting change.

Satan's attraction for the reader might thus be said to grow out of Milton's ability to reenact the terrors of deviant reality. Milton confronts the reader with a condition which he may fear more than evil itself: the fear of being separated from the group, of being isolated and excluded from others. Such a condition is associated with and perceived to be as terrifying as death itself.

Paradise Lost presents us with stages in the creation of a deviant reality. The various metamorphoses of Satan, noted by critics as indicative of Satan's moral degeneration, also represent the evolution of a deviant, with all the characteristics we associate with deviance.[17] In order to trace Satan's role and its affinity with deviant reality we must follow Satan, Adam, and Eve as they experience themselves as deviants after the Fall. The dominant quality of deviance that Milton ascribes to Satan is a sense of separateness from others, the feeling of not belonging. He is portrayed as having a compulsion to oppose. He carries with him a personal sense of injury and pain, expressed in suicidal or homicidal fantasies or actions. He is reputed to look different; obvious physical and psychic transformations distinguish him from others. The ultimate consequence of his actions is his actual experience of exile. Moreover, Satan's situation, like the deviant's, is described as self-inflicted. No one assumes responsibility for the deviant's existence: he creates his own misery, we are told. Since everything in Milton's world is based on choice rather than determinism, Milton presents Satan as one who self-consciously creates his own suffering and his own differences from others.

Books I and II of *Paradise Lost* throw us abruptly in Satan's way. Without prior reference or preparation we confront Hell and the image of creatures who we learn have removed themselves from Heaven. Milton stresses Satan's alienation in such a way as to equate tainted character and tainted environment:

> Such place Eternal Justice had prepar'd
> For those rebellious, here thir Prison ordained
> In utter darkness, and thir portion set
> As far remov'd from God and light of Heav'n
> As from the Center thrice to th' utmost Pole.
> O how unlike the place from whence they fell!
> There the companions of his fall, o'erwhelm'd
> With Floods and Whirlwinds of tempestuous fire.   (I, 70–77)[18]

Satan is like a mourner who is recently bereaved. He grieves over his loss, but he can only articulate the loss in a confused and angry way:

"for now the thought / Both of lost happiness and lasting pain / Torments him" (I, 54–56). Milton rivets the reader's attention on Satan's aggression and on the terrifying conditions in Hell. By choosing to begin the epic *in medias res* with Satan, Milton shows him not in his original splendor but as already degenerate. Thus Milton immediately challenges the reader to confront Satan's rebelliousness, isolation, and frustration. Though we are aware of changes that have taken place in Satan's situation, in his appearance, and in his environment, Milton does not provide contrasting or mitigating images of his condition. Initial contact with Satan and his world therefore provokes curiosity and— possibly even more—the fear of contagion which is often generated by the sight of the deviant. The only possible frame of reference the reader has to understand the character of Satan at this stage is his own knowledge and fear of the existence of individuals who have disregarded the rules and are therefore outside the boundaries of normal social discourse. Moreover, Milton also plays on the reader's fear of his or her own deviance.

Milton marshals all the characteristics of deviance in order to make Satan's behavior appear unacceptable and frightening. For example, Satan's speech in Book I ("Fallen cherub to be weak is miserable") and his rhetorical strategies in speaking to the Council in Book II emphasize his narcissism and the unpleasant conjunction between his sense of personal injury, his self-pity, and his compulsion to pass on these uncomfortable feelings to others. Milton never misses the opportunity to equate Satan's actions with criminality. He describes Satan as an "archthief," a "felon," and as such deserving of containment. Ideas of criminality are always germane to concepts of deviance. The deviant is a victim of guilt by association, and the label of deviant is often enough to produce feelings of fear and revulsion in others.

The comparisons of Satan to various animals, all animals with negative associations such as wolves, cormorants, toads, and serpents, are also familiar in constructions of deviant reality. The deviant is thus removed from human consideration and relegated to an alien reality. The allegory of Sin and Death at the end of Book II distances the terrifying reality of the devil by associating him with the most frightening aspect of human existence, death.[19] Association with the deviant thus becomes a threat to one's physical and social well-being. Satan's confrontation with Sin and Death also reminds us of the physical transformations he has undergone. Satan asks: "Do I seem / Now in thine eye so foul, once deem'd so fair?" (II, 747–48.)

Books III and IV corroborate for the reader Satan's isolated and alienated condition. Milton provides the reader with contrasts between positive and negative images of community, in Heaven and on Earth. He develops the contrast between Satan's situation and Adam and Eve's prelapsarian life. Satan appears an intruder in Paradise, only too aware of his isolation.

As an intruder, he struggles with his rage, entertains his differences from God, and reaffirms his unwillingness to express gratitude, submission, and cooperation. He articulates his desperate condition thus: "Which way shall I fly / Infinite wrath and infinite despair" (IV, 72–73). Satan's speeches affirm his separateness and the reality of his exile: "All hope excluded thus, behold instead / Of us out-cast, exil'd" (IV, 105–06). His alienation from the paradisal environment is further conveyed through the narrator's distinction between the pleasant "Sabean odors" of Paradise and Satan's association with the fishy fumes of Asmodeus and later with the stench of cities. Milton's comparison of Satan to a wolf, and immediately thereafter to a thief, reinforces the conjunction between the antisocial and the nonhuman:

> As when a prowling Wolf,
> Whom hunger drives to seek new haunt for prey,
> Watching where Shepherds pen thir Flocks at eve
> In hurdl'd Cotes amid the field secure,
> Leaps o'er the fence with ease into the Fold:
> Or as a Thief bent to unhoard the cash
> Of some rich Burgher, whose substantial doors,
> Cross-barr'd and bolted fast, fear no assault,
> In at the window climbs, or o'er the tiles:
> So clomb this first grand Thief into God's Fold. (IV, 183–92)

Having established the world of the outsider as Hell and Satan as an exile from Heaven, Milton uses these similes to establish more firmly that Satan penetrates yet does not belong in human company. The demarcations between inside and outside, beast and man, natural and artificial are visible here. Moreover, the description of "this place, / A happy rural seat" (IV, 246–47), and the contrast with the dolorous and disorganized Hell which Satan brings with him, make the reader even further aware of his unwanted presence. The "arch-felon," the "Fiend" who "overleap'd all bound," does not belong in this company, and yet he is essential to the scene. His presence enables the reader to be aware of his own dual role as participant and observer. The reader is both involved and distanced as a result of Satan. Satan not only crystallizes the difference between his reality and that of Paradise as characterized by Adam and Eve, but he makes concrete the differences between isolation and belonging. Satan's deviant condition of isolation can be assimilated now.

Death *is* in Paradise, and is represented by Satan with his predatory, bestial, and antisocial behavior. Satan's isolation strikes a familiar chord, for in human society isolation from the group is akin to the isolation of the grave. In his prose writings on marriage, in his political tracts as well as in his poetry, Milton places the highest value on community, fit discourse, justice, stability, and concord. The isolated existence of the deviant and his working to isolate others—Adam and Eve from God, each from the other—mark Satan as the ultimate embodiment of political and social subversion. It is Satan's fate now to be the archetypal social misfit, while Adam and Eve's sociability is unambiguous:

> Henceforth an individual solace dear;
> Part of my Soul I seek thee, and thee claim
> My other half.   (IV, 486–88)

In contrast, Satan, the classic subverter, states:

> Live while ye may,
> Yet happy pair; enjoy, till I return,
> Short pleasures, for long woes are to succeed.   (IV, 533–35)

Milton endows Satan with characteristics of deviance still found in the twentieth century. He attributes degenerate sexual desires to Satan; Satan is a common political agitator, an irresponsible radical and an opportunist. He is a sower of domestic discord. His appearance is different from others. He smells, lives in chaos and filth, observes no limits, and has no respect for rules. He will attack the defenseless, even violating people in their sleep as in his violation of Eve's dream.

The reader of Books V and VI has a fairly solid idea of Satan's environment and behavior and can by now recognize similarities between Satan's deviance and his own knowledge of deviant reality. What remains for the reader to observe is the genesis of deviance through Milton's description of the War in Heaven. While Milton has made Satan accessible to human intelligence in the first four books of the epic, the War in Heaven stamps Satan as the archetypal deviant, especially in the scenes between Abdiel and Satan, where we confront the Miltonic distinction between appropriate and inappropriate defiance of the group. Abdiel, too, is shown as standing alone, yet his resistance, unlike Satan's, is in the service of the heavenly community. If we felt Satan's attraction earlier, because of our sympathy for the misfit, our tendency to be compassionate in the face of pain and isolation, these reservations are diminished by Milton's picture of Satan as hardened, blinded, incapable of change, and deserving of removal from the ranks of the divine community. Abdiel confronts Satan with the specific character of his deviance:

> O alienate from God, O Spirit accurst,
> Forsak'n of all good; I see thy fall
> Determin'd, and thy hapless crew involv'd
> In this perfidious fraud, contagion spread
> Both of thy crime and punishment.   (V, 877–81)

Abdiel articulates the key determinants of deviance: alienation, determinism, crime, and contagion. He confirms God's and the Son's descriptions of Satan in Book III.

The idea of law, of the rigid containment of antisocial behavior, is central to *Paradise Lost* and to an understanding of Satan's negative functions. Milton portrays the law as more than an abstract system of rewards and punishments. In Milton, law represents much more than force. It represents the existence of human order and of justice, conditions fundamental to the maintenance of social values. Law differentiates positive moral values from destructive values and behavior.[20] But the practice of the law in institutional terms is only one aspect of justice. More significantly, the examples of crime and punishment—the "knowledge of good and evil"—influence and shape daily life, acting as reminders of the consequences of transgression.[21] The operation of justice in formal terms comes into play only when the law is broken.

The social role of the deviant is more significant than the law as a deterrent to transgression. Satan and—to a lesser extent—Adam and Eve after the Fall are significant for the reader as models to be avoided so as to eliminate the necessity of open violence and punishment whenever possible. Deviant behavior should evoke shame or guilt on the part of others and serve as an incentive to avoid socially undesirable behavior. The fear of isolation, more than the fear of capital punishment, should direct the individual to socially acceptable actions. In speaking of man's relationship to the law, God equates disloyalty and deviance with death:

> Man disobeying,
> Disloyal breaks his fealty, and sins
> Against the high Supremacy of Heav'n,
> Affecting God-head, and so losing all,
> To expiate his Treason hath naught left,

> But to destruction sacred and devote,
> He with his whole posterity must die,
> Die hee or Justice must; unless for him
> Some other able, and as willing, pay
> The rigid satisfaction, death for death.   (III, 203–12)

This speech is quite legalistic and frightening in its emphasis on rigid punishment for infraction of the rules. Equally terrifying, because immediate and concrete, is Milton's description of Death, the true essence of Satanic reality exemplified in Adam's and Eve's suffering after the Fall and their expulsion from Paradise. Satan is the author of Death. In his description of Death, Satan's offspring, Milton emphasizes the shapelessness, ugliness, and arbitrariness of such a condition. Death is the enemy of all forms of social creativity, including artistic creation. Milton describes the "Universe of death" as breeding "perverse, all monstrous, all prodigious things, / Abominable, inutterable" (II, 622, 625–26) and describes Death as: "The other shape, / If shape it might be call'd that shape had none" (II, 666–67).

The description of Death, the association of Sin and Death with criminality and the law, and their conjunction with images of bestiality, serve to stigmatize behavior as antisocial and politically undesirable. Milton uses these constructions in *Paradise Lost* to present a world where distinctions can and must be made between rebellion and change. Seen in this way, death is not merely a biological fact to be understood and accepted; it is a reality to be manipulated in order to interpret and direct social behavior.[22]

Milton contrasts the Son's and Satan's attitudes toward Death. Satan minimizes the threat of death, in contrast to the Son, who offers "to be mortal to redeem man's mortal crime" (II, 214). The Son will pay the "rigid satisfaction, death for death" (II, 212). He has perfect faith in God's powers of grace and redemption, and he believes in the "rigid threat of Death." Satan, however, tells Eve:

> Queen of this Universe, do not believe
> Those rigid threats of Death; ye shall not Die:
> How should ye? by the Fruit? it gives you Life
> To Knowledge: By the Threat'ner? look on mee,
> Mee who have touch'd and tasted, yet both live,
> And life more perfet have attain'd than Fate
> Meant mee, by vent'ring higher than my Lot.
> Shall that be shut to Man, which to the Beast
> Is open? or will God incense his ire
> For such a petty Trespass?   (IX, 684–93)

His words and behavior demonstrate his nonchalance and even more his disrespect for all rules. His disregard for death, especially, epitomizes his deviance. Milton thus exposes Satan's lack of seriousness. Without a sense of the urgency of time and choice conveyed by a knowledge of death, Satan has no motivation, no responsible sense of action, purpose, or history. He is committed to forms without content, movement without progress. His cyclical movement from Hell and back to Hell reinforces the static reality attributed to him. He deserves to be mistrusted, watched, and ultimately confined.

III. SATAN AND SOCIETY

Milton, like Dante and like Shakespeare in his history plays, was profoundly involved with contemporary problems of political stability, and his art both reflects and addresses these problems. J. H. Plumb asserts that "the contrast between political society in eighteenth- and seventeenth-century England is vivid and dramatic. In the seventeenth century men killed, tortured, and executed each other for political beliefs; they sacked towns and brutalized the countryside. They were subjected to conspiracy, plot, and invasion. This uncertain political world lasted until 1715."[23] Milton's choice of the epic mode is a creative response to the unstable world Plumb describes. Milton faced the problem common to other Puritan writers of balancing individual behavior against that of the group in order to establish the reasonableness of political dissent within permissible boundaries.

More particularly, Christopher Hill has characterized the 1640s as a formative period for English radical thinking, and for Milton, citing particularly the class conflicts which surfaced, especially the "fierce popular hostility to gentry and to aristocracy and to the monarchy which protected them."[24] Milton's opposition to the court, the king, and the bishops is amply documented in his prose. His relationship to Puritanism and to radicalism has also been documented. But, as Hill and other Milton critics point out, Milton had his reservations about radical ideas of egalitarianism.[25] His position as an "eclectic" was an independent one; his work is permeated by a recognition of the existence and necessity of conflict but also by his attempt to reconcile oppositions between elitist views and democracy, the individual and society, privilege and merit, past and present, tradition and iconoclasm. Milton's portrait of Satan embodies the conflict of opposites without reconciliation. He uses Satanism both to dramatize extremes and to engage in them without resorting to external controls. Given his fierce emphasis on liberty and individualism, he had to find a psychological mode for internalizing necessary restraints on freedom. The threat of deviance, the fear of death and isolation, provide a proper internal restraint. While Milton's Satan appears to be an advocate of change, to be politically active and concerned, to espouse ideas of freedom and equality, Milton identifies his behavior as conservative and as a product of self-constructed determinism. He is an enemy of the ideal commonwealth, of responsible government, and of proper individualism.

In place of the rituals of exorcism and excommunication characteristic of Catholicism, Puritanism depends on the internalization of shame, guilt, and deviance to control behavior in a society that moves progressively away from external rituals in religion and authoritarian controls in politics, and toward social and parliamentary regulation and individual conscience. Hence Milton's use of Satan as deviant reflects the need of the society for ways, other than physical force or arbitrary legislation, to contain political change and individual prerogatives. Milton can thus stigmatize undesirable change as he does in his prose by typifying his opponents, while still adhering to the idea of the necessity of change, in the hope that the process of making proper distinctions will be internalized. It is important, therefore, that Satan is never totally removed from the community. He must coexist with others because of the importance in the Miltonic world of constantly and concretely distinguishing deviance from acceptable behavior. Particularly, Satan dramatizes the consequences of alienation from the wisdom inherent in daily life. Prior to the Fall, Raphael explains to Adam the importance of centering oneself in daily life and the importance of checks and limits on the imagination. His admonition can be taken, too, as a description of the Satanic consciousness, of freedom and autonomy:

> But apt the Mind or Fancy is to rove
> Uncheckt, and of her roving is no end;
> Till warn'd, or by experience taught, she learn
> That not to know at large of things remote
> From use, obscure and subtle, but to know
> That which before us lies in daily life,
> Is the prime Wisdom; what is more, is fume,
> Or emptiness, or fond impertinence,
> And renders us in things that most concern
> Unpractic'd, unprepar'd, and still to seek.   (VIII, 188–97)

Lost in the unchecked rovings of the mind, Satan has lost contact with his immediate world, the necessary context for making judgments and responsible decisions. Milton portrays Satan as lost in abstraction, in great designs divorced from moral considerations, and, above all, lost in subjectivity.

IV. HUMAN DEVIANCE

Turning to Adam and Eve after the Fall, we find further evidence of Milton's awareness of the social and political strategies of deviance. But in dramatizing Adam and Eve's straying, Milton creates significant departures from Satan's role and behavior. Their initial flirtation with "deviance" is, as God prophesies in Book III, not self-initiated as with Satan, but the result of fraternizing with the deviant. Eve shares with Adam the propensity to stray, but she is not yet a deviant; she experiences deviant reality only after the Fall. Though both human beings have the potential, Eve's tendency toward deviance is greater, since she is portrayed as being weaker than Adam and in need of his instruction. Yet Adam too needs, is given, and disregards angelic instructions. Eve's potential for deviance is obvious in her impatience with constraint. She alludes to their lives as being threatened by the "narrow circuit strait'n'd by a Foe" (IX, 323), in reference to the necessity of the strait and narrow gate to grace from which she is about to deviate. Eve's frailty, her vanity, and her inadequately assimilated ideas of equality, in Milton's terms, make her vulnerable to Satan's rationalizations about freedom and the inconsequentiality of death. It is appropriate, given her subordinate status, that she is the first to exemplify human deviance.

After she eats the fruit, Eve takes on the qualities of the deviant. Her appearance changes; she appears "lost, how on a sudden lost, / Defac't, deflow'r'd, and now to Death devote" (IX, 900–01). Moreover, her condition appears to be contagious. Her language changes. In order to subvert Adam, she presents all the spurious reasons she has acquired from Satan about why he should eat, though Adam actually eats so as not to lose her company. Both Adam and Eve experience the terrors of being different. They now share another deviant quality, licentiousness. They indulge their new experience of lust, which invites another new experience, "this newcomer, Shame" (IX, 1097).

From shame, they move to guilt as they recognize what has happened to them and begin to reproach one another. Unlike Satan, they are capable of experiencing shame and guilt, which proves them capable of self-examination and conversion. For them, the experience of deviancy operates in a positive direction to motivate them to reject its taint. They struggle against the stigma of the deviant and regain their sense of self-esteem before God and themselves. They accept their responsibility for transgressing, and accept their sentence of death as a necessary prologue to their struggle to overcome death. They work to restore community with each other and with God so as not to remain forever outcasts.

In Eve's contemplation of suicide, which would involve race suicide, the taint of deviance remains, but tempered by a movement toward contrition. Adam and Eve's conflict with one another, their "mutual accusation," is another sign of deviant reality, the presence of conflict and disorganization. Their isolation from each other and their humiliated condition in relation to the Son convey poignantly their altered situation and the work they must perform in order to become acceptable in the eyes of God. Most significantly, their descriptions of themselves, like the changes in their environment, reveal their recognition of change, but change that marks them as different and unattractive:

> Love was not in thir looks, either to God
> Or to each other, but apparent guilt
> And shame, and perturbation, and despair,
> Anger, and obstinacy, and hate and guile.   (X, 111–14)

The reader witnesses not only changes in Adam and Eve, but also the transformation of Satan into a serpent, which prefigures his final condition when the Son of God will "obstruct the mouth of Hell / For ever, and seal up his ravenous Jaws" (X, 636–37). The oral image recalls Hell, the shapelessness of Death, the contagious nature of deviance which demands its exclusion, and the need for silencing subversive language.

Again, Milton differentiates Satan's fate from Adam's and Eve's. Satan's exile is final, a sign of the abandonment of all hope, whereas Adam's and Eve's expulsion from the Garden, coming as it does after their remorse, penitence, contrition, and prayer, and also after their instruction by Michael about their history and the history of humanity, signifies a new beginning, their restored potential to live in a harmonious community, and their renewed potential for choice. If man conforms to the moral path outlined, he will be able to defeat death and isolation:

> The World was all before them, where to choose
> Thir place of rest, and Providence thir guide:
> They hand in hand with wand'ring steps and slow,
> Through *Eden* took thir solitary way.   (XII, 646–49)

The image of openness is a positive indication of their situation in contrast to Satan's closed fate. Having fully experienced the pains of deviant reality, they are portrayed as capable of exorcising those feelings.

Reinforced in their efforts by Michael, God's emissary, they are removed from the demonic, connected to others through history, and, though excluded from Paradise, not permanently excluded from the possibility of grace.

The threat of deviance remains, nonetheless. In Adam's and Eve's exclusion from Paradise, and in Satan's regression to an inarticulate, bestial, and exiled condition, Milton capitalizes on the reader's worst fears of isolation, ostracism, and alienation as embodied in the figure of the deviant. For the manipulation of deviant reality to be socially and politically effective, deviance must remain a threat, and it must draw repeatedly and directly on the fear of death and isolation.

The creation of deviants is a powerful method, as later history will attest, for ensuring political stability. Divorced from Milton's humanistic context, such a process, as we have seen in the twentieth century, produces destructive conformity; but Milton's use of the threat of deviancy is inextricable from the religious, politically progressive, and humane context of *Paradise Lost*. In all his work, Milton tested his own and others' attitudes toward social change. Consistent with his emphasis on self-determination, he makes the role of Satan function as a vehicle for examining, differentiating, and exemplifying appropriate and inappropriate views of conformity and nonconformity, continuity and change.

University of Pittsburgh

NOTES

1. Lynn White, "Death and the Devil," in *The Darker Vision of the Renaissance*, ed. Robert S. Kinsman (Berkeley, 1974), pp. 25–26.

2. Bronislaw Malinowski, *Magic, Science and Religion and Other Essays*, ed. Robert Redfield (New York, 1948), p. 47.

3. Christopher Hill, *Milton and the English Revolution* (New York, 1977), p. 248.

4. Ibid., p. 114.

5. Peter Berger, *The Sacred Canopy: Elements of a Sociological Theory of Religion* (Garden City, N.Y., 1969).

6. Thompson, *The Making of the English Working Class* (New York, 1963); Foucault, *Discipline and Punish: The Birth of the Prison* (New York, 1977).

7. *Deviant Behavior* (London, 1973), p. 35.

8. Ibid.

9. William Empson, *Milton's God* (Norfolk, Conn., 1961); R. J. Zwi Werblowsky, *Lucifer and Prometheus* (London, 1952); A. J. A. Waldock, *"Paradise Lost" and Its Critics* (Cambridge, 1947).

10. Roland Mushat Frye, *God, Man, and Satan* (Princeton, 1959); E. M. W. Tillyard, *The Miltonic Setting* (Cambridge, 1938), and *Studies in Milton* (London, 1951); Douglas Bush, *"Paradise Lost" in Our Time* (Ithaca, 1945); Burton O. Kurth, *Milton and Christian Heroism* (Berkeley, 1957); John Steadman, *Milton and the Renaissance Hero* (Oxford, 1967).

11. Fish, *Surprised by Sin: The Reader in "Paradise Lost"* (London, 1967); John R. Knott, *Milton's Pastoral Vision: An Approach to "Paradise Lost"* (Chicago, 1971); Anne Davidson Ferry, *Milton's Epic Voice: The Narrator in "Paradise Lost"* (Cambridge, Mass., 1963).

12. Rock, *Deviant Behavior*, p. 21, describes the role of typification thus: "Law structures a society's systems of typifications. It affects a population's stock of knowledge about the nature, extent and distribution of deviancy. It establishes patterns of guilt, shame and motivation. Yet it cannot be universal without coercion because it is an imperialistic code whose very existence presupposes dissent. It depends upon supporting coercive agencies for its effectiveness."

13. Trans. Richmond Lattimore (Chicago, 1951).

14. Irenaus Eibl-Eibesfeldt, *Love and Hate: On the Natural History of Basic Behaviour Patterns* (London, 1971).

15. Georges Balandier, *Political Anthropology* (New York, 1972).

16. Peter Berger and Thomas Luckmann, *The Social Construction of Reality: A Treatise in the Sociology of Knowledge* (Garden City, N.Y., 1967).

17. C. S. Lewis, "Satan," in *Milton: Modern Essays in Criticism*, ed. Arthur Barker (New York, 1965), p. 201.

18. All references to *Paradise Lost* are from *John Milton: Complete Poems and Major Prose*, ed. Merritt Y. Hughes (New York, 1957).

19. White, "Death and the Devil."

20. Ted Honderich, *Punishment, the Supposed Justifications* (Harmondsworth, Eng., 1971), p. 15.

21. Daniel J. Boorstin, *The Mysterious Science of the Law: An Essay on Blackstone's Commentaries* (Gloucester, Mass., 1973), pp. 62–63.

22. Herbert Marcuse, "The Ideology of Death," in *The Meaning of Death*, ed. Herman Feifel (New York, 1965), pp. 64–78.

23. *The Growth of Political Stability in England, 1675–1725* (Harmondsworth, Eng., 1973), p. 13.

24. *Reformation to Industrial Revolution* (Baltimore, 1969).

25. *Milton and the English Revolution*, p. 93.

THE LIMBS OF TRUTH: MILTON'S USE OF SIMILE IN *PARADISE LOST*

Linda Gregerson

MY SPECIFIC topic is the Miltonic simile, the materials that compose it, the ends it serves. The figure of speech is a turn of the mind; the simile's ground is epistemology. The artist makes both an artifact and an instrument with which to see, like the Tuscan artist's glass. The figure made from the language of men goes into the making of an artifact called *Paradise Lost*. To know the function of figure and poem, we must know how Milton believes we come to know.

We and the poem and the author live after the Fall; that limits our means. Stanley Fish has written a book about reading after the Fall, and his point is, first, that reading is not an innocent act. This seems to me to be indisputable. The reader is not innocent of what he reads, but is implicated, called to judgment, to render and receive. Judgment is a placing of the self in relation to the thing seen. And where do we find ourselves while reading *Paradise Lost?* In sin, says Fish; and the way we know is one of our sins. So he posits the poem as a *via negativa*, provoking, one by one, our perceptual habits that we may regard them in the light of faith and discover them to be impasses, props that characterize and maintain us in the fallen state. The next step is presumably to cast them off.

Among the movements of mind that seem to us to render the world articulate is the drawing of likenesses, which give voice at once to division and to a unity of structure or plan. "The superfluousness of the simile as an instrument of perception is, I believe, part of Milton's point. . . . those who walk with faith . . . are able, *immediately*, to discern the unity in diversity."[1] In this portion of his thesis, Fish seems to ignore a great deal of Milton's poem. God, it is our premise, sees everything as one and at once. But the angels, for example, cannot discern hypocrisy; their unity of vision, if such it be, fails to admit such doubleness and is therefore incomplete. Man, even before the Fall, is further still from divine omniscience; Adam's "sudden apprehension" (VIII, 354) of the animals he names is exceptional:

135

Immediate are the Acts of God, more swift
Than time or motion, but to human ears
Cannot without procéss of speech be told,
So told as earthly notion can receive.   (VII, 176–79)[2]

The discrepancy need not be mere impediment: "what surmounts the reach / Of human sense, I shall delineate so, / By lik'ning spiritual to corporal forms" (V, 571–73). Raphael's analogical method of instruction is presumably endorsed by the underlying coherence and continuity of creation. The forms of understanding itself are potentially part of a gradual, uninterrupted sequence: "In contemplation of created things / By steps we may ascend to God" (V, 511–12). The angel's expressed uncertainties about relation simply underscore its potency. On the one hand, the tale related may "unfold / The secrets of another World, perhaps / Not lawful to reveal" (V, 568–70); the story of understanding may be wrongfully abridged. On the other hand, relations drawn by the narrator may have a fuller ontological warrant than we yet divine: "though what if Earth / Be but the shadow of Heav'n, and things therein / Each to other like more than on Earth is thought?" (V, 574–76).

The Fall, in any case, is not an utter corruption of God-like apprehension. For man, understanding has always proceeded in time: before the Fall, the requisite time is that of discourse, and of perfection in obedience; after the Fall, time is invaded by death and becomes the time of history. When Satan rebels, he receives a "discontinuous wound" (VI, 329); when man rebels, his progress toward God becomes discontinuous, at least as perceived by human sense. In Michael's narration, the divine pattern must now be fulfilled by death and rebirth; Adam, too, must repeatedly die to one form of consciousness and awake to another. His senses are scattered by Michael's tidings (XI, 294) and restored by the angel's mild words to Eve; he sinks into a trance on the Hill of Paradise (XI, 420) and is then recalled; his mortal sight begins to fail (XII, 9), and henceforth pictures are made with words. The path has been broken at intervals but exists after as before the Fall. "Those who walk with faith" do not reach God at once, but must journey to him.

Raphael advises Adam to "be lowly wise" (VIII, 173) but does his best to "lift / Human imagination" to the "highth / Of Godlike Power" (VI, 299–301). Adam is to curb his inquiry into the motions of the stars, but only that he may better address his steps to the course which will lead him by degrees to God. He is warned against eating the fruit, but is encouraged to know himself (VIII, 437 ff.), having known the beasts. The boundaries he discovers are the boundaries of ordered progress, not the pattern of stasis. When Adam reiterates to Michael the limits "Of knowledge, what this Vessel can contain; / Beyond which was my folly to aspire" (XII, 559–60), he repents, not of inquiry in general, but of the sin of disobedience and the pride of the "worldly wise" (XII, 568). Man's longing may be for immediate apprehension, but his sinning lies in false abbreviation: by plucking the fruit, to take the walls of heaven by storm; by worldly wisdom, to erect the walls where he stands.

Raphael expounds the angelic and human modes of understanding:

> Fancy and understanding, whence the Soul
> Reason receives, and reason is her being,
> Discursive, or Intuitive; discourse
> Is oftest yours, the latter most is ours,
> Differing but in degree, of kind the same.   (V, 486–90)

The Latin root *discurrere* means to run to and fro. The similes in *Paradise Lost* have been characterized as errant, wanderings off the path. But discourse, even before the Fall, goes to and fro. Nor does the eye go straight down the page, but back and forth, like Spenser's plowman, who is also the penman.

The Miltonic similes portray knowledge as problematic; they do not suggest we throw away the tools we have and wait for grace as for rain. The rain does no good if the field or the page is not plowed. "To be still searching for what we know not by what we know . . . this is the golden rule"(*Areopagitica*, p. 742). This calls for motion in two respects: first, because the truth historical man achieves is by nature incomplete. To rest in the accomplished truth is to be guilty of pride or even of heresy, for we pretend to be as God:

Our faith and knowledge thrives by exercise, as well as our limbs and complexion. Truth is compared in scripture to a streaming fountain; if her waters flow not in a perpetual progression, they sicken into a muddy pool of conformity and tradition. A man may be a heretic in the truth. (*Areopagitica*, p. 739)

Secondly, what we must know is precisely what we do not know. Our course, since the Fall, is discontinous. We must step beyond the confines of our understanding, and must do so continually, for the point is neither to domesticate otherness nor to resolve it into terms we already know. Malvolio reads according to an error of this kind ("If I could make that resemble something in me!") and is trapped. In *Paradise Lost*, we proceed by perceived alliance (with a Pilot, with a peasant, with Adam and Eve), but not by assimilation. If we seek to place ourselves in the poem, it is not to eradicate what is elsewhere, but precisely to engage it. The fallen angels are trapped in the limits of the conceivable ("For who can yet believe, though after loss . . ." I, 631) and thus compound their sin. There is more in this world than we may conceive, and that we may not forget it we must tackle the limit repeatedly. The figures in the poem are markedly anachronistic, oxymoronic, and this is to bring us to a verge. As we get in place, the sands shift. Only in movement can we be oriented toward God, who is with us but is not assimilable.[3]

The figures from which my examples are drawn are primarily those of Book I, where they fall as thick as autumnal leaves. Though similes are unevenly distributed in *Paradise Lost*,[4] I do not believe they alter in kind as the poem proceeds. They develop in relation to one another, as well as to the surrounding text, so the first book, with its impacted figurative language, is simply a convenient source. The work the similes do is of five kinds.

I. On the simplest level, the vehicle conveys real information about the tenor, or locates it in an experiential realm.

a. It may do this by stimulating the sensual memory: "As when the Sun new ris'n / Looks through the Horizontal misty Air / Shorn of his Beams" (I, 594–96). T. S. Eliot says that the visual imagination is "at no period . . . conspicuous in Milton's poetry."[5] The generalization has its point, but sacrifices certain detail. The image above is not, like the light from Eden, vision remembered and generalized. The phenomenon is particular and rendered with such accuracy as to invent for the community of readers a shared remembrance. Lucifer's radiance, diminished, has a body by which we may know it.

b. A subject may be modified by means of its analogue; the attributes of the latter attach to the former. Thus Satan is like a vulture on Immaus bred because he too is after prey (III, 431 ff.). The fallen angels are like locusts, not simply because of their number, but because they threaten to plague the earth as locusts once plagued Egypt (I, 338 ff.).

c. And similes may be mimetic; they may induce in the reader an experience which characterizes the subject. The vulture's flight begins a sentence which extends for forty-five lines, proceeds across lands we know by hearsay alone to light on an oxymoron, a windy Sea of Land (III, 431 ff.). And twenty lines of a second sentence pass before the place is named. The grammatical suspension gives the reader a little sampling of Limbo itself.

II. The simile may be proleptic.[6] Those in *Paradise Lost* are anachronistic by nature, appealing as they do to the myths and experience of men not yet created at the time of the Fall. They often prefigure subsequent events in the story. Thus Satan is compared to Leviathan (I, 201ff.), and the fate of the small night-foundered skiff forecasts our own, and that of Adam and Eve. References to Pharaoh and to the Flood remind us that the biblical story extends beyond the Fall. All events are one in the eye of God, but the unity requires translation if it is to be apprehended by man. Hence the tradition of parallels between the Fall and the Passion:

> Man for man, tre for tre,
> Madyn for madyn; thus shal it be.
>   . . . .
> Angell must to mary go,
> ffor the feynd was eue fo.
>
> ("The Annunciation," Towneley cycle)[7]

The tradition of reading in one event the prefiguration of another, of reading in the second a fulfillment of the first, is distinguished from other signifying systems (from allegory, from symbolism) by the nature of its existence in human time. The historicity of figural interpretation, one of Erich Auerbach's major points,[8] accords with the interpreter's temporal medium, but lodges necessity outside time, in the eternal. If, as in "The Annunciation," the relation between events seems causal, the cause is sheerly the will of God. The similes in *Paradise Lost* seldom invoke the Passion as a direct fulfillment of the Fall; they rather invoke the intervals between scenarios of completion: the time between the Fall and the Incarnation, the time between the comings of Christ, times when the Fall is enacted again and again.

The root of *interpret* corresponds to the Sanskrit *prath*—to spread abroad. Between what is spread abroad, the interpreter moves. The figure of speech, like the figurative event, stands for what elsewhere is unity. In *Ars amoris* (2,679), *figurae* are the positions of lovemaking.[9]

Discussions of "ornament" therefore mislead insofar as they conjure optional, detachable figures of speech.[10] There is no straighter rendering; we have only the translation into time. The text (in Bacon it is nature) has not the same form as the reader's mind.[11]

III. The poem is addressed to fallen man and points beyond the fallen state, both backward in time to the prelapsarian state and outside of time to divine omniscience. We seek, not more of the same, but what we know not by what we know: the perceptual task is demanding. The

similes put us in training of a sort, give us sometimes a running start and
sometimes the edge of the cliff:

> His Spear, to equal which the tallest Pine
> Hewn on Norwegian Hills, to be the Mast
> Of some great Ammiral, were but a wand.   (I, 292–94)

This is not altogether the radical undoing which Stanley Fish takes it to
be. The pine, to be sure, is not commensurate in stature to the spear,
but, as James Whaler has affirmed, a definite proportional relation is
suggested: the spear is to the pine as the pine is to the wand.[12] Whaler's
general point is well taken: there are coherent relations other than
equivalence. His paraphrase also, I think, captures the sense we extract
from the image, insofar as we continue to attend to size. The stricter
grammatical cues, of course, tell us that the pine transformed to a mast
is as a wand to the spear when an effort is made to equate the pine and
the spear. This effort is hardly made by the tree; it no more seeks to be
equal than it seeks to be a mast. Another perspective has entered and, I
would argue, as far outweighs the question of size as the spear outweighs the wand. The projections of human intentionality and imagination have become the subject; man navigates on the ocean as he navigates
in conceptual space. "Were but a wand" does not undo the project, but
strips away its simplest guise to reveal its proper dimension. The dimension at stake is not of a spear.

A wand, though small, is rich in connotation. It may be, for example, a walking stick or a magic rod. As the former, it modulates oddly
back into the extrametaphorical territory. The pine, generated within
the simile and transformed there to a mast, is compared to a wand, and,
when we return to the tenor (spear), we find it being used as a walking
stick (wand): "a wand / He walkt with to support uneasy steps" (I, 294–
95). This is not, of course, its proper use. It is a measure of Satan's fall,
in one respect, that he should use his weapon of war to support uneasy
steps. It is not just the pine but the spear itself which is "but a wand."
The spear, so far above our imaginative powers, falls below the image
we have summoned to be its correlative, as far below it as a wand is
to a pine.

As a magic rod, the wand has precedents. In the Towneley cycle,
Moses perplexes Pharaoh with his "wand."[13] Milton himself used the
word in Comus: "Nay Lady, sit; if I but wave this wand, / Your nerves
are all chain'd up in Alabaster" (Comus, 659–60). The spear, less than
fifty lines after it emerges from simile, is used to assemble the fallen angels as Moses' "potent rod" called up the locusts (I, 338 ff.). So a wand is
more than a negligible item, even when compared to a pine tree or to

Satan's spear. The transformation of the middle term, the pine, to a mast that can move a ship, is awesome but not incomprehensible.[14] It bespeaks specifically human creativity and will. The nature of the spear is not so easily read. The magic stick used as a walking stick is, once more, a measure of diminishment, but we cannot assume that its powers are wholly gone.

In the fallen angels' new abode the powers of heaven undergo not mere erasure but a radical translation. "As one great Furnace flam'd, yet from those flames / No light, but rather darkness visible" (I, 62–63). Much of Hell is described in oxymoronic or paradoxical terms: "a fiery Deluge, fed / With ever-burning Sulphur unconsum'd" (I, 68–69). The normal exchange between earth and air (consummation) is abrogated, as is the normal antipathy between water and fire. The image makes no concessions to the familiar patterns of synthesis, but is not therefore a systematic disparagement of postlapsarian perceptual equipment. The mind does not stop before the paradox—that's the important thing. It rather gains new energy, as subatomic particles are accelerated in cyclotrons by being made to jump magnetic fields.

There are many ways of creating a verge to be jumped. There are only two requirements: that the elsewhere be neither assimilated nor so radically severed as to make what is here and now appear intact. Cut off from Eden, the realm of man is neither autonomous nor whole. The limbs of truth have been torn from her trunk and scattered (*Areopagitica*, pp. 741–42); this severance keeps the other in mind. The similes in *Paradise Lost* generate temporal and geographical maps in which the boundaries are both barriers and passageways. The fallen angels are

> A multitude, like which the populous North
> Pour'd never from her frozen loins, to pass
> Rhene or the Danaw, when her barbarous Sons
> Came like a Deluge on the South, and spread
> Beneath Gibraltar to the Lybian sands.   (I, 351–55)

The Rhene and Danaw give way before barbarian hordes as the Red Sea gave way before the Israelites. Fifty lines earlier, the fallen angels are as thick bestrown as the floating carcasses and broken chariot wheels of Pharaoh's men when the passageway becomes boundary again. North has flowed into south and the west for a time opened into the east. Norwegian pines make their entry amidst pictures of the Tuscan landscape. The four corners of the world are invoked in such a way as to assure us they are separate but not intact. "Pour'd never from her frozen loins": the event that did not take place is ambiguously insemination and birth; the Israelites, after wandering in the desert, beget a nation. As in "were

but a wand," the logically extractable meaning is that the Vandal mul-
titudes can no more be compared to fallen angels than a pine can be
compared to Satan's spear. As in "were but a wand," the point is not
mere size, but the quality of human imagination. We are certainly not
encouraged to think we can embrace the numbers of the angels with our
minds. "Comprehension" here is not containment, but an act which
may be intuitively provoked. Comparison does not mean equation. We
are taken to our conceptual limits as to the Red Sea, and told we must
go beyond.

But "never" is a temporal modifier and is placed next to "pour'd."
Unlike "were but a wand," the term of negation is placed, as it were,
midstream. The Vandals never poured, but the subordinate passage ex-
trapolates the deluge as though it had occurred, as indeed we know it
did: "and spread / Beneath Gibraltar to the Lybian sands." The tension
between "never" and "once" (in the mind, on the page) parallels the tension between north and south; they do not merge but interpenetrate.
We have no more seen the Vandals pour than we have seen "Chineses
drive / With Sails and Wind thir cany Waggons light" (III, 438–39).
The process by which we know the events of human history and the
reaches of human activity is not different in kind from the way in which
we know the angels. We embody neither.

Barriers may be erected in the poem as in a landscape. When they
are erected around similes, the figure will still inform the surrounding
text:

> The Pilot of some small night-founder'd Skiff,
> Deeming some Island, oft, as Seamen tell,
> With fixed Anchor in his scaly rind
> Moors by his side under the Lee, while Night
> Invests the Sea, and wished Morn delays.   (I, 204–08)

The story is cut off before the morn, and menace looms all the larger.
Lest chaos be come again, there is a movement to contain the threatening power within the "will / And high permission of all-ruling Heaven"
(I, 211–12). The very suddenness of the closure underscores its inade-
quacy. Not that we doubt Providence, but that the level on which it is
ordered is not the level on which we have anchorage. The rescue from
night at sea has been rendered ominously ambiguous. Wished morn will
presumably disclose to the pilot his doom.

IV. The similes focus attention upon the act of perception itself
and make us aware that we are not looking alone. Whaler accounts for

the introduction of "extraneous" human points of view by identifying this as a digressive device, a form of pleasant distraction.[15] Geoffrey Hartman talks of the observer "on the shore," who confirms by his presence the suspended quality internal to many of the similes, a quality that constitutes a "counterplot" about divine imperturbability.[16] It is not clear in the poem, however, that we have landed with perfect safety on the shore. The benignity Hartman points to exists in certain specific terms: the angels thick as autumnal leaves, the scattered sedge, the carcasses and chariot wheels so thick bestrown are alike in that they portray devastation as benevolent (I, 302ff.). But the shore from which the chosen people watch their enemies borders on the desert as well as on the Red Sea, the desert in which the Israelites will wander for forty years. No shore, till Christ come and come again, is the final refuge. We are offered the image of safety in order that we may not despair, may know that our state is different from that of Satan, who cannot repent. The images of danger remind us that we are not safe in an armchair as in a harbor when we read, but are active as on a ship.[17] We navigate by means of perceived alliances: with a pilot, a peasant, an astronomer. The patterns of alliance shift, because anchor is unsafe. The human figures planted within the poetic figures are part of a larger phenomenon of corroborative vision. We see through allusion and direct borrowings from previous traditions. Language itself is a medium of inherited, endowed imagination. What is logically condemned may be poetically affirmed. Those who look with us and what they see are no less present because the images that house them are condemned as "mere fabling." Hartman's point is that the "counterplot" of *Paradise Lost* is manifested by means other than overt theme, plot, and subplot. I would qualify his account of the subtext but see no reason to doubt the method by which it comes into being. The reading experience is not primarily governed by preexistent ordering structures, theological or otherwise. We are embroiled, for example, in simile. We form judgments by means of recognition.

a. The observer *ab extra*.[18]

> As when the Sun new ris'n
> Looks through the Horizontal misty Air
> Shorn of his Beams, or from behind the Moon
> In dim Eclipse disastrous twilight sheds
> On half the Nations, and with fear of change
> Perplexes Monarchs.
>
> (I, 594–99)

The sun looks as we look upon it, but is not, as is usual, the light by which we see. This is Satan, shorn of half his brightness, that half of the sun (his beams) which normally lights our way. His fall has introduced disastrous division into the world. The sun from behind the moon sheds half light on half the nations. The monarchs, too, presumably look, and are perplexed. They read the event for implications, as does the peasant who sees, or dreams he sees, the revels of faery elves: "At once with joy and fear his heart rebounds" (I, 788). The moon above the peasant "sits Arbitress." The epithet is an odd one. Not simply the mistress of revels, the moon is arbitress, the one who goes between. The peasant sees by the moon and is judged by what he sees. Interpretation is difficult ("with joy and fear," "perplexes").

We look at and by the sun and the moon; the light is divided and reflected to boot. We look at and by the simile:

>   his ponderous shield,
> Ethereal temper, massy, large and round,
> Behind him cast; the broad circumference
> Hung on his shoulders like the Moon, whose Orb
> Through Optic Glass the Tuscan Artist views
> At Ev'ning from the top of Fesole,
> Or in Valdarno, to descry new Lands,
> Rivers or Mountains in her spotty Globe.
> His Spear, to equal which the tallest Pine
> Hewn on Norwegian hills, to be the Mast
> Of some great Ammiral, were but a wand,
> He walkt with to support uneasy steps.   (I, 284–95)

The syntax is such that the shield and the spear attain a large degree of temporary independence from Satan. He throws the shield behind him; it changes from object to subject in the next clause, and its analogue, the moon, becomes the object of vision. The observer is observed by us: we locate the artist in Fesole *or* in Valdarno as he locates new lands, rivers *or* mountains in his glass. The spear generates an analogue that extends the purview to Norwegian hills and an Ammiral. The project, in several forms, is human navigation; it's the movement that maps a globe. And yet the structure is pendant to Satan's navigation in his fallen state; he is moving toward the shore. The globe is spotty, the monarchs perplexed with fear of change. The change that heralds others has already occurred.

    b. *Obiter dicta*.[19]

The simplest form is a phrase, "as Seamen tell" (I, 205), or a verb that makes us aware that others have looked or are looking as well: "So numberless were those bad Angels seen" (I, 344). More complex is to look by means of previous versions of experience:

he stood and call'd
His Legions, Angel Forms, who lay intrans't
Thick as Autumnal Leaves that strow the Brooks
In Vallombrosa, where th'Etrurian shades
High overarch't imbow'r; or scatter'd sedge
Afloat, when with fierce Winds Orion arm'd
Hath vext the Red-Sea Coast, whose waves o'erthrew
Busirus and his Memphian Chivalry,
While with perfidious hatred they pursu'd
The Sojourners of Goshen, who beheld
From the safe shore thir floating Carcasses
And broken Chariot Wheels; so thick bestrown
Abject and lost lay these, covering the Flood,
Under amazement of thir hideous change.   (I, 300–13)

The landscape immediately contrasts with that in which Satan is walking: his torrid clime is vaulted with fire, the Tuscan valley embowered with shade trees. Brooks and autumn are cool, as is evening, in which the Tuscan artist, fifteen lines ago, looked through his optic glass. But the contrast is not complete. The Etrurian shades may be spirits of the older (Etruscan) civilization, thus reinforcing what Merritt Hughes takes to be an allusion to Dante: spirits numberless as autumn leaves.[20] Orion armed has scattered the sedge as Orion, in Virgil, has risen with the winds that force the Trojans to land on Dido's Libyan shores. Virgil is to Dante as the Etruscans are to Tuscans. The landscape is old.

With the scattering of Pharaoh's men, we move from classical to Hebrew history, to greater violence and a more visible will in the simile. It is in relation to this will that we seek to orient ourselves. Men are wont to read their own mortality in the falling of leaves, but the cycle of seasons consoles us. The seas that shipwrecked Aeneas were raised by Juno's malevolent will, but the allusion is indirect and the will submerged. The exodus, on the other hand, is evoked directly: we know who made the Red Sea waters close. As Christians, we inherit the divine benevolence that overthrew the Memphian chivalry. As Britons (Trojans via Rome), we are part of a line that continued *despite* the raising of the wind. We seem to have arrived on the shores of simile as a chosen people, but back in the tenor the angels cover a flood. We are reminded of another flood, which was sent when men had wandered from God, as the Israelites are again about to do. When Satan's spear is raised to summon the angels, they swarm like the plague of locusts. The fallen angels will threaten men as the locusts threatened Egypt. A subsequent passage tells us how: the angels are named by the names they received from the sons of Eve, who fell into false belief. Our status as survivors, as the chosen, is complicated more than once.

       c. The instrument sees.

> As when by night the Glass
> Of Galileo, less assur'd, observes
> Imagin'd Lands.   (V, 261–63)

> But now my Oat proceeds,
> And listens to the Herald of the Sea.   (*Lycidas*, 88–89)

As with the sun, the thing we see by also sees. As with the poem, the thing we make is an instrument of perception. The eye dominates *Paradise Lost* as the ear dominates *Comus* and *Lycidas*. In the masque, characters are forewarned of one another by the sound of footsteps or songs. In the elegy, the birth of the final persona follows conception through the ear. Early attempts to enter are made and rejected: Phoebus "touch'd my trembling ears" (77); St. Peter comes as a "dread voice" (132). Lycidas' arrival in heaven is celebrated by an "unexpressive nuptial Song" (176), and the poet is finally freed for transformation by the song he sings himself.

    Ear becomes eye as speech moves to the page. *Comus* was of course written to be spoken aloud. The convention of the sung lyric still obtains in *Lycidas*, but is minimal in *Paradise Lost*. The word sees as the pipe once heard; this is the twofold nature of bearing witness. The witness perceives and testifies, is wholly implicated. Stanley Fish considers the act of composition primarily by implication, but his theory seems to me to maximize the difference between Milton's experience of the poem and that of the reader. Where the poet has received the understanding and control not granted to fallen man is never explained: presumably from his heavenly Muse. But dialogue with the Muse sounds strangely like a single voice; she answers quickly, for one thing: "Who first seduc'd them to that foul revolt? / Th'infernal Serpent; he it was" (I, 33–34). The Muse hasn't even a verse paragraph to herself. The voice is not distinct from numerous others that enter the poem; the inspiration is patently plural. I would posit the poet as a reader rather than a puppeteer, his poem a rendered reading of another text which he contemplates by our side. "And albeit whatever thing we hear or see, sitting, walking, travelling, or conversing, may be fitly called our book" (*Areopagitica*, p. 733). The inherited myths, the inherited structures of language are our book. The similes, highly allusive, heavily based upon classical and biblical texts, inhabited by suns and peasant and an artist who look, do much to foreground the act of reading. Milton's humanism seems to dominate his Puritanism on this point: we read in the company of those who have read before.

V. The navigation does not by itself get us to the other side; the landing on shore calls for grace. Milton's similes inculcate agility of mind: points diverse in human and divine history, in ordered philosophy, fable, nature observed, points which seem merely disparate to a man too comfortably lodged in his own space and time, are seen to have mutual relevance. There is an agility that is cultivated for purposes of evil (Satan's "ambivalent words"), and there is another that keeps us strong ("our faith and knowledge thrives by exercise, as well as our limbs and complexion," *Areopagitica*, p. 739). That which we cannot resolve but must continually posit is there for our good as well.

Galileo's astronomy is a going forth, an intellectual and creative project. The Copernican revolution was presumably long established but, in *Paradise Lost*, as elsewhere in Renaissance literature, the Copernican and Ptolemaic schemata are used alternately as sources for poetic image. Milton invokes the Prutenic tables in *Doctrine and Discipline of Divorce*,[21] though they had already been surpassed by Kepler's. Merritt Hughes (*Complete Poems*, p. 706n.) says that the perpetual revision of human understanding is precisely the point. However structured the wheel of day and night, it "needs not thy belief" (VIII, 136). The distances of celestial space are "inexpressible / By Numbers that have name" (VIII, 113–14). The unnamable has a singular potency. The power to name belongs in the created world to man alone, and is rightly the source of major confidence. When Adam named the animals, he knew at once their inmost natures. The significance of names extends beyond the human: the fallen angels have their names erased from the Book of Life, and we are to regard this as a dire consequence. We know them only by the names they have assumed as seducers of men. To be without name in the Book of Life is to have all opportunity for recovery of their heavenly state denied. The vessels that housed their former essences have been broken; they exist only as fallen. The creatures without name, like the spaces between the stars, their movements and patterns of subordination, so difficult to read, are not for naught. They exist "That Man may know he dwells not in his own" (VIII, 103).

As the space between celestial bodies instructs, so the space between vehicle and tenor instructs. There's slippage here, and space we cannot wholly resolve into either term. The poem resists complete synthesis in order that the reader may know there is more in the world than can be owned (made into himself) by man. Disjunctions are built into the figurative text to remind us of the space and our dependence. The starry lamps in Pandemonium yield light "as from a sky" (I, 730). The metaphor embodied in an adjective (starry) has encouraged this analogue, and the simile, paradoxically, calls attention to the falseness of the image. As from a sky: not only is there no sky in Pandemonium, there is no sky in Hell; there are only the vaults of fire. We think of any landscape as beneath a sky. The image betrays our assumptions, articulates as exceptional an analogue we tend to take for granted. Similarly, the angels spring up "as when men wont to watch / On duty, sleeping found by whom they dread, / Rouse and bestir themselves ere well awake" (I, 332–34). A homing instinct predisposes us to compare all things with ourselves. "As when men," oddly, warns us to respect the distance.

> and how he fell
> From Heav'n, they fabl'd, thrown by angry Jove
> Sheer o'er the Crystal Battlements: from Morn
> To Noon he fell, from Noon to dewy Eve,
> A Summer's day; and with the setting Sun
> Dropt from the Zenith like a falling Star,
> On Lemnos th'Aegean Isle: thus they relate,
> Erring.   (I, 740–47)

The error is identified as an error in dating: he fell much earlier than men relate. The laminations of time get complicated: Mulciber fell, not before Jove threw him, but before there were men to make up stories about the gods. One of the functions of this and similar anachronisms is to insist on the temporal precedence of the Christian God. Another is to cast doubt on the nature as well as the timing of myths. Achieved suspension is the quality that unites Pandemonium and the fall of its architect, as portrayed in classical myth. "From the arched roof / Pendant by subtle Magic many a row / Of Starry Lamps and blazing Cressets . . . yielded light" (I, 72–79); "From Morn / To Noon he fell, from Noon to dewy Eve, / A Summer's day," which is the longest day. We make a turning at the end of a line and encounter "Erring." The suddenness of the judgment is difficult to assimilate. Milton the poet has derived clear benefit from the classical image, has recreated it, and another to match, in distinctly attractive form. Time and space are extended as if to offer repose and consolation. "Nor aught avail'd him now / To have built in Heav'n high Tow'rs" (I, 748–49). The towers are built again in the poem, as the fall is built in fable and the capitol in Hell; their material is nostalgia, a longing backward to the forms of heaven. We are not to take up lodging in these structures, but to use them for moving on. "The light which we have gained, was given us, not to be ever staring on, but by it to discover onward things more remote from our knowledge" (*Areopagitica*, p. 742). We are warned, lest we be too much consoled.

The insubstantiality of Pandemonium is made even clearer by analogy to a straw-built citadel. The angels, even before their "actual" transformation in size, are like bees. But weakness and diminution are not the only points. A straw-built hive is built by the beekeeper, not by bees; their sweetness is all dependent. "When the sun in Taurus rides . . ." (I, 769): having dismissed the fable of the ancients, does Milton expect us to read Taurus as devoid of classical allusion? Or the earth's giant sons as less to be doubted than Mulciber's fall? Surely not.

> they but now who seem'd
> In bigness to surpass Earth's Giant Sons
> Now less than smallest Dwarfs, in narrow room
> Throng numberless, like the Pigmean Race
> Beyond the Indian Mount, or Faery Elves,
> Whose midnight Revels, by a Forest side
> Or Fountain some belated Peasant sees,
> Or dreams he sees.
>   . . . .
>   they on thir mirth and dance
> Intent, with jocund Music charm his ear.   (I, 777–87)

The "seem'd" casts doubt, not on the earth's giant sons, but on the relative size of the angels. The possible elves may be dreamt, but they take on enough reality to dance in the poem. If we, like the peasant, are belated because attached to the myths of earlier times, surely Milton is too. He employs the beauty and momentum of two constructs, and undoes them only to substitute others with similar materials. The warning may partly be, of course, that beauty formed without thought of God is no beauty to be trusted. Hartman affirms that we don't undo the work of the simile by being restored to "better judgment." The poem may caution us about the appetites to which similes appeal, the pleasures derived from stories, from the senses, but the figures are not therefore disposable. Milton builds with inherited stories and words. To read "dreams he sees" and "Erring" as signals of univocal control is like reading Othello's "It is not words that shakes me thus" as unparadoxical.

Raphael introduces the process of human understanding by means of a vegetative image:

> So from the root
> Springs lighter the green stalk, from thence the leaves
> More aery, last the bright consummate flow'r
> Spirits odorous breathes.   (V, 479–82)

If similes in *Paradise Lost* at times remind us of Eve's hair in wanton ringlets (IV, 306), they are trained to the elm of our greater inquiry.

We may look for unity too soon, or in the wrong place, miscalculating either our self-sufficiency or our helplessness, and thereby turn from God. Straight paths do exist. When Raphael stands at the opened gates of Heaven, he travels first with his eye: "From hence, no cloud, or, to obstruct his sight / Star interpos'd, however small he sees" (V, 257–58). Then, in borrowed shape he "Sails between worlds and worlds" (V, 268). Man's path, except to destruction, is "less assur'd." Satan, leading Eve to mischief swift, "made intricate seem straight" (IX, 632). The highway forged between Hell and Earth by Sin and Death is straight:

> a Bridge
> Of length prodigious joining to the Wall
> Immoveable of this now fenceless World
> Forfeit to Death; from hence a passage broad,
> Smooth, easy, inoffensive down to Hell.   (X, 301–05)

They have stopped all flux to pave their route:

> As when two Polar Winds blowing adverse
> Upon the Cronian Sea, together drive
> Mountains of Ice, that stop th'imagin'd way
> Beyond Petsora Eastward, to the rich
> Cathaian Coast.   (X, 289–93)

The way is not less crucial because it is imagined:

> As when by night the Glass
> Of Galileo, less assur'd, observes
> Imagin'd Lands and Regions in the Moon:
> Or Pilot from amidst the Cyclades
> Delos or Samos first appearing kens
> A cloudy spot.   (V, 261–66)

The imagination, though liable to fog or mirage, is our light. The truth, though single once and continuing so in the mind of God, is not so to her human friends. They must gather her scattered limbs as Isis gathered those of Osiris (*Areopagitica*, p. 742). We must not take the part for the whole; to do so is to despair of God and to ally with Belial, making hell

The Limbs of Truth 151

more livable. We may not, on the other hand, treat as indifferent all earthly modes of understanding. The gathering is the way we wait for grace. Gatherers in a field do not walk in a single straight line, but their steps are not therefore unguided.

Stanford University

NOTES

1. Stanley Fish, *Surprised by Sin: The Reader in "Paradise Lost"* (New York, 1967), p. 311.

2. Page and line references to Miltonic texts are derived, unless otherwise noted, from *John Milton, Complete Poems and Major Prose*, ed. Merritt Y. Hughes (1957; rpt. Indianapolis, 1977).

3. The writer/persona of *Sonnet 19* hears in "stand and wait" his profoundest task in the service of God. But the mind and language are hardly at rest in the poem. Structures of stasis may encourage—indeed, require—movement within. The structure of the sonnet contributes to the accelerated momentum of enjambment. The consequent submergence of rhyme accentuates the starkness of the final demand, and withholds the comfort of resounding closure.

4. James Holly Hanford, "Milton's Style and Versification," in *A Milton Handbook*, 4th ed. (New York, 1946), p. 319.

5. "Milton I," in *Selected Prose of T. S. Eliot*, ed. Frank Kermode (New York, 1975), p. 259, first published in *Essays and Studies of the English Association*, 1936.

6. James Whaler names this function in "The Miltonic Simile," *PMLA*, XLVI (1931), 1034, 1036, 1048–52, 1071.

7. *The Towneley Plays*, ed. George England and Alfred W. Pollard, *EETS*, ES LXXI (1897; rpt. London, 1966), Play X, lines 33–34, 61–62.

8. "Figura," trans. Ralph Manheim, in *Scenes from the Drama of European Literature* (Gloucester, Mass., 1973). The essay first appeared in *Neue Dantestudien* (Istanbul, 1944).

9. Ibid, p. 23.

10. To better illuminate the function and valence of ornament, Angus Fletcher revives the Greek term *kosmos* and reminds his readers of the etymological connection between such words as *cosmic* and *cosmetic*. See his discussion of the cosmic image in *Allegory: The Theory of a Symbolic Mode* (Ithaca, 1964), pp. 108–17.

11. See especially Aphorisms XXIII and XLV in Book I of *Novum Organum*, trans. James Spedding, in *The Works of Francis Bacon*, VIII, ed. James Spedding, Robert Ellis, and Douglas Heath (Boston, 1863).

12. P. 1064.

13. See "Pharaoh," in England and Pollard, *The Towneley Plays*, lines 160, 232, 247, 257, 388.

14. The periphrasis, moreover, has a history. The Roman poets commonly referred to the Argo as the "pine of Pelion." See Ernst Robert Curtius, "The Ship of the Argonauts," in *Essays on European Literature*, trans. Michael Kowal (Princeton, 1973), first published as *Kritische Essays zur europäischen Literatur*, 2nd ed. (Bern, 1954).

15. "The Miltonic Simile," p. 1057.

16. "Milton's Counterplot," *ELH*, XXV (1958), 8.

17. The comparison of poetic composition to a voyage by sea was a commonplace among the Roman authors and continues in such later poems as the *Paradiso* (II, 1–15) and *The Faerie Queene* (VI, xii, 1). In a short thesaurus of "nautical metaphors," E. R. Curtius surfaces only one direct reference, however, to the reader's part in the navigation (*European Literature and the Latin Middle Ages*, trans. Willard R. Trask, Bollingen Series XXXVI [New York, 1953], pp. 128–30; originally published as *Europäischen Literatur und lateinisches Mittelalter* [Bern, 1948]). In "The Ship of the Argonauts," Curtius traces a related theme from the Greeks to Goethe. Of special interest here is the emergence of an attendant figure: the observer on shore who finds the ship mysterious and attempts to "read" its nature and significance. Thus, though the Argo itself is not explicitly summoned as an image for the writing of the poem, it does figure as a stimulus to and representative of human inquiry.

18. The term is Hartman's, "Milton's Counterplot," p. 8.

19. The term is Whaler's, "The Miltonic Simile," p. 1060.

20. *Complete Poems*, p. 219n. The allusion to Virgil is documented here as well.

21. *The Doctrine and Discipline of Divorce*, in *Complete Prose Works of John Milton*, II, ed. Ernest Sirluck (New Haven, 1959), p. 243.

MILTON'S SECRET GARDEN: STRUCTURAL CORRESPONDENCES BETWEEN MICHAEL'S PROPHECY AND *PARADISE REGAINED*

Mary Wilson Carpenter

THE THEMATIC relationship between *Paradise Lost* and *Paradise Regained* is clearly established by the title and induction of the latter poem: *Paradise Regained* is to be in every respect a sequel, a completion of *Paradise Lost*. Arnold Stein even suggests that the induction is something of a literary joke, for it implies that *Paradise Regained* is, after all, the *real* epic, rather than the tale of the "happy Garden" lost.[1] Indeed, Milton's nephew reported that his uncle "could not hear with patience" those who felt that the shorter epic was in any way inferior to the longer.[2] Milton's own conception of the exact relationship between the two poems, however, has remained an unknown quantity which has long exercised critics and students. This essay will seek to demonstrate a hitherto unexplored dimension of the relationship between the two poems: a carefully ordered and elaborately symmetrical series of thematic correspondences between the ten temptations in *Paradise Regained* and ten sections of Michael's prophecy in Books XI and XII of *Paradise Lost*.

In an article in *Milton Studies*, Richard Jordan pointed out not only that there are precisely ten temptations in *Paradise Regained*, but that the number of temptations in each of the four books matches the number of the book:

Book I: Stones-to-bread temptation

Book II: Banquet temptation
            Riches temptation

Book III: Glory temptation
            Throne-of-Israel temptation
            Parthia temptation

153

Book IV: Rome temptation
            Learning-of-Greece temptation
            Storm temptation
            Pinnacle-of-temple temptation[3]

Jordan proposes that the primary comparison in the poem is between
Adam and Christ, or fallible and infallible man, and that the numerological structure is a symbolic representation of the contrast between
man under grace (represented by the number four, for the four Gospels)
and man under the Law (represented by the number ten, for the Ten
Commandments).[4]

     The numerological design which he demonstrates, however, ap-
pears to be only part of an intricate, mathematically balanced, interlocking structure with the last two books of *Paradise Lost*, which further supports the comparison and contrast between fallen man and
perfect Son of God. Within each of the ten temptations as characterized
by Jordan are themes and images that correspond to the parallel section
of Michael's prophecy. For example, after the third scene portraying
the temptations of music, metals, and the marrying of richly dressed
women, Michael warns Adam against the self-indulgent pursuit of pleasure and "effeminate slackness" (*PL* XI, 634). After the third temptation in *Paradise Regained*, the temptation to "Get Riches first," Christ
replies in accents similar to Michael's that riches only "slacken Virtue"
and are "the toil of Fools" (*PR* II, 452–54). Similarly, in the eighth
section of Michael's prophecy, the archangel instructs Adam in the
meaning and purpose of the Law, while Christ responds to the eighth
temptation with a statement on the significance of the Law. Following
his fifth temptation, Satan wishes he could fly to the forgiving shade of
Christ's brow, while Adam interprets the rainbow in Michael's fifth
scene as the sign of God's forgiving brow. Each temptation can be
similarly matched with a corresponding theme at the same point in Michael's prophecy.

     But there may be an even more elaborate and subtle symmetry be-
tween the two works, emanating from the symbolism of vision. The ten
sections of each work can be divided at the point where Michael pro-
fesses to end visual presentation ("I perceive / Thy mortal sight to fail
. . . Henceforth what is to come I will relate," *PL* XII, 8–11) and at the
point where Satan begins to emphasize it, removing Christ to the "specular mount." That these shifts in technique occur at the same point in
both works—between the first and last five revelations or temptations—
suggests that Michael's first five, "visual" revelations may correspond to

Satan's second five, "visual" temptations and vice versa. This in fact appears to be the case. The particularly "visual" halves of each work balance each other like matching windows above an altar. The more nonvisual halves similarly appear to balance along the more abstract continuum of the search for truth, although correspondences between these sections are harder to discern and less convincing. The correspondences I propose between Michael's prophecy and *Paradise Regained* nevertheless constitute a display of numerical balances and symmetry even more ingenious than the numerical balancing of temptations and book number in *Paradise Regained* demonstrated by Jordan.

Jordan's analysis of a numerological design for Milton's brief epic is not the first evidence of Milton's fondness for what Arthur Barker has described as "dealing with poetic material in clearly defined and precisely balanced blocks."[5] James Whaler, in *Counterpoint and Symbol*, demonstrates a mathematical construction of verse paragraphs in *Paradise Lost* based on the same numerical design as the temptation structure in *Paradise Regained:* 1-2-3-4 or 4-3-2-1.[6] John T. Shawcross not only proposes a balanced bipartite structure and a pyramidal construction but discusses the existence of numerological relationships in *Paradise Lost*.[7] In "The Apocalypse Within *Paradise Lost*," Michael Fixler proposes a sevenfold structure for Milton's great epic, based on the sevenfold structure of Revelation, or the Apocalypse of St. John of Patmos.[8] More recently, Galbraith Crump has proposed a "circular" construction for *Paradise Lost*, or a precisely balanced structure of concentric rings, in which Book I balances Book XII, Book II balances Book XI, and so on, with the structure moving toward a point in the center at which Christ ascends to heaven.[9] Both Fixler and Crump, moreover, propose Milton's extensive use of inverted, as well as corresponding, parallels.

Critics have also discovered correspondences between *Paradise Regained* and *Paradise Lost* based on the "triple equation," a group of three temptations which appears in the same sequence in both works. Elizabeth Pope first demonstrated that Satan tempts Christ to intemperance, vainglory, and ambition, just as Adam and Eve were earlier tempted in *Paradise Lost*.[10] Barbara Lewalski has in addition shown that Michael's prophecy is stuctured on this same triple equation.[11] Although the appearance of the triple equation three times in the two works is not, strictly speaking, evidence of numerological design, it does tend to confirm the averred Miltonic interest in numerical schemes.[12]

It is not inconsistent with Milton's already demonstrated practice, then, that there should be a precisely balanced series of ten correspondences between *Paradise Regained* and Michael's prophecy, or even a further elaboration of that balance into a perfectly reversed symmetry. I would like further to point out that, at the time *Paradise Regained* was published (1671), *Paradise Lost* was still in the form of ten books. Michael's prophecy was at that time contained entirely in the tenth book. As the pair of epics first existed, then, the interlocking structure I propose would have consisted of the four-by-ten numerological structure in *Paradise Regained* and a corresponding tenfold division in the tenth book of *Paradise Lost*. Milton's epics would thus have been linked by a cryptic, numerological design based on the number ten, which in Pythagorean terms represented perfection or completion. In Christian terms, the design would have posited Michael's vision of man under the Law as a ten-part structure symbolically representing that condition, while Christ's subjection to the ten temptations would have been "broken" by the number symbolically representing the New Covenant.[13]

The hypothesis that the epics are numerologically linked seems the more acceptable when we realize that the series of correspondences appears to have the same effect Arthur Barker has proposed for Milton's change of structure in *Paradise Lost:* the reduction of emphasis on Satan's work. The only difficulty with the four-times-ten numerological structure of *Paradise Regained* is that the brief epic may thus be interpreted as having a "satanic" design, or a structure controlled by Satan's ten temptations. Reduced to diagrammatic form, the structure is, as we should expect, asymmetrical, lopsided, and obviously doomed to fall:

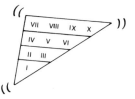

If, as Barker contends, Milton saw the need to rearrange *Paradise Lost* into twelve books in order "to reduce the structural emphasis on the Fall of Man and to increase the emphasis on his restoration," it seems unlikely that the poet would not have felt a similar need to balance with some divine symmetry this top-heavy structure apparently dictated by the ten temptations.[14] The system of correspondences between the temptations in *Paradise Regained* and the ten sections of Michael's prophecy appears to provide exactly this balance: temptations are shown to correspond to revelations, suggesting that both are actually the work of God. Although Satan may believe the earth to be his kingdom, and the believer may feel himself subject to the temptations of the devil, the subtle, hidden parallels between angelic prophecy and satanic temptation reveal that even Satan unwittingly carries forth the divine will. In this unwritten, prophetic dimension created by the correspondences between Milton's two epics, divine perfection overbalances earthly imperfection—and Satan sinks, disappears from the equation entirely.

II

Book XI of *Paradise Lost* does not begin immediately with Michael's prophecy, nor does *Paradise Regained* begin immediately with Satan's temptations. Nevertheless, there are striking correspondences between the opening sections of Book XI of *Paradise Lost* and Book I of *Paradise Regained*.[15] Book XI opens with the account of Adam's and Eve's repentance for their sins, and Book I opens with the account of John the Baptist calling the people to repentance and to baptism as a symbol of the washing away of their sins. Book XI continues with a divine council, in which the Son intercedes with the Father for Adam and Eve and is heard by the Father with serene and unclouded joy. Book I continues with a satanic council, in which Satan announces the sudden appearance of the Son on earth, and is heard by his "infernal crew" with dismay and fear. In *Paradise Lost*, God instructs the archangel Michael with his plans for Adam and Eve, namely their expulsion into the wilderness and their preparation for that experience; in *Paradise Regained*, he instructs the archangel Gabriel with his plans for the Son, namely his exercising in the wilderness and his final preparation there for his eventual conquest of Satan. Then follows Christ's entry into the wilderness, while in *Paradise Lost* Adam ascends the mount with Michael.

Such opening correspondences in themselves strongly suggest that the angelic instruction will in some sense parallel the satanic temptation. There is in addition the explicit comparison of Michael's mount to Satan's:

> It was a Hill
> Of Paradise the highest, from whose top
> The Hemisphere of Earth in clearest Ken
> Stretcht out to the amplest reach of prospect lay.
> Nor higher that Hill nor wider looking round,
> Whereon for different cause the Tempter set
> Our second *Adam* in the wilderness,
> To show him all Earth's Kingdoms and thir Glory. (XI, 377–84)

We cannot tell from this comparison which mountain is higher, or whether more can be seen from one than the other. Although the Tempter set Christ on his mount "for different cause," the suggestion is strong that the view is much the same from Mt. Niphates as from the hill of Paradise.

In the accompanying table I have detailed both the ten temptations in *Paradise Regained* and the corresponding ten sections of Michael's prophecy. Although the temptations are clearly demarcated, there is room for dispute over the precise number of divisions in Michael's prophecy. The divisions I have made, however, are simply those which appear to correspond to the temptations in *Paradise Regained*. In Book XI, each of these sections is marked by an introductory line such as "His eyes he op'n'd, and beheld . . ." (XI, 429), or "He look'd and saw a spacious Plain . . ." (XI, 556), indicating Adam's visual perception of a new scene, or a new, spatially defined region on earth. The first scene, beginning line 429, is a field in which Adam beholds a "Reaper" fell a Shepherd. The second, beginning line 497, is a lazar house in which he beholds all manner of disease. The third, beginning line 555, is a plain on which he beholds men living in riches and luxury and marrying beautiful women. The fourth, beginning line 638, is a "Territory" on which he first beholds men fighting in a "cruel Tournament" and then, "the face of things quite chang'd" (712), beholds them living in sinful merriment, in the midst of which they are engulfed by the Flood. Although Adam sees the men of this scene at different times, engaged in different occupations, everything appears to take place in the same "Territory." The fifth scene, beginning line 840, is the vision of the ark coming to rest on a mountain peak, and of the rainbow which Adam rightly interprets as the promise of God's forgiveness. These five scenes reveal striking correspondences to Satan's first five temptations in *Paradise Regained*.

The first angelic vision presents an unnamed farmer who offers "unculled" fruits on an altar, followed by a shepherd who offers the "choicest and best" of his flock. Heaven consumes the second offering with fire and "grateful steam," but the first offering is ignored because it "was not sincere." The farmer then kills the shepherd by smiting him in the midriff with a stone.

The vision represents Adam's first knowledge of death, and he responds to it with dismay and horror, but little else. He jumps to the conclusion that all death occurs in this manner and that he himself may die violently, so the angel quickly moves on to the second vision where he displays other kinds of death. Adam has missed the point, for he has failed to recognize a mirror image of his own lost innocence. The farmer's attempt to disguise his insincere offering mimics Adam's and Eve's attempt to hide their disobedience from God. Adam also fails to see that insincerity, or dissembling before God, is a root cause of human evil. Perhaps most significantly of all, Adam responds to the vision of human death with a fear which leads him into the sin of distrust. After the second vision of death, he rails against God's purpose in creating man in his Maker's image only to subject him to physical suffering:

> Why is life giv'n
> To be thus wrested from us? rather why
> Obtruded on us thus?
>   .   .   .   .
>   Can thus
> Th'Image of God in man created only once
> So goodly and erect, though faulty since,
> To such unsightly sufferings be debas't
> Under inhuman pains?   (XI, 502-11)

As Barbara Lewalski has pointed out, the first temptation in *Paradise Regained* cannot realistically be considered a temptation to gluttony, as Christ is not hungry yet.[16] Rather, it conforms to the Protestant interpretation of this first temptation as a temptation to distrust, or lack of faith. The first temptation in *Paradise Regained* therefore does not fit into the triple equation scheme discernible in the pattern of revelations in Michael's prophecy. It is the more interesting, then, that in the first temptation Satan's action appears to duplicate the farmer's in *Paradise Lost*, although Satan (as we should expect) adopts a new disguise.

Michael's scene shows the farmer—a type of Adam, and therefore of mankind after the Fall—murdering the good shepherd, a type of Christ.[17] Motivated by envy (of Abel's greater favor with God), Cain turns a stone into a weapon and kills his brother with it—by hitting him "in the Midriff," oddly enough. In the first temptation, Satan appears in what Stewart Baker has called an "outrageously literal parody" of the Good Shepherd, and he too attempts to turn the stones of the desert into weapons against the true Good Shepherd by tempting Christ to turn them into bread.[18] He attempts, in short, to hit Christ "in the Midriff"— the seat of hunger—with a stone. However, since Christ does not as yet experience hunger, Satan's temptation actually aims at the greater sin of distrust, tempting Christ not to accept hunger and even death as the will of God. In this respect, Christ's response is the opposite of Adam's, for he replies, "Man lives not by Bread only, but each Word / Proceeding from the mouth of God" (I, 349-50).

TABLE OF CORRESPONDENCES

Opening correspondences	
Adam and Eve's repentance	John calls the people to repentance
Divine council: the Son intercedes with the Father	Satanic council: Satan confers with his Powers
God instructs Michael	God instructs Gabriel
Michael and Adam "ascend in the Visions of God"	Christ enters the wilderness

Revelations	*Temptations*
1. The farmer kills the "good shepherd" with a stone	1. Satan tempts Christ to turn stones into bread
2. Lazar-house vision of physical deformity and death: demonstration of consequences of intemperance, particularly in eating	2. Banquet temptation: temptation to intemperance
3. Vision of the "spacious Plain" with music, metals, and fair women: demonstration of sensual intemperance	3. Temptation to riches, or to intemperate greed
4. Vision of "wide Territory" with "cruel Tournament"; two just men singled out by God	4. Temptation to military glory; Christ cites Job and Socrates as examples of those who suffered for truth's sake
5. Vision of ark on mountain; Adam interprets rainbow as "God's brow" and sign of forgiveness	5. Temptation to Kingdom of Israel for "zeal and duty"; Satan desires to fly to Christ's brow, but can't accept forgiveness

Cessation of angelic visions
(Michael "relates" only)

6. Michael relates stories of a "mighty Hunter" and Tower of Babel as examples of unlawful attempts at political dominion

7. Adam permitted to see the Promised Land

8. Michael's discourse on the Law: prophecy of Christ's lineage and birth

9. Michael's prophecy of Christ's suffering, death, and Resurrection; teaches about baptism, false signs and portents

10. Adam learns to obey, and to suffer for truth's sake

Michael and Adam descend, Adam and Eve take their "solitary way" into Eden and the world

Christ and Satan ascend "specular mount"
(Satan displays elaborate visions)

6. Satan tempts Christ to political dominion, exhibits Parthian warriors with "Steel Bows and Shafts"

7. Christ shown the earthly empire of Rome by Satan's "strange Parallax or Optic skill"

8. Greek idyll; Christ discourses on the Law

9. Satan prophesies Christ's suffering and death; torments Christ with storm, false signs, and portents

10. Christ balances on the pinnacle, Satan falls

Christ returns to his mother's house in "private" and "unobserv'd"

The first temptation in *Paradise Regained* therefore contains the same symbolic elements as the first scene in Michael's prophecy—stones which become the weapons of temptation, the good or True Shepherd, and the individual who tries to deceive God with an insincere offering. Everything about Satan demonstrates the same fundamental sin manifested by Cain, insincerity before God: his pretense of admiring recognition; his attempt to trick Christ into a superficial kind of "shepherd-hood," in which he would feed a few of the hungry while neglecting universal spiritual hunger; his disguise as a good shepherd himself; and above all, his lengthy speech after Christ recognizes him—a speech that is one long tissue of lies. Satan does in the first temptation precisely what Cain does in the first angelic scene: he pretends sincerity before God, and he attempts to usurp the place of the Good Shepherd, one way or another.

Finally, Adam's response is the opposite of Christ's: he fails to have faith in God, while Christ responds to all Satan's dissimulations and to the reality of deprivation and physical death with perfect faith. Insincerity and the temptation to distrust serve as the crux in both angelic scene and satanic temptation.

The second and third angelic scenes represent the sins of intemperance as related specifically first to Eve's weakness—intemperance in eating—and second to Adam's—intemperance of the passions.[19] The second and third temptations also are appeals to intemperance, first to sensual indulgence and then to riches and the power generated by wealth. Michael first shows Adam a "Lazar-house" in which all kinds of human diseases are represented, explaining to him that these result from intemperance "In Meats and Drinks." Next he shows Adam a plain, where men live in wealth and pleasure, composing music, molding metals at a forge, and marrying "fair Women" richly and alluringly dressed. Adam responds to the lazar-house vision by protesting the deformity of God's image in man's physical deformities and diseases. Michael tells him that it is *man* who deforms his "Maker's image" in himself, not God. It is man's own intemperance which leads to spiritual and physical deformity. But Adam reveals his spiritual blindness even more in the third scene, when he exclaims to the angel: "True opener of mine eyes, prime Angel blest, / Much better seems this Vision" (XI, 598–99). Perhaps not unexpectedly for a recent inhabitant of Paradise, he equates surface beauty and pleasure with goodness. Michael patiently explains that the "females" he saw were "empty of all good wherein consists / Women's domestic honor and chief praise," and that their superficial attractiveness can lure good men away from their religion. At this, Adam falls again, concluding that the moral of the angel's lesson is that "the tenor of Man's woe / Holds on the same, from Woman to begin" (XI, 632–33). It is here that Michael rather brusquely replies, "From Man's effeminate slackness it begins," pointedly insisting that human misery derives from failure to control the passions and sensual appetites.

Satan's second temptation, the banquet scene, clearly tempts Christ to the sin of intemperance in eating. Not only is Christ explicitly hungry now (II, 246–47), but Satan proudly contrasts his sumptuous banquet with "the crude Apple that diverted Eve!" (II, 349). The banquet scene also includes both beautiful women and boys, and is in every way intensely alluring to the senses. Yet Christ "temperately" restrains his right—as the Son of God—to whatever he desires. Even Satan has to admit, grudgingly, that Christ displays "temperance invincible" and in the third temptation cleverly makes no appeal to the senses. Instead, he urges Christ to "get Riches first," an argument that rhetorically parallels the third angelic scene of wealth, women, and luxurious living. Christ, however, apparently discerns that the temptation to "get Riches first" merely aims more subtly at the sin of intemperance. His reply echoes Michael's emphasis on control of the passions and avoidance of "slackness":

> Extol not Riches then, the toil of Fools
> The wise man's cumbrance if not snare, more apt
> To slacken Virtue and abate her edge
> Than prompt her to do aught may merit praise.
> . . . .
> Yet he who reigns within himself, and rules
> Passions, Desires, and Fears, is more a King;
> Which every wise and virtuous man attains:
> And who attains not, ill aspires to rule
> Cities of men, or headstrong Multitudes,
> Subject himself to Anarchy within,
> Or lawless passions in him, which he serves. (II, 453–72)

The first three sets of angelic revelations and satanic temptations, then, present the same evils—insincerity, the temptation to distrust, and intemperance—and display an instructive contrast between fallen man and perfect Son of God. Adam is still spiritually blind: he responds to the angelic scenes with undisciplined passions and lack of faith. Christ, however, responds to Satan's dissimulation with perfect perception of divine truth and with invincible faith, just as he responds with "temperance invincible" to sensory and mercenary temptations.

In the fourth pair of revelation and temptation scenes, both Christ and Michael denounce glory as humanity understands it—that is, *military* glory. Indeed, Michael's and Christ's statements are nearly identical in substance at these corresponding points. Michael first shows Adam a "wide Territory" in which "Giants of mighty Bone, and bold emprise" carry on a "cruel Tournament," perpetrating "slaughter and gigantic deeds." He then explains:

> For in those days Might only shall be admir'd,
> And Valor and Heroic Virtue call'd;
> To overcome in Battle, and subdue
> Nations, and bring home spoils with infinite
> Man-slaughter, shall be held the highest pitch
> Of human glory, and for Glory done
> Of triumph, to be styl'd great Conquerors,
> Patrons of Mankind, Gods, and Sons of Gods,
> Destroyers rightlier call'd and Plagues of men.
> Thus Fame shall be achiev'd, renown on Earth,
> And what most merits fame in silence hid.   (XI, 689–99)

In the fourth temptation, Satan urges Christ that it is not too late yet for him to achieve glory such as that of "Macedonian Philip," to which Christ replies:

> They err who count it glorious to subdue
> By Conquest far and wide, to overrun
> Large countries, and in field great Battles win,
> Great Cities by assault: what do these Worthies,
> But rob and spoil, burn, slaughter, and enslave
> Peaceable Nations, neighboring or remote,
> Made Captive, yet deserving freedom more
> Than those thir Conquerors, who leave behind
> Nothing but ruin wheresoe'er they rove,
> And all the flourishing works of peace destroy,
> Then swel with pride, and must be titl'd Gods,
> Great Benefactors of mankind, Deliverers,
> Worship't with Temple, Priest and Sacrifice?
> . . . .
> But if there be in glory aught of good,
> It may by means far different be attain'd,
> Without ambition, war, or violence;
> By deeds of peace, by wisdom eminent,
> By patience, temperance.   (III, 71–92)

Another striking parallel is that both angel and Son of God characterize the temptation to military glory as *vainglory*, or the desire to become as gods. Both prophecy and temptation thus follow the triple equation, progressing from intemperance to vainglory at identical stages.[20]

But there are other, and deeper, correspondences here. It is in response to the fourth scene that Adam, for the first time, weeps for his own and mankind's sins. "All in tears," he turns to Michael and asks:

> O what are these,
> Death's Ministers, not Men, who thus deal Death
> Inhumanly to men, and multiply
> Tenthousandfold the sin of him who slew
> His Brother. (XI, 675–79)

After explaining the wrongful conception of glory, Michael shows how the people engaged in violence turn to equally sinful merrymaking, and then how all are swept away in a flood. Adam responds with terrible anguish, recognizing for the first time the full extent of his own evil and its dreadful consequences. He also sees for the first time two examples of just men who foreshadow Christ. The first just man, arguing alone against the violence of his fellows, is snatched up by a cloud and translated into heaven. The second, who also admonishes his fellows, is instructed by God to build an ark, in which he will save a remnant of mankind from the Flood. Adam has thus for the first time truly repented his sins and begun to have some understanding of how a single just man could be singled out by God. The two just men both function as types of Christ, one prefiguring his reward in heaven after trials on earth, and the other his freedom from the sins of mankind and consequent salvation for all mankind.

It is during the fourth temptation that Christ also first begins to perceive that his mission will involve suffering. Interestingly, he does not cite messianic prophecy, but instead draws on biblical and secular history for examples or types, just as the angel teaches Adam by means of messianic types. He speaks of Job and of Socrates, who "For Truth's sake suffering death unjust, lives now / Equal in fame to proudest Conquerors" (III, 98–99). Christ seems to consider for the first time whether the kind of glory God intends for him may be not only a nonmilitary but even an otherworldly glory:

> Shall I seek glory then, as vain men seek
> Oft not deserved? I seek not mine, but his
> Who sent me, and thereby witness whence I am. (III, 105–07)

In both angelic and satanic sequences, then, the concept of suffering as divine mission appears after the first three-stage instruction in faith and temperance. Adam's progress in spiritual insight now parallels Christ's, prefiguring the availability of salvation to all men who perceive God's purpose.

In the fifth angelic scene, Adam sees the ark resting on a mountain-top and the dove alighting on it, symbolic of the gift of the Holy Spirit, as in baptism. Here Adam's religious joy begins, as he perceives that God will raise another whole world for the sake of one just and perfect man. Looking on the rainbow which Michael describes as a token of "peace from God, and Cov'nant new" (XI, 867), Adam demonstrates his faith and belief in God's forgiveness as he attempts to interpret the sign:

> But say, what mean those color'd streaks in Heav'n,
> Distended as the Brow of God appeas'd,
> Or serve they as a flow'ry verge to bind
> The fluid skirts of that same wat'ry Cloud,
> Lest it again dissolve and show'r the Earth?
>   To whom th'Arch-Angel. Dext'rously thou aim'st;
> So willingly doth God remit his Ire.   (XI, 879–85)

The angel compliments Adam for his spiritual "aim" at the meaning of the divine sign: the rainbow does indeed mean that God is appeased and his "Ire" remitted, through the grace of one just man.

Identical imagery appears in the fifth temptation in *Paradise Regained*, but here it indicates Satan's inability to believe in Christ's salvation, or the reverse of Adam's condition. After urging Christ to be moved by "Zeal / And Duty" and to consider himself bound to free his country from "Heathen servitude," Satan reveals his own self-imprisonment in his conviction that the "Father's ire" will not be remitted for him:

> My error was my error, and my crime
> My crime; whatever, for itself condemn'd,
> And will alike be punish'd; whether thou
> Reign or reign not; though to that gentle brow
> Willingly I could fly, and hope thy reign,
> From that placid aspect and meek regard,
> Rather than aggravate my evil state,
> Would stand between me and thy Father's ire
> (Whose ire I dread more than the fire of Hell)
> A shelter and a kind of shading cool
> Interposition, as a summer's cloud.   (III, 212–22)

Where Adam perceives the rainbow as God's "Brow" now "appeas'd," and holding back the "rain" of his justice, Satan believes that whether Christ "reigns" or reigns not, he will be punished. The use of homonyms in the two passages suggests a religiously meaningful pun lying in the "unwritten" dimension created by the correspondences between the two poems: God's reign contains both the meaning of vengeful justice, as expressed in the Flood, and of forgiveness offered to all men in Christ. Although Satan seems to experience glimmerings of the knowledge that Christ's "gentle brow" really could protect him from the "Father's ire," paralleling the metaphor of the rainbow which "binds" the cloud of God's justice in *Paradise Lost*, he cannot quite bring himself to accept this "interposition."

There also seems to be a precise imagistic balance between Adam's perception of the ark resting on a mountain peak and Satan's despairing statement that "worst is my Port." After the symbolically significant imagery of the Flood, a type of baptism, Adam attains the divine heights of belief in God's forgiveness. Satan, whose presence in the desert mirrors his spiritual dryness, will end up at the bottom of things, "worst" being his ultimate port and harbor.

In the first five pairs, then, Adam and Christ have begun very differently but come out near the same spiritual peak. Satan, however, has descended to a point where his lack of spiritual insight and faith is shown to be greater than that of the fallen Adam at the beginning of Michael's instruction. Both temptations and revelations have revealed the same five stages in salvation: the need for faith, the control of the passions, the rule of man's inner self, the perception of suffering as divine mission, and belief in God's forgiveness, or faith.

After his first five unsuccessful temptations, Satan removes Christ to the "specular mount," the better to tempt him with elaborate visual panoramas. At the corresponding point in *Paradise Lost*—the beginning of Book XII—the archangel denies physical sight to Adam:

> Much thou hast yet to see, but I perceive
> Thy mortal sight to fail; objects divine
> Must needs impair and weary human sense;
> Henceforth what is to come I will relate,
> Thou therefore give due audience, and attend.   (XII, 8–12)

Adam apparently has progressed beyond physical sight: now able to perceive divine truths figuratively, he no longer needs his "weary human sense." Satan's presentation of the Parthian, Roman, and Greek scenes moves in the contrary direction: he attempts to dazzle Christ's sight and keep his eye fixed on earthly visions. Angelic and satanic techniques are thus reversed at this point, yet revelations and temptations continue to reveal corresponding themes and images.

The first section of Michael's continuing revelation in Book XII describes the building of the Tower of Babel, a tower men erect in order to "reach to Heav'n" (XII, 44), and which stands as a physical embodiment of their attempt to usurp God's power and authority over men. One among these men, of "proud ambitious heart" (XII, 25), will be styled "A mighty Hunter" who will hunt men rather than beasts. But God derides the futile efforts of these ambitious men, confounding their language and making the building itself ridiculous.

In the sixth temptation, Satan does his best to trick Christ into the same kind of attempt at political domination. From his "specular mount" he first exhibits a catalogue of empires and then focuses on a specific example of successful military dominion: the Parthian kingdom. Urging Christ to utilize "means" to gain the kingdom foretold for him, Satan shows Christ the Parthian host hunting their enemies with "Steel Bows and Shafts," doubtless an advance over the weaponry employed by the "mighty Hunter" Michael describes. Satan's Cecil B. DeMille panorama also shows "laboring Pioneers" who follow the horsemen and

> lay hills plain, fell woods, or valleys fill,
> Or where plain was raise hill, or overlay
> With bridges rivers proud, as with a yoke.   (III, 332–34)

This enterprise not only strongly resembles the overly ambitious construction plans of the Tower of Babel builders, but is undertaken with the same purpose: the unlawful attempt to dominate other men politically. Satan, however, emphasizes the theme that Christ would merely be utilizing "means" to gain what is lawfully his anyway—a diabolically subtle misinterpretation of messianic prophecy.

Michael's instruction on, and Christ's response to, these highly similar "scenes" (Michael's is, of course, only narrated, not displayed visually) sound the identical theme: political liberty is lost through man's failure to rule his *inner* self, not through tyranny or captivity. Michael emphasizes the loss of "right Reason":

> Therefore since hee permits
> Within himself unworthy Powers to reign
> Over free Reason, God in Judgment just
> Subjects him from without to violent Lords.   (XII, 90–93)

Christ emphasizes lack of repentance and the worship of false gods:

> Should I of these the liberty regard,
> Who freed, as to their ancient Patrimony,
> Unhumbl'd, unrepentant, unreform'd,

> Headlong would follow, and to thir Gods perhaps
> Of Bethel and of Dan? No, let them serve
> Thir enemies, who serve Idols with God.   (III, 427–32)

But both archangel and Son of God repeat the theme that Paradise, or
God's kingdom, cannot be restored until man learns to rule his inner
kingdom.

The seventh revelation-temptation pair similarly points to Christ's
kingdom as a kingdom not of this world, and we see a comparison between the Promised Land, which foreshadows heaven, and the great
secular kingdom of Rome. Michael relates the story of God leading Israel into the Promised Land, permitting Adam—in an exception to his
rule of "relating" only—to glimpse the landscape. Since Adam sees the
Promised Land but cannot enter it, his experience prefigures Moses'
view from Mt. Pisgah. The story of the Promised Land thus becomes
another symbol of the heavenly kingdom God promises to his people,
and Adam significantly interrupts the angel at the point in his narration
where the people of Israel finally regain Canaan, exclaiming "now first
I find / Mine eyes true op'ning" (XII, 273–74). These lines suggest a
prophetic foreshadowing of the song of Simeon when he first sees the in-
fant Christ.

Satan's vision of Rome demonstrates a great secular empire in contrast to Michael's catalogue of Abraham's journey into the Promised
Land;[21] and where Adam achieves another stage of spiritual illumina-
tion in response to Michael's narration, the narrator in *Paradise Regained* comments on Satan's "strange Parallax or Optic skill" (IV, 40).
Parallax denotes the view of a heavenly body as changed by different
perspectives and, when unmodified, refers specifically to a geocentric
perspective. Clearly, the angelic and the satanic visions of earthly land-
scapes are directly opposed in meaning, one pointing toward the heavenly kingdom and the other focused narrowly on the earth. Christ
responds to Rome's magnificence, however, by prophesying that his
own kingdom will

> be like a tree
> Spreading and overshadowing all the Earth,
> Or as a stone that shall to pieces dash
> All Monarchies besides throughout the world,
> And of my Kingdom there shall be no end.   (IV, 147–51)

Both the sixth and the seventh revelation and temptation pairs, then,
develop the concept of the Promised Land as a kingdom not of this
world. Although Adam beholds the Promised Land with his own eyes,

he perceives it as a symbol of God's Covenant with his people, and Christ similarly describes his kingdom in metaphorical terms, indicating its extratemporal nature.

After Michael's narration of the descent of Moses from Abraham, and the establishment of "Laws and Rites" in Moses' time, Adam ingenuously inquires why God gives "So many and so various Laws" (XII, 282). Michael's answer emphasizes that while the Law is imperfect in itself, it leads men to look for that "better Cov'nant" of which it is only a forerunner. The Law, in essence, is prophetic: it points toward those greater truths which lie beyond flesh and "shadowy Type." The archangel then continues with a prophecy of the rise of "the Woman's seed to thee foretold," who will be born of the royal house of David but will be barred from his rightful throne because of Israel's internal strife and dissension. Adam responds to Michael's prophecy with an inspired salute to the "Virgin Mother," and in the succeeding section the archangel emphasizes that Christ will fulfill the Law of God "Exact" (XII, 402).

Just as the subject of Michael's eighth section of revelation is the Law, so the focus of Christ's response to Satan's eighth temptation is the Law. Where Michael explains the significance of the Law as type of the "better Cov'nant" which will succeed it, Christ affirms the superiority of the Law over classical learning, stating that the Law *precedes* the classics. He flatly rejects Satan's third vision from the specular mount, the surpassingly beautiful "Olive Grove of Academe," stating that classical learning is a "false resemblance" only of wisdom. The Greek arts are derived from the Hebrew "Law and Story," and the Prophets teach "solid rules of Civil Government" better than "all the Oratory of Greece and Rome" (IV, 334–64). This much commented-upon rejection of classical literature takes on new meaning when seen with its parallel in Michael's prophecy, for the emphasis is clearly on the divine inspiration of the Law, not on classical literature, whatever its merits or demerits. The Law is seen both as prior to the wisdom of Greece and Rome and as pointing beyond it, to the fulfillment of the Kingdom of God. Filled with "light from above," it is superior to literature which can reveal only the "light of Nature," despite the shadowy and imperfect character of the Law. Seen in this double framework, Milton's statements about the Law constitute a restatement of some of Du Bartas' arguments for Christian poetry in *L'Uranie*.[22]

A further parallel between the two passages is that, where Michael moves from his dissertation on the Law as type of greater truths to the prophecy of one who will fulfill that Law "exact," Christ characterizes himself at this point as "he who receives / Light from above, from the fountain of light" (IV, 288–89). He is then himself the embodiment of that light, the fulfillment of the Law prophesied by Michael.

The correspondence between the ninth revelation and temptation focuses once again on Christ's suffering but relates it to the problem of false prophecy, and false teaching even in Christ's church. Both Michael and Satan, in these ninth sections, prophesy Christ's suffering and death, but Michael also foretells Christ's Resurrection and Ascension. He then continues with instruction as to how the faithful will be given "spiritual Armor," so that they can resist Satan's "fiery darts," and how the Spirit will be poured forth first on the apostles and then on all the baptized. Nevertheless, "Wolves shall succeed for teachers, grievous Wolves," and the truth will be tainted with superstitions by false spiritual leaders.

Following the eighth temptation, Satan also presumes to foretell Christ's future, predicting:

> Sorrows, and labors, opposition, hate,
> Attends thee, scorns, reproaches, injuries,
> Violences and stripes, and lastly cruel death.   (IV, 386–88)

In predicting Christ's sufferings and death, his prophecy corresponds closely to Michael's:

> For this he shall live hated, be blasphem'd,
> Seiz'd on by force, judg'd, and to death condemn'd
> A shameful and accurst, nail'd to the Cross
> By his own Nation, slain for bringing Life.   (XII, 411–14)

We note, however, that Satan merely predicts Christ's sufferings as an augury of cruel fate, or what is written in the stars, while Michael emphasizes that Christ's sufferings result from men's injustice and evil. And where Michael further prophesies Christ's Resurrection and Ascension, explaining how he will "bruise the head of Satan," defeat Sin and Death, drag Satan in chains through heaven, and eventually dissolve the entire world and turn it into Paradise, Satan either does not know or pretends not to know when Christ's kingdom will come:

> A Kingdom they portend thee, but what Kingdom,
> Real or Allegoric I discern not,
> Nor when, eternal sure, as without end,
> Without beginning; for no date prefixt
> Directs me in the Starry Rubric set.   (IV, 389–93)

Satan then subjects Christ to the storm in the desert, in which he pours down "Fierce rain with lightning mixt," a meteorological version

of the "fiery Darts" Michael prophesied for the faithful. Christ withstands the storm serenely, however, and meets Satan again the next
morning. Satan now proceeds to bombard Christ with false portents
and confusing oracles, first assuring him that the storm meant nothing
and was a harmless natural event, and then insisting that it was "a sure
foregoing sign" of the troubles Christ is bound to have if he does not listen to Satan's predictions of the proper *times* to do things. Christ replies
only briefly, informing Satan that he was neither frightened nor harmed
by the storm and that he recognizes such signs as "false portents, not
sent from God, but thee" (IV, 491).

In the storm scene, then, Satan enacts the false teaching and false
portents Michael predicts, and the storm itself is a symbolic counterpart
of the persecution and sufferings of the faithful, also foretold by Michael. Christ's resolute and calm resistance enrages Satan, who still
maintains that he cannot tell whether Christ is the Son of God, and if so
in what sense, since Satan himself is also a Son of God—or was. With
that, he snatches up Christ and flies to the pinnacle, there to test finally
whether he is the Son of God.

In this final temptation, Christ is placed on the highest pinnacle of
the temple in Jerusalem. Satan once more attempts to turn stones into
weapons by suggesting that Christ should command the angels to bear
him up lest he dash his foot against a stone when he falls. Instead, of
course, Satan falls, and angels then arrive and restore Christ to a new
Paradise, an outward counterpart of the inner paradise or kingdom
now founded "For Adam and his chosen Sons."

In the final scene of *Paradise Lost*, Adam attains a spiritual pinnacle with his insight that "to obey is best" and that "suffering for
Truth's sake / Is fortitude to highest victory, / And to the faithful
Death the Gate of Life" (XII, 569–71). But Adam then must descend
from the mountain and with Eve depart into the wilderness. Like
Christ, who "private return'd" to his Mother's house, Adam and Eve
take their "solitary way" through Eden and into the world. In both
works, then, the tenth and last section implies an ascension into a spiritual kingdom followed by a solitary, unheralded return to the real world.

III

In *Paradise Regained* and the last two books of *Paradise Lost*, I
have suggested a system of correspondences between same-numbered
pairs of temptations and revelations. Let me sum up the major themes
of those correspondences as I have described them:

1. Insincerity and lack of faith
2. Intemperance
3. Rule of the inner self
4. Perception of suffering as divine mission; rejection of vainglory
5. Faith in God's forgiveness; belief in New Covenant won by one just man

   Angelic and Satanic shift in visual presentation

6. False pinnacle of man's military and political ambition
7. Earthly empire as opposed to "Promised Land"
8. Classical literature and art as opposed to the Law and the Prophets
9. True and false prophecies of Christ's suffering; the storm as type of Christ's suffering and the persecution of the faithful
10. Adam's ascension to spiritual insight and Christ's balancing on the pinnacle; Christ's regaining of Paradise and Adam's descent from the mount; private and solitary return of both to the world

From this summary it appears that the second group of five revelation-temptation pairs recapitulates the themes of the first in some degree. The first three pairs of both groups cluster around spiritual obstacles to the true understanding and achievement of the kingdom within, while the last two pairs of both groups deal first with Christ's suffering and death, then with his Resurrection and Ascension, or types of those events. Both groups, then, present interpretations of the Kingdom of God as an inner paradise moving from man's emptiness to Christ's fulfillment. Both works are essentially prophetic: temptations are the equivalent of revelations in pointing toward the Kingdom of God and prophesying its attainment for fallen man and perfect Son of God alike.

The symbolism of vision, however, suggests not only a parallel, but a reversed, correspondence. I have earlier pointed out that Satan and Michael exchange methods of visual presentation at the same point in both sequences: between the first and the last five temptations or revelations. It is after the first five temptations that Satan removes Christ to the "specular mount," and during the seventh temptation that the narrator comments on the "strange Parallax or Optic skill" (IV, 40) by which Satan presents his visions to Christ's eyes. The phrase suggests a corollary to the purging of Adam's "visual Nerve" and removal of the

film from his eyes, since "he had much to see" (XI, 415), at the beginning of Michael's prophecy. This positioning of emphasis on visual perception, and the evidence gathered so far of a generally symmetrical
structure of correspondences between the two works, suggests that the
angel's and the devil's visual presentations may correspond, and, conversely, so may the "nonvisual" halves of each work. Of course, neither
half of either work is, in the strictest sense, entirely visual or nonvisual.
Although Michael characterizes his second five revelations as relation,
he nevertheless permits Adam to see the landscape of the Holy Land.
Similarly, Satan's first and second temptations are visually perceived by
Christ, while the storm and the pinnacle temptations take place after
Christ has been removed from the "specular mount." Yet the "visual"
and "nonvisual" halves of each work are consistent in a metaphorical
sense of the terminology of sight, for what Adam perceives in the first
half of the angelic revelation is what Satan strives hardest to bind Christ
to in the second half of the temptations—earthly appearances. Therefore, what may be characterized as the "visual shift" in the middle of
the two works does suggest a reverse correspondence between the first
section of one work and the last section of the other.

And indeed, Satan's second five temptations match Michael's first
five scenes so well as almost to appear double images for the same subject and theme. The first three of these double images depict man's
depravity: the first murder balanced by the portrayal of advanced warfare (Cain killing Abel, the Parthian scene); a gruesome depiction of
diseases caused by physical self-indulgence, and a scene of luxurious
and idolatrous feasting (the lazar house and the Roman scene); and a
scene of the Israelites feasting, marrying pagan women, and casting
idols balanced by a scene of secular art and beauty, equally irreligious
(the "spacious Plain" and the Greek idyll). The latter pair suggests a deliberate comparison between the Renaissance elevation of classical literature and art and the idolatry practiced by the Israelites.

The last two double images depict Christ's suffering and death, his
Resurrection and Ascension, in typological imagery; that is, Adam is
depicted as a type of Christ. In the fourth scene, Adam views the Flood
as it rolls over the entire world, while in the corresponding scene in
Paradise Regained Christ is inundated by Satan's storm. The narrator,
as if looking on these two images in devout meditation, responds with
markedly similar tone and feeling to both:

> How didst thou grieve then, Adam, to behold
> The end of all thy Offspring, end so sad,
> Depopulation; thee another Flood,

Of tears and sorrow a Flood thee also drown'd,
And sunk thee as thy Sons; till gently rear'd
By th'Angel, on thy feet thou stood'st at last,
Though comfortless, as when a Father mourns
His Children, all in view destroy'd at once;
And scarce to th'Angel utter'd'st thus thy plaint.   (XI, 754–62)

        ill wast thou shrouded then,
O patient Son of God, yet only stood'st
Unshaken; nor yet stay'd the terror there.
Infernal Ghosts, and Hellish Furies, round
Environ'd thee, some howl'd, some yell'd, some shriek'd,
Some bent at thee thir fiery darts, while thou
Satt'st unappall'd in calm and sinless peace.   (IV, 419–25)

Both flood and storm are types for the suffering of death, as Adam sinks to the ground and Christ is ill "shrouded" in the wilderness. While Adam is appropriately felled by his grief, however, Christ remains "Unshaken" and "unappall'd." But Adam is raised by the angel, who then presents the vision of the ark as symbol of God's New Covenant, in which God will save the world for the sake of one just man. Christ rises afresh with the new morning, an act which a later comment of Michael's serves to gloss as a type of the Resurrection: "the Stars of Morn shall see him rise / Out of his grave, fresh as the dawning light" (XII, 422–23). Then, in the final scene in *Paradise Regained*, Christ balances on the pinnacle, as the ark balances on the mountaintop in the final image of Book XI.

These pairs of brilliantly visual images depict a progression from man's depravity or deformity to Christ's perfection, a progression exemplified by Adam's protest after the lazar-house scene, that "his Maker's Image" is deformed in man, and the narrator's comment after the pinnacle scene that Christ is the "True Image of the Father."

The correspondence between the "visual" halves of Michael's prophecy and Satan's temptations seems to me remarkable. The correspondence between the "nonvisual" halves is less dramatically apparent, yet it is possible to detect a series of parallels along the continuum of truth as theme. In Michael's first revelation in Book XII, the Tower of Babel built as a sign of man's domination over man also exemplifies the confusion of tongues. From the tower arises a "jangling noise of words unknown" and "a hideous gabble" (XII, 55–56). This can be seen as a correspondence in fallen men to Satan's verbal insincerity and lies in the first temptation, suggesting that man and Satan alike are devoid of the spirit of truth.

Michael's next revelation concerns Israel's entry into the Promised Land, which Adam greets with the words, "now first I find / Mine eyes true op'ning, and my heart much eas'd" (XII, 273–74). In Satan's second temptation, Christ views the "pleasant Grove" from the top of a hill, an action which suggests a parallel to Adam's "Mt. Pisgah" view of the Promised Land. But Christ actually enters Satan's land of promises, and is there tempted by very real sensual delights, while Adam's mere sight of the Promised Land far off seems intended to be received as a prophecy of God's heavenly kingdom. The comparison between the two scenes suggests that Satan creates many false versions of the Promised Land on earth, and man must learn to distinguish the false from the true kingdom, as Christ does. It may also be a deliberately instructive difference that the archangel restricts Adam's vision to the bare landscape alone, apparently fostering prophetic vision or figurative reading rather than physical sight, while Satan multiplies visual and sensory details in a clear attempt to distract Christ from his spiritual condition.

In the eighth angelic revelation, Michael's homily on the Law merges into his prophecy of Christ's royal lineage. Michael's genealogy several times refers to the inheritance of wealth along with royal birth, but shows that by the time Christ is born he will be "Barr'd of his right" to both throne and wealth. Satan's third temptation is to "get Riches first" as necessary to rule. Christ, however, goes beyond Michael and Satan by rejecting wealth in order to affirm an inner kingdom of control over the passions. Here Christ distinguishes even between one interpretation of messianic prophecy and another, for he rejects the royal heritage Michael suggests is rightfully his as well as the search for riches urged by Satan. In these three pairs there appears to be a progression from the fundamental concept of truth itself (as opposed to Satan's lies and man's babble) to the discrimination of shades of truth concerning Christ and his kingdom.

In the ninth revelation, Michael prophesies Christ's suffering and death, stating that he will fulfill the Law "exact" through "coming in the Flesh / To a reproachful life and cursed death" (XIII, 405–06). He also prophesies his Resurrection and Ascension to heaven, where he will "enter into glory" and achieve his final triumph over Satan (XII, 451–65). In the fourth temptation Christ rejects military glory and proposes Job as an example of a man who, though he suffered on earth, received "true glory and renown" because God made him "Famous" in heaven. He cites also Socrates, who "For Truth's sake suffering death unjust, lives now / Equal in fame to proudest Conquerors" (III, 98–99). As already pointed out, it is at this stage in *Paradise Regained* that Christ first seems to gain insight into his divine mission to suffer (or, alternatively, makes his first statement of it), and in the corresponding nonvisual revelation, Michael similarly prophesies both his suffering and his reward in heaven.

And in the last section of *Paradise Lost*, Adam has learned that "to obey is best," and that "suffering for Truth's sake / Is fortitude to highest victory" (XII, 561, 569–70). Here Adam parallels almost exactly Christ's response to the fifth temptation (to the kingdom of Israel), that this is the time, not for him to gain a kingdom, but to suffer and obey.

The correspondences between the second five revelations and the first five temptations—the "nonvisual" halves—thus may be seen as a progression from man's emptiness of truth to Adam's and Christ's expressions of divine truth. This is, of course, a progression toward the kingdom within, or the inner paradise. The "spiritual" pinnacle achieved by both Adam and Christ in the last pair overbalances the material or "real" Tower of Babel in the first pair, which marks a false elevation of mankind. Note how perfectly appropriate this progression is also in its employment of visual imagery. The most visual scenes—the Tower of Babel, Satan's "Good Shepherd" and banquet temptations—exemplify lies, the opposite of truth, while the progression toward the inner kingdom of truth is more and more nonvisual.

Both the "visual" and "nonvisual" halves of Michael's prophecy and *Paradise Regained* begin with the deformities of man and move toward the perfection of Christ. They also, like the progression in the ten correspondences, may be seen as man's need for a kingdom progressing to Christ's conquest of that kingdom. Milton's dimensions within a dimension thus reflect the same image—the Kingdom of God.

IV

The very complexity of the correspondences between Michael's prophecy and *Paradise Regained* provokes resistance. Yet similarly complex, interlocking structures, conceived as overlapping arcs and circles, are found in Renaissance exegesis of Revelation. Joseph Wittreich, in "'A Poet Amongst Poets': Milton and the Tradition of Prophecy," points out that "With few exceptions, the Book of Revelations was regarded as 'a certayne and distincte order,' all of whose parts are 'knit together' so as to be 'coherent and correspondent.'"[23] Although different commentators perceived different divisions in the work, its structure was generally described as "nonlinear, patterned according to a system of synchronisms: events, instead of succeeding one another, were made to mirror one another." Joseph Mede's diagram of Revelation (fig. 1) il-

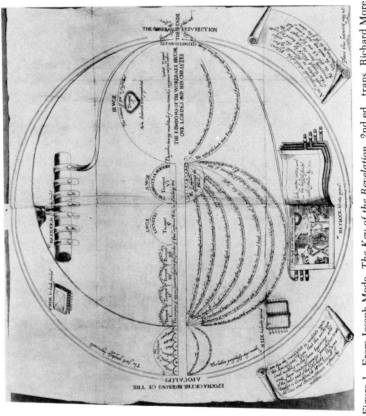

Figure 1. From Joseph Mede, *The Key of the Revelation*, 2nd ed., trans. Richard More (London, 1650), between pp. 26 and 27. Reproduced by permission of the Henry E. Huntington Library and Art Gallery.

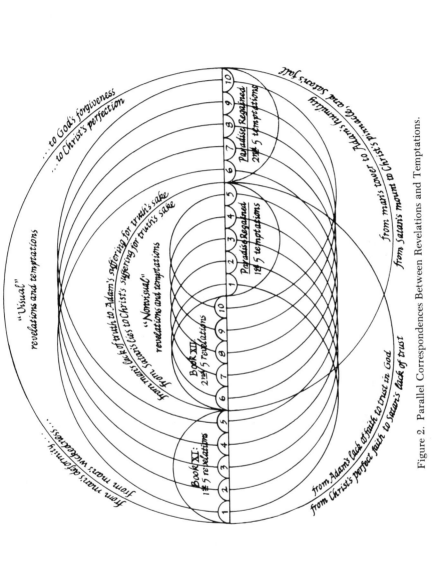

Figure 2. Parallel Correspondences Between Revelations and Temptations.

Book XI: 1ª 5 revelations

Book XII: 2ⁿᵈ 5 revelations

Paradise Regained 1ª 5 temptations

Paradise Regained 2ⁿᵈ 5 temptations

"Visual" revelations and temptations

"Nonvisual" revelations and temptations

from man's deformity ... from man's wickedness ...

from man's (lack of truth) to Adam's suffering for truth's sake to Christ's suffering for truth's sake

... to God's forgiveness ... to Christ's perfection

from Adam's lack of faith to trust in God from Christ's perfect faith to Satan's lack of trust

from man's tower to Christ's pinnacle from Satan's mount to Adam's pinnacle, and Satan's fall lustrates the complexity of structure which one Renaissance commentator perceived in this work.

It is possible to diagram the correspondences between Michael's prophecy and *Paradise Regained*, as I have interpreted them, in a very similar manner, thus demonstrating a quintessentially Renaissance harmony (fig. 2). The unifying correspondences are visualized as four great arcs, each encompassing two sets of five temptations and revelations that mirror or balance each other. This harmonizing structure, like the temptations in *Paradise Regained*, also emphasizes the numbers four and ten, yet where Satan's inverted pinnacle is doomed to fall, here each of the four great arcs embodies Christ's ultimate victory in a series of five-plus-five.

In the last analysis, however, a merely numerical assessment of Milton's astonishing architectonics seems—and is—inadequate. The hidden structure of these correspondences must be appreciated in the context of the prophetic mode, for only a prophetic intention can justify its deliberate obscurity and difficulty. Wittreich's explanation of the prophet's objective illuminates the function of such ingenious structures: "he assaults the mind by opening the doors of perception and enlarges its perimeters by imposing upon it not one but many perspectives."[24] The relationships I have explored, though based on numerical correspondences, all create different perspectives on the same unmathematical concept: the idea of the kingdom within, or the inner paradise. Toward that end Milton seems to have structured his works so that the reader, in "private return," may create a secret garden of contemplation. Here, in that incorporeal dimension to be found only *between* the poet's "happy garden" and "happy garden lost," lies hidden a model of that timeless, immeasurable kingdom.

Brown University

NOTES

1. *Heroic Knowledge* (New York, 1957), p. 6.
2. Edward Phillips, "The Life of Milton," in *John Milton, Complete Poems and Major Prose*, ed. Merritt Y. Hughes (Indianapolis, 1957), p. 1036.
3. "*Paradise Regained* and the Second Adam," *Milton Studies*, IX, ed. James D. Simmonds (Pittsburgh, 1976), p. 269.
4. P. 262. Jordan notes that Christ is compared to other types of himself as well, most notably Job, as demonstrated by Barbara Lewalski in her *Milton's Brief Epic* (Providence, R.I., 1966).

5. "Structural Pattern in *Paradise Lost*," in *Milton: Modern Essays in Criticism*, ed. Arthur Barker (Oxford, 1965), p. 145.

6. (Copenhagen, 1956).

7. "The Balanced Structure of *Paradise Lost*," *Studies in Philology*, LXII (1965), 696–718.

8. In *New Essays on "Paradise Lost*," ed. Thomas Kranidas (Berkeley, 1969). In his earlier book, *Milton and the Kingdoms of God* (Evanston, Ill., 1964), Fixler suggests a relationship between *Paradise Regained* and *Paradise Lost*, stating that "doctrinally and dramatically the mission of Jesus in *Paradise Regained* is to overcome the consequences of Adam's disobedience by his own obedience and faith" (p. 249). In a more recent article, "Plato's Four Furors and the Real Structure of *Paradise Lost*," PMLA, XCII (October 1977), 952–62, Fixler proposes a new conception of prophetic structure in *Paradise Lost* based on the sequence of invocations in Books I, III, VII, and IX.

9. *The Mystical Design of "Paradise Lost*," (Lewisburg, Pa., 1975). In addition to the critics cited in the body of my text, Gunnar Qvarnström discusses the chronological scheme and other structural aspects of *Paradise Lost* in *The Enchanted Palace* (Stockholm, 1967), and Maren-Sofie Røstvig discusses numerology in relation to Milton in *The Hidden Sense: Milton and the Neoplatonic Method of Numerical Composition* (Oslo, 1963). Both Douglas Bush and Ernest Sirluck question the value of Røstvig's work and of numerological studies in general in "Calculus Racked Him" and "Recent Studies," in *SEL*, VI (1966), 1–6 and 190–91. Røstvig's reply appears in VII (1967), 191–94.

10. *"Paradise Regained": The Tradition and the Poem* (Baltimore, 1947).

11. "Structure and the Symbolism of Vision in Michael's Prophecy: *Paradise Lost*, Books XI–XII," *PQ* XLII (1963), 26.

12. Both the number nine and three-times-three are repeatedly used in connection with Satan and the fallen angels, as in the description of the gates of Hell: "And thrice threefold the Gates; three folds were Brass, / Three Iron, three of Adamantine Rock" (*PL* II, 645–46).

13. My hypothesis that Books XI and XII of *Paradise Lost* accommodate a tenfold division is offered in addition to, rather than in competition with, traditional interpretations that Michael's prophecy is based on a sevenfold structure related to the Augustinian division of history into seven ages of restoration balancing the seven days of Creation, for which see Lewalski's "Structure and Symbolism" and George Whiting, *Milton and this Pendant World* (Austin, 1958), pp. 175–83, or Fixler's proposal that *each* book is divided into seven parts. As Arthur Barker suggests in his outline of the structure of the *Aeneid*, epic structure implies a multiple organization, a capacity to accommodate meaningfully more than one division into parts ("Structural Pattern," p. 143). This perception does not resolve the possibility raised by both Crump and Fixler, however, that since there is considerable evidence of a general symmetry between Michael's prophecy and the first two books of *Paradise Lost*, any correspondence between Michael's prophecy and *Paradise Regained* should also suggest the possibility of a similar linkage between Michael's prophecy and the first two books of *Paradise Lost*. It seems unlikely to me, nevertheless, that Milton consciously intended a precisely symmetrical correspondence between the first and last two books of *Paradise Lost*, such as I have proposed between Michael's prophecy and *Paradise Regained*, inasmuch as Books I and II were originally just as they are now, whereas Books XI and XII were originally only one book. It seems more probable that Milton's perception of a general symmetry between his account of the fallen angels and Michael's prophecy may have prompted, in part, his division of Book X into two books, for as Crump notes, "the division of Book X into XI and XII allowed the 'historical' nature of those books

about fallen man to be seen in comparison with that of the opening two books about the fallen angels" (*Mystical Design*, p. 77). The possibility that Milton deliberately constructed a series of correspondences between *Paradise Regained* and Michael's prophecy does not, therefore, necessarily entail a similarly precise, deliberate series of correspondences between Michael's prophecy and the first two books of *Paradise Lost*, or between *Paradise Regained* and those books. I feel there are, nevertheless, some striking correspondences between the first two books of *Paradise Lost* and the temptation structure of *Paradise Regained*, most noticeably in the inverse order suggested by Crump's view of the "circular" construction of *Paradise Lost*, and that these merit further investigation.

14. "Structural Pattern," p. 151.

15. Note that hereafter "XI" and "XII" refer to Books XI and XII of *Paradise Lost*, while "I," "II," "III," and "IV" refer to the books of *Paradise Regained*, unless otherwise identified.

16. *Milton's Brief Epic*, pp. 202–03.

17. Although the men and events presented in the angelic scenes of Book XI are clearly taken from the Old Testament, and are recognizable as following the recapitulation of the Old Covenant given in Hebrews, chapter xi (as Lewalski demonstrates in "Structure and Symbolism"), the angel mentions no names before Abraham. Presumably this indicates a universalization of the events depicted in Book XI—that they are intended to be taken as types of all mankind, rather than just of the people of Israel. With Abraham, however, the archangel begins the specific history of God's chosen people, Israel, and therefore uses proper names.

18. "Sannazaro and Milton's Brief Epic," *CL*, XX (1968), 125.

19. "Structure and Symbolism," p. 27.

20. Ibid.

21. Since Eden stretched from Haran (see note for *PL* IV, 211, Hughes edition) eastward, it is likely that Michael's catalogue not only traces Abraham's journey into Canaan but also names the approximate region of the Garden of Eden. The angel's catalogue then would stand in even more striking opposition to Satan's Roman Empire, balancing the lost Paradise and the Promised Land against a secular empire.

22. Du Bartas' argument for a Christian muse for poetry, and for the superiority and precedence of biblical poetry over all other, is discussed in Lily B. Campbell's *Divine Poetry and Drama in Sixteenth-Century England* (Cambridge, 1959), pt. I, chap. 9, as well as in Lewalski's *Milton's Brief Epic*, pp. 69–71.

23. In *Milton and the Line of Vision*, ed. Joseph Anthony Wittreich, Jr. (Madison, Wis., 1975), p. 107. Prof. Wittreich's more recent *Visionary Poetics* (Huntington Library, 1979) greatly expands his discussion of Renaissance exegesis of Revelation, and of prophetic structure in Milton's work, focusing particularly on *Lycidas*.

24. *Milton and The Line of Vision*, p. 103.

THE DOUBLE SET OF TEMPTATIONS
IN *PARADISE REGAINED*

William B. Hunter, Jr.

I T H A S long been recognized that the construction of *Paradise Regained* presents one of the most difficult problems in the entire field of Milton interpretation. There is no agreement, for instance, about how many temptations Satan offers Jesus (to say nothing of what they mean). Despite efforts by some of our most perceptive critics to find organizing principles in the work, a wealth of internal evidence— repetitions and self-contradictions—proves that something is seriously askew which cannot be explained away.[1] An associated problem is the divisions between Books II and III, and between III and IV, which seem merely to interrupt the narrative, not to organize it or to clarify the stages of its development. I propose as the best explanation of such anomalies the hypothesis that Milton developed two different conceptions of the temptation in the wilderness which he combined without complete success. But first an account of some of the repetitions and self-contradictions is necessary.[2]

Following a brief invocation, the story begins with Christ's Baptism. The narrator tells it first in I, 18–32. Then Satan repeats the information in almost the same language in lines 70–85. Finally, Jesus himself reflects upon the experience at lines 268–86. Besides the similar length of the three passages, the words themselves are almost identical, as the conclusion to each statement shows:

on him baptiz'd
Heaven open'd, and in likeness of a Dove
The Spirit descended, while the Fathers voice
From Heav'n pronounc'd him his beloved Son.   (I, 29–32)

[I saw] on him rising
Out of the water, Heav'n above the Clouds
Unfold her Crystal Dores, thence on his head
A perfect Dove descend, what e're it meant,
And out of Heav'n the Sov'raign voice I heard,
This is my Son belov'd, in him am pleas'd.   (I, 80–85)

as I rose out of the laving stream,
Heaven open'd her eternal doors, from whence
The Spirit descended on me like a Dove,
And last the sum of all, my Father's voice,
Audibly heard from Heav'n, pronounc'd me his,
Me his beloved Son, in whom alone
He was well pleas'd.   (I, 280–86)

The main information added to the original account is that Satan was uncertain what the episode meant.[3] His repetition seems to some extent defensible as he informs the devils of what has happened, but for a reader Jesus' recapitulation of the event is merely otiose.

Then there is the duplicate account of Jesus' life up to his Baptism. He himself recalls, for instance, his teaching in the Temple (I, 211–14), information repeated by Mary in II, 96–99, as she too details his birth and youth.[4] But the worst confusion of the whole poem is generally acknowledged to be the time when Jesus first becomes hungry and when the first night falls. In Book I, for "Full forty days" he did not feel hunger "Till those days ended" (303–09), whereupon Satan appears disguised as a shepherd. He promptly offers the first biblical temptation, that Jesus turn stones into bread, and is rejected. After 150 lines of dialogue he leaves and night falls. But in Book II he reports his failure of Book I to the devils, who authorize him a second time to proceed (a duplication of their authorization in Book I), whereupon attention shifts to Jesus who, "Now hungring first" (244), is not tempted by Satan but, seeing night come on, lies down to sleep and dreams about food. The difficulty here is really impossible to overcome. It has led to such diverse interpretations as Dunster's that two different days are involved or Lewalski's that "Christ does not actually experience hunger until Book II," although this ignores the biblical account that Jesus was hungry before the first temptation.[5]

But there are further troubles. Most obviously, the temptation from hunger in Book I seems to be duplicated in the temptation from hunger by the banquet in Book II. Indeed, having failed in the former, Satan is a simpleton to propose the latter. Moreover, in the second conference of the devils Belial proposes that Satan should "Set women in his eye and in his walk" (153), a suggestion which Satan utterly rejects in a long and caustic attack (173–224). But then seductive women help serve up the banquet; indeed, Jesus has a choice between virgins or more experienced ladies, those "of th' *Hesperides*, . . . Fairy Damsels" (357–58), worthy of Lancelot and other knights like him whose sexual activities are scarcely beyond reproach.

After the banquet scene, however, the duplications disappear as two nonbiblical temptations follow, those of wealth and glory. But then Satan offers to restore Jesus to the throne of David, the last nonbiblical temptation of this series—a duplication which seems to differ only in geographical extent from his offer of all the kingdoms of the world which follows, the second of the biblical temptations. In the kingdoms temptation itself there are no serious duplications, nor are there any in the third biblical temptation, that on the pinnacle of the Temple (except for the two summaries of Greek philosophy, which will be considered below as part of this temptation).

Such narrative flaws in *Paradise Regained* as have been presented here forcefully pose the question of what has happened to the poet who had conclusively proved his ability to organize and control huge amounts of material in *Paradise Lost* in a way unmatched by any other English writer. I think it likely that he has combined, without complete success, two different versions of the same event, written perhaps at different times. One version, the "biblical," derives from the account in Luke; the other, which I call the human, derives from the baptismal service. It will be useful to consider separately the two different accounts, beginning with the three biblical temptations.

First, Milton distinguished them by having each take place on a different day without any biblical authority at all. It seems quite unlikely that he was consciously paralleling in them the three days of the Passion and Resurrection, for the narration of the third day in *Paradise Regained* begins not at dawn but later in the morning.[6] More probable is the parallel with the three days of Adam and Eve's life narrated in *Paradise Lost* up until their disobedience, with which the obedience of Christ, the second Adam, is frequently contrasted. In any case, the three-day division is a convenient narrative device. Having created it, however, Milton proceeds to unbalance it seriously by having the first day occupy the first book, and the second day most of the second book, all of the third, and the fourth down to line 397. Finally, the short third day reaches through to the end of the poem. The account of the second day, that is, is longer than the other two put together, perhaps a match for the very long account of Adam and Eve's second day, which lasts in *Paradise Lost* through one-third of the whole poem, Books V–VIII, whereas their first day occupies only a part of Book IV and their third (to the Fall and the rest of that afternoon) only Book IX. Such a comparison, however, may not be immediately recognized by a reader as validation for the unbalanced organization of *Paradise Regained*.

For another approach to this problem, let us consider the number of lines composing each of the biblical temptations, not the days in which they occur, and let us begin with the second because it is the most clearly delineated. This one, in which Satan offers Christ the kingdoms of the world, begins at III, 251, and runs through IV, 194—a total of 387 lines of which 193 are in III and 194 in IV. The division of the books at the midpoint of the central "biblical" temptation must be deliberate. The third temptation, on the pinnacle of the Temple, runs from about IV, 212, to line 580, a total of some 368 lines.[7] The first, that of turning the stones into bread, is somewhat harder to delimit in this way. The temptation itself appears at I, 342–50, having been preceded by Jesus' long reflection about his past (183–341) and being followed by a dialogue with Satan to the end of the book. This whole section totals about 320 lines.[8] That is, the three biblical episodes taken by themselves each occupy somewhat the same space in the poem, and each climaxes on a different day, facts which suggest that Milton at one time considered them as a unit, the subject matter of *Paradise Regained* consisting at that point of approximately equal sections devoted to each of the biblical temptations, to each of which is allocated a day, and this sequence paralleling in time that in which Adam and Eve move in *Paradise Lost*. Such a whole may or may not have been preceded by the present invocation and coda (I, 1–17; IV, 581–639). All together it would be something over a thousand lines long, about half the present poem. It is not clear whether Milton thought of it as divided into books or not. If he did, there would be only three of them, none so long as any of the present ones.

What then of the rest of the poem—the extrabiblical temptations of the banquet, wealth, glory, and the throne of David which occupy most of Book II and over half of III? For them Milton developed a second and independent interpretation of the episode in Luke, his authority perhaps being the more general report of Mark i, 13: "he was there in the wilderness forty days tempted of Satan." This series is not divided by days. It begins, of course, with the Baptism by John in the River Jordan. Milton certainly was aware that in his day every person baptized, or, if a baby, his adult representative, was asked, according to the Book of Common Prayer, "Dost thou renounce the devil and all his works, the vain pomp and glory of the world, with all covetous desires of the same, and the sinful desires of the flesh; so that thou wilt not follow, nor be led by them?" Jesus, the exemplary man, would be expected to abide by the same promise, a fact Milton makes perfectly explicit when he has the Father in heaven tell Gabriel that the Son's "weakness shall o're-come Satanic strength / And all the world, and mass of sinful flesh" (I,

161–62), listing the temptations here in the same order as they are in the baptismal service.[9] Accordingly, Milton invented human temptations for Jesus to face which would supplement and parallel the superhuman biblical ones listed in Matthew and Luke, his authority being such a passage as Hebrews iv, 15: Jesus "was in all points tempted like as we are, yet without sin." Indeed, such a temptation as turning stones into bread is hardly a real one for mankind at large, but such a one as resisting the banquet and its attendant delights is.

Following the night (II, 260–79) that marks the end of the fortieth day in the wilderness when Jesus at last becomes hungry (Luke iv, 2), Milton introduces his original set of human temptations elaborated from the warnings of the Prayerbook (thus this introductory nightfall has no relationship to those of Books I and IV). First is the temptation of the flesh, depicted in the banquet scene of Book II.[10] The episode tests far more than gluttony (as it is sometimes interpreted as a duplication of the stones/bread temptation of Book I). Beautiful music plays, accompanying "*Arabian* odors . . . and *Flora's* earliest smells" (II, 362–65). The sexuality of the attendant ladies has already been mentioned, and there are pederastic youths as well, "of fairer hew / Then *Ganymed* or *Hylas*" (II, 352–53), hardly in agreement with Satan's recent statement that Jesus can be tempted only by "Lawful desires of Nature, not beyond" (II, 230). Because Milton is writing from a different perspective from that of Book I, Belial's rejected suggestions made at the devils' conclave can be and are adopted here. This generalized temptation of the flesh is clearly conceived in a very different fashion from that of the limited biblical one of the stones/bread.

Second are the temptations of the world. As has been seen, the Prayerbook warns of them in two aspects: of "the vain pomp and glory of the world, with all covetous desires of the same"—that is, of pomp and glory, and of wealth. Accordingly, Satan next tempts Jesus with covetousness or wealth (II, 412–end): "Money brings Honour, Friends, Conquest, and Realms" (422), to which Christ responds that riches are "the toyl of Fools / The wise man's cumbrance" (453–54). The other phase of the temptation of the world, according to the Prayerbook, is that of glory, which opens Book III. Satan now invites Christ to

> The fame and glory, glory the reward
> That sole excites to high attempts the flame
> Of most erected Spirits.   (25–27)

In the next 125 lines Milton employs the word *glory* twenty-seven times, leading to Christ's distinction between the true glory which is God's and "the vain pomp and glory" of the world which Satan offers. It is surely significant that the book division of II and III separates the two parts of the human temptation of the world (avarice and glory) just as that of III and IV separates the equivalent worldly biblical temptation of the kingdoms. These divisions between books, that is, appear respectively in the middle of the central temptation of both the human series and the biblical series.

The final temptation of the human series is that of "the devil" himself, the equivalent of the biblical test upon the pinnacle of the Temple. What is the temptation of "the devil"? As Milton answers in this episode (III, 150–202), Satan invites Christ to exercise his "Zeal, / And Duty" (III, 171–72) to overthrow the government and free his "Country from her Heathen servitude" to those who have supplanted him upon the throne of David. Underlying the invitation seems to be a subtle form of antinomianism. This is, of course, the same temptation to which Satan himself had surrendered as he led the fight against divine authority in *Paradise Lost.* Although perhaps not sufficiently appreciated today, the point is the central one for Milton's religious beliefs as he expressed them in action: man is never to undertake anything until directed by God to do so, and God has not directed Christ to overthrow the rulers of Palestine (an issue to recur, according to the Bible, near the end of his life).[11] Christ's answer accordingly is that one must patiently accept the given circumstances, leaving innovative activity to God's direction, for man may not rightfully arrogate to himself this kind of decision. Such beginnings

> The Father in his purpose hath decreed,
> He in whose hand all times and seasons roul.
> .   .   .   .
>   [For] who best
> Can suffer, best can do; best reign, who first
> Well hath obey'd.   (III, 186–96)

This is exactly equivalent to the response that Jesus quotes from Deuteronomy in rejecting Satan's biblical temptation to save himself when placed upon the pinnacle of the Temple: "Tempt not the Lord thy God" (IV, 561): obey; do not appropriate to yourself the divine prerogatives.[12]

Thus, in the set of what I have called human temptations, Milton has created a series equivalent to the biblical ones in Luke and parallel with them, both exemplifying the baptismal warnings of the Prayerbook. It remains to show that the temptation on the pinnacle actually begins earlier than the third day in that it also includes within a single larger unit the temptation of pagan wisdom and the night of physical terror which follows. Finally, it is necessary to show how this unified set of episodes relates to the human temptation to rebellion and repossession of the throne of David.

As has been mentioned, Milton actually wrote two versions of the temptation of wisdom. They are not entirely consistent with each other. First Satan exhibits

the Olive Grove of *Academe*,	
Plato's retirement;	Plato
. . . .	
within the walls then view	
The schools of antient Sages; his who bred	
Great *Alexander* to subdue the world,	Aristotle
Lyceum there, and painted *Stoa* next.	Stoics
	(IV, 244–53)

Following the offer of the wisdom of these philosophical schools, Satan moves on to other areas of Greek culture which do not concern us here: lyric and epic poetry, the dramatists, and the orators. But at line 272 he begins the list of philosophers all over again, now a more inclusive group:

To sage Philosophy next lend thine ear,	
From Heaven descended to the low-rooft house	
Of *Socrates*, see there his Tenement,	Socrates
Whom well inspir'd the Oracle pronounc'd	
Wisest of men; from whose mouth issu'd forth	
Mellifluous streams that water'd all the schools	Platonic
Of Academics old and new, with those	academy
Sirnam'd *Peripatetics*, and the Sect	Aristotle
Epicurean, and the Stoic severe.	Epicureans, Stoics
	(IV, 272–80)

This time no mention of other aspects of Greek culture follows.

In his rejection of this pagan wisdom Christ responds first and primarily to these schools of philosophy. He includes all the members of both lists, adds yet another group, the skeptics, and singles out for extended rejection the dangers of the last school in both lists, the Stoics:

The first and wisest of them all profess'd	Socrates
To know this only, that he nothing knew;	
The next to fabling fell and smooth conceits,	Plato
A third sort doubted all things, though plain sence;	Skeptics
Others in vertue plac'd felicity,	Aristotle

> But vertue joyn'd with riches and long life,
> In corporal pleasure he, and careless ease,   Epicureans
> The Stoic last in Philosophic pride,   Stoics
> By him call'd vertue; and his vertuous man,
> Wise, perfect in himself, and all possessing
> Equal to God, oft shames not to prefer,
> As fearing God nor man, contemning all
> Wealth, pleasure, pain or torment, death and life,
> Which when he lists, he leaves, or boasts he can,
> For all his tedious talk is but vain boast,
> Or subtle shifts conviction to evade.
> Alas what can they teach, and not mislead;
> Ignorant of themselves, of God much more.   (IV, 293–310)

In singling out the Stoic for such special attention, "perfect in himself . . . , Equal to God," Milton clearly has in mind the fact that this group consciously trained themselves to be inwardly self-sufficient, dependent not upon any exterior being for decisions but solely upon themselves. They "in themselves seek vertue, and to themselves / All glory arrogate, to God give none" (314–15). It is just this failure to depend upon God's revealed will, this attempt at full self-sufficiency, which marks the Stoics for Milton as fundamentally disobedient, even as it had marked Satan throughout his career. In contrast, Christ's obedience—his leaving decisions in God's hands—will save him on the pinnacle the next day.[13] He certainly does not save himself there. The night racked by storms and demons shows yet another instance of how the obedient Christian can put his faith in God and achieve thereby an inner trust, peace, and certainty which Milton believes the Stoic, despite all his self-control, can never really experience.

The rejection of pagan wisdom and especially of the self-sufficiency which was the Stoic goal in favor of Christian trust and obedience thus marks the events of this entire section of the poem, molding the wisdom–night terrors–pinnacle episodes as three different manifestations of the same faith in God, the same decision that Jesus not take matters into his own hands so as to resolve them. Satan had trusted in himself and in his own powers; so had Adam and Eve, and they were all disobedient. By not asserting himself in the temptation to resume the throne of David because God had not directed him to do so, Jesus had demonstrated in human terms how one obediently puts one's trust in God and not in oneself. The same happens in his response to the terrors of the night and to the biblical temptation on the pinnacle. Rejection of these "temptations of the devil," then, in both the human and the biblical episodes, is a rejection of self-sufficiency, of pride. This is the paradise lost by Adam which Jesus regains (IV, 608).

Interpreted in this light, *Paradise Regained* exhibits an interesting and original construction in its three-day pattern of the biblical temptations from Luke, within which Milton elaborates three parallel human temptations developed independently from the admonitions of the baptismal service of the Prayerbook. This is not to overlook the flaws of the poem that have been pointed out. No attempt to explain them away has ever been successful (many critics prefer to ignore them), for they seem to be the result of two different conceptions of the subject which Milton telescoped without full success at every juncture. Surely much of the difficulty lay in his blindness. Perhaps for some reason that we do not know he was hurried and indeed wrote it "in a wonderful short space," as Edward Phillips reported.[14] Just which lines originally belonged to which set of temptations is sometimes difficult or perhaps now impossible to establish. It seems probable that the preliminary reflections of Jesus in the wilderness (I, 183–293), including those upon his Baptism, and the second conference of the devils (II, 115–241) belong with the biblical set, as do the lines down to nightfall which end Book I. The passages concerned with the first account of the Baptism, the first devilish colloquy, and the colloquy in Heaven (I, 29–182), the search for Jesus by Andrew and Simon and Mary's reflections (II, 1–108), and the second account of his hungering at the first nightfall (II, 242–78) seem, on the other hand, better related to the human ones. In any case Milton has created a convincing set of human temptations (climaxed by that of "the devil" interpreted as disobedience or self-interest, against which the baptismal service warns) that parallel the biblical set. Seen from this perspective the divisions of Books II and III, and of Books III and IV, do not seem merely capricious, but derive from a principle different from that governing the separation of Books I and II. Finally, the double and parallel sets of temptations proposed here exemplify a far simpler and subtler principle of organization of the poem than any offered hitherto.

University of Houston

NOTES

1. Patrick Cullen's *Infernal Triad* (Princeton, 1974), pp. xvi–xviii and esp. chap. 4, surveys previous analyses of the problems considered here and various interpretations of

them. The hypothesis I shall develop is quite different from any earlier ones and far simpler.

2. William R. Parker, in *Milton: A Biography* (Oxford, 1968), II, 1139–42, also uses some of this evidence to argue for two different times of composition: for an early form of the poem as a play which Milton then adapted to the form of the short epic, with some consequent duplication. Although I shall be demonstrating two different levels of composition, my evidence does not necessarily support an early dramatic form nor does it support any particular dates. It interestingly corroborates some of the conclusions of John Shawcross in "The Chronology of Milton's Major Poems," *PMLA*, LXXVI (1961), 345–58, especially for Book III and for much of Book I.

3. As for the Baptism itself, he realized that it did not signify the washing away of Jesus' sin, for he had none, but was "The testimony of Heaven, that who he is / Thenceforth the Nations may not doubt" (78–79), the same interpretation as that of Calvinist exegetes. See John Downham, *Annotations upon All the Books of the Old and New Testaments* (London, 1651), *ad* Matt. iii, 13, and William Ames, *The Marrow of Theology*, trans. J. D. Eusden (Boston, 1968), I, xxi, 30.

4. A separate problem of continuity appears at I, 259, where Jesus, having been repeating Mary's story with her as first person, suddenly and confusingly shifts that person to himself.

5. Charles Dunster, ed., *Paradise Regained*, 2nd ed. (London, 1800), p. 88; Barbara Lewalski, *Milton's Brief Epic* (Providence, R.I., 1966), p. 202.

6. I have argued that this is the substance of the central episode in *Paradise Lost*. See "The War in Heaven: The Exaltation of the Son," in *Bright Essence* (Salt Lake City, 1971), pp. 115–30. Milton may, however, suggest the future exaltation by locating Jesus on a hill on both the second and third mornings in *Paradise Regained*: II, 285, and IV, 447; for on the authority of Psalm ii Milton associated the positioning of the Son on a hill with his exaltation. See *Paradise Lost* V, 604. "Days" should generally be considered here in the Hebrew fashion as beginning at nightfall.

7. I am, of course, including the temptation of pagan wisdom and the terrors of the subsequent night in this episode, as I shall explain below.

8. The second colloquy of the devils, in which Belial's suggestion and rebuke fit so lamely with the banqueting scene which actually follows, could much better come directly before the temptation of the kingdoms, for Satan concludes the colloquy by asserting that the next temptation must be based on "honour, glory, and popular praise; / Rocks whereon greatest men have oftest wreck'd" (II, 227–28)—hardly applicable to the banquet.

9. Because of the occasion Milton follows the baptismal statement rather than the more familiar prayer for delivery "from all the deceits of the world, the flesh, and the devil" of the Litany. He treats them in reverse order in *Paradise Regained* because they must correspond to and parallel the biblical temptations in Luke. The fact that Jesus was an adult certainly must be associated with Milton's interpretation of baptism expressed in his *Christian Doctrine* I, xxviii.

10. If, as is argued here, Milton has introduced this and the following episodes into the parallel structure of the biblical temptations, he adds a few lines of adjustment. Satan, for instance, now appears "Not rustic as before" (II, 299) in the stones/bread temptation, and he refers (II, 302) to the permission to return granted by Jesus at the conclusion of that temptation (I, 494–95).

11. See the final paragraph of my study, "John Milton: Autobiographer," *Milton Quarterly*, VIII (1974), 103. The concept is especially prominent in the Gospel of John, e.g., vii, 6.

12. Ultimately Milton had in mind Paul's words in Romans xiii, 1–2: "Let every soul be subject unto the higher powers. For there is no power but of God: the powers that be are ordained of God. Whosoever therefore resisteth the power, resisteth the ordinance of God: and they that resist shall receive to themselves damnation."

13. Indeed, in order to emphasize this interpretation, Milton somewhat alters the biblical temptation, in which Satan only invites Christ to throw himself down, for God's angels will keep him from harm (IV, 554–59), adding an alternative: "There stand, if thou wilt stand; to stand upright / Will ask thee skill" (IV, 551–52). In other words, Satan presents Christ on the pinnacle with alternative actions, standing or throwing himself down. Apparently they are a choice, but in one way they require the same response: whichever he chose he would himself initiate the action. Christ neatly avoids the dilemma by refusing both alternatives, leaving the matter to God: "Tempt not the Lord thy God" (561); do not force God's hand.

14. *The Early Lives of Milton*, ed. Helen Darbishire (London, 1932), p. 75.

WHY IS *PARADISE REGAINED* SO COLD?

Alan Fisher

P^ARADISE REGAINED disappointed its first readers, and their disappointment made Milton angry. Edward Phillips, who tells us about this, thought the poem was "sublime" enough, but general opinion found it "much inferior" to *Paradise Lost*. Milton "could not hear with patience any such thing when related to him," and Phillips, with a problem on his hands, attempted to resolve it judiciously. "The subject may not afford such variety of invention," he concedes, but "the most judicious" find it "little or nothing inferior to the other for style and decorum."[1] It is the familiar situation of experimental art: an audience expects a certain range of pleasures it knows an author can give; the author deliberately gives his audience something else; audience is disappointed, author is angry, and the hopeful critic is left feebly to explain the misunderstanding. Always, in these instances, "the most judicious" see farthest into the matter—and agree with the author.

In some disputes, the opinion of the judicious few becomes the orthodoxy of the next generation. When this happens, the dispute may smolder for a while, but its extinction seems assured enough that the problem can be declared resolved. When this does not happen, the problem persists, and critics have three ways to deal with it: (1) solve it, with a judiciousness that has escaped their predecessors; (2) confess that it is there, that it will not go away, and treat it as an "unintended consequence"[2] of the author's design; (3) treat the matter as uninteresting. This third strategy has two tactical branches: the explicit dismissal, in which the critic mentions the problem in an aside as an avoidable, and therefore unimportant, lapse; and the implicit dismissal, in which the critic ignores the problem altogether, as though the issue *he* is talking about renders the problem irrelevant. The second branch of the third strategy is the approach we see most frequently.

With *Paradise Regained*, the problem is three centuries old. At this late date, the critic has little hope of happening upon some truly judicious, definitive solution which has eluded predecessors. Strategies 2 and 3, of course, do not dislodge the problem at all. But if a problem cannot entirely be removed, it can be budged and made to present a new face to those who must face it. That is the course this essay shall at-

195

tempt to follow. The "problem" of *Paradise Regained* will not go away, but perhaps it was never meant to go away; the "judicious reader" would then be the one who accepted the problem for what it was and asked not "How can I make this disappear?" but "What possible use could the author have had for it?" I do not pretend that readers will like *Paradise Regained* any better for contemplating it in the way I am about to propose, though I would be disappointed if none did. But I can hope that the exercise of doing so will enable them to see Milton and what he stood for a little more clearly.[3]

I

The first task is to specify the problem. Phillips hinted that it has to do with "invention," and critics agreed with him for the next century or so. Richard Bentley declared that the temptation in the wilderness was an inadequate subject; the proper subject was the whole life of Christ, ending grandly with the Resurrection. This, he said, "would have been a copious and sublime subject for a second poem. The wonders then to be described would have erected even an ordinary poet's genius; and in episodes he might have introduced his conception, birth, miracles, and all the history of his administration while on earth." Bentley was "grieved" about Milton's actual choice, for the temptation alone was "a dry, barren, and narrow ground to build an epic poem on." So Bentley could praise the "dignity" of Milton's poem, but he had to regret his "being cramped down by a wrong choice, without the expected applause."[4] Little question for Bentley, in other words, that Milton chose deliberately—and perversely—*not* to be "copious" and "sublime."

The century that raised this complaint also brought forth answers to it. Thomas Thyer, who agreed that the temptation was an "odd" subject for an epic poet to choose, also points out that Christian doctrine would support the choice: "Paradise, *regained* by our Saviour's resisting the temptations of Satan, might be a better contrast to Paradise, *lost* by our first parents too easily yielding to the same seducing spirit." And Charles Dunster, who remembered that Milton had talked about "brief epic" in one of his pamphlets, pointed out that an epic did not have to be vast or even sublime: "however the subject which he selected may have been considered as narrow ground, and one that cramped his genius, there is no reason to imagine that it was chosen hastily or inconsiderately." Indeed, the *brief* epic is meant for teaching, and a vehicle for teaching is supposed to be plain. William Hayley, whom Dunster quotes in support of this point, saw the poem as "rich in moral sentiment, and sublime in its mode of unfolding the highest wisdom that

man can learn; for this purpose it was necessary to keep all the orna-
mental parts of the poem in due subordination to the precept."[5]

Its "invention" and overall format could be defended, then, but
the objection to "narrowness" would not melt away. As critics began to
shift their attention from themes and overall actions to characters, their
sense of something wrong in *Paradise Regained* found something new to
focus upon. Where before it had been narrowness of design, it now became the narrowness of its hero. Northrop Frye sums up these objections this way: "*dramatically*, Christ becomes an increasingly unsym-
pathetic figure, a pusillanimous quietist in the temptation of Parthia,
an inhuman snob in the temptation of Rome, a peevish obscurantist in
the temptation of Athens." We must not succumb to this "dramatic" impression, Frye goes on to argue. If saying no in the face of Satan's
"energy and resourcefulness" is an "ungracious dramatic function" for
any character, we must look past this problem and see that "the real
source of life and freedom and energy" in the poem remains with "the
frigid figure at the center."[6] Looking past the "dramatic" impression of
a character takes a special effort, however, and special efforts tend to be
suspect. The poem that needs one is a poem with a flaw. The blunt
"harshness" of Jesus, says Louis Martz, is "out of line with the charity of
a Savior"[7]—in other words, a mistake. "The condemnation of man's
failings ought to be gentle and compassionate as possible," says Elizabeth Marie Pope, and "there is certainly some degree of coldness and in-
sensitivity in Milton's failure to realize" as much.[8] Some critics so resent
this aspect of the poem as to feel that the poem is ruined by it. The "success" of *Paradise Regained*, W. W. Robson says, "depends on the
reader's willingness to imagine himself in sympathy with certain religious and ethical doctrines. To a reader without this sympathy, or
without the capacity for it, *Paradise Regained* is indeed a frigid work.
And the fair criticism of the poem here is that Milton, by his presentation of Christ, has done something to disturb that sympathy where it already exists, and to hinder its attainment where it does not."[9]

"Narrowness," "harshness," "coldness": whatever one calls it, something about *Paradise Regained* refuses to allow us the feelings we think
appropriate to its theme. We should like to rejoice, in other words, but
the poem "hinders" us. These hindrances are too well planned and too
prominent to be accidental. But if their effect is calculated, we should
look at them directly, and not in a spirit of hostility. We should try to
determine what they contribute to the poem. It will help, I think, if we
begin with one very important and rather startling assumption: every
person resists salvation, passionately as he or she may also desire it. Odd

as this idea must seem, Milton took it as given. Because the Fall had corrupted human affections, the terms upon which salvation could please our affections could not be the terms upon which God would offer it. *Paradise Regained* presents salvation, then, but presents it in such a way as will stir up one's natural resentments of it. Milton would not have us avoid these feelings, I think, but have us face them; he would lead us through them, not around them. How he does so is the subject of the analysis that follows.

II

To conduct this analysis, I must keep track of "the reader's" response, and this, of course, is a speculative undertaking. Actual readers, as opposed to the hypothetical reader I shall talk about, feel varying degrees of uneasiness over being told what their responses "are"; this I cannot avoid, and I must hope that the "experience" I construct is one a reader will at least consider having. But I can clear away at least one objection by presenting evidence that thinking about readers' responses is an appropriate way of thinking about Milton. He himself had designs on the reader's response, and the critic who talks of what readers "must" feel here and "cannot avoid" feeling there is, at least, dealing in matters Milton consciously understood and calculated.

Readers, as Milton imagined them, were very much caught up in the books they read and yet, at the same time, they could, if they were doing their job, keep their active wills free of this involvement. Milton's notion of the reader's relation to a book, in other words, was contradictory. It combined the commonplace fear "that there is no adequate defence against eloquence at the moment of impact"[10] with an opposing idea, dear to Milton, that reason is choice and that choice may stay free from any "impact," if the chooser will have it so. Milton sets all this forth in the *Areopagitica*, where he says that reading books is like eating food. "For books," he says, "are as meats and viands are—some of good, some of evil substance, and yet God in that unapocryphal vision said without exception, 'Rise, Peter, kill and eat,' leaving the choice to each man's discretion." Freedom of reading is as fundamental as freedom of diet; Christian liberty allows them both together. "I conceive," he continues, "that when God did enlarge the universal diet of man's body, saving ever the rules of temperance, he then also, as before, left arbitrary the dieting and repasting of our minds; . . . How great a virtue is temperance, how much of moment through the whole life of man! Yet God commits the managing so great a trust, without particular law or prescription, wholly to the demeanor of every grown man." The reason is plain: "those actions which enter into a man, rather than issue out of him, and therefore defile not, God uses not to captivate under a perpetual childhood of prescription."[11] Milton seems to mean this literally. "*Actions*" truly "*enter into* a man": as food provides the body with vital energy, substance for the actions of the body, so books nourish the mind, providing *it* with energy in the form of "actions" it ingests in the act of reading. If so, the impact of eloquence cannot be evaded. But just as one may choose what ends to serve with the body's energy, so also may one choose purposes for the energy of the mind. Books, like food, become literally part of us, but they do not—or should not—determine what we are.

If these ideas stand behind *Paradise Regained*, and there is no reason to think otherwise, then one of its chief peculiarities may immediately be explained. *Paradise Regained* is almost wholly speeches; epic action, in the usual sense, is at a minimum. The way to recover Paradise is to say no in the face of an "impact" that insists on yes. No is said, again and again, until suddenly and miraculously the need to say it disappears. Critics complain about this, and with reason: listening to someone else—even Jesus—say no is not exciting. The reader who regards his job as mere detached listening to denials cannot fail to be bored, no matter how well he understands their didactic purpose. But the evidence shows that Milton did not think his readers would be detached listeners. Speechmaking implies the same attention he described as the "ingesting" of books—indeed, a book, for Milton, is an oration in print. The effect he imagines books having on readers is the same effect speakers have upon listeners. To fill an epic with speeches is to address the reader's concernment directly, by the most vivid means at hand, for speeches, if we allow them to do so, have a capacity to exert more force on readers than even the most grandiose action can do. Milton may have overestimated the power of speeches, but for better or worse he could not have imagined that mainstay of so much modern criticism, the silent, passive book with its active reader sorting out its text from some secure "ironic distance."

Distance, in fact, was a special effect. Milton deliberately inserts that effect for contrast. Establish distance, he cheerfully confesses, and the action of *Paradise Regained* becomes sheer monotony. Satan proposes, Jesus denies, and aside from God's subsequent intervention, that is all there is to it. "Still will [Satan] be tempting him who foils him still," says Milton at a moment of summary, when the poem is three-fourths done. At this distance emphasis falls, first and last, upon the adverb *still*. Similes enhance the emphasis:

> as a swarm of flies in vintage time,
> About the wine-press where sweet must is pour'd,
> Beat off, returns as oft with humming sound;
> Or surging waves against a solid rock,
> Though all to shivers dash't, th'assault renew,
> Vain batt'ry, and in froth or bubbles end;
> So Satan, whom repulse upon repulse
> Met ever, and to shameful silence brought,
> Yet gives not o'er though desperate of success,
> And his vain importunity pursues.   (IV, 15–24)

Milton sets up this distance after putting us through a long, intimate involvement with the give-and-take of speeches—as though he supposed that this declaration of monotony might come as some surprise.

Endless energy to annoy, endless patience in the face of annoyance, and no end in sight: this may, in fact, be the "plot" of *Paradise Regained*, but it ought not to be the plot of our experience with it. If the point of this passage is to suggest this notion as a new idea to readers caught up in an experience of a different kind, then getting at this different experience requires us to ask the questions suggested by Milton's parallel of books and food: What *are* the "actions" his book has been thrusting into our minds? What *is* the experience we cannot avoid—but can, as we exercise our capacity of choice, apply to good ends and not bad?

Every analysis of "the reader's" response requires that we imagine our reader stopping at some point to register his awareness of the direction his mind has been taking. There has been debate over just when these self-reflecting halts occur. In all theories, they occur when a "unit of sense" has been completed, but theories differ over just what a "unit of sense" might be. At one extreme, the unit is as small as a sentence or phrase or even a single word, while at the other, the unit cannot be less than the completed whole work.[12] I do not see any way for abstract methodology to resolve this debate, and I suppose that the appropriate "unit of sense" must vary from work to work. If *Paradise Regained* is filled with speeches, at any rate, and if Milton is calculating the impact of those speeches upon his readers, then let us say that the unit of sense appropriate to this poem is the completed speech. I shall imagine the reader as taking stock of his experiences at the conclusion of each whole speech.

I am encouraged to do this by a special fact about this particular poem. The speakers are Jesus and Satan. For any reader who is a Christian, or can imagine being one in order to become the "reader" of a Christian poem, a temptation speech from Satan has a special impact and carries with it a special responsibility. Out there in the wilderness, Jesus put the Devil behind him, but this, to a lesser degree, is also the responsibility of every well-affected Christian. A temptation speech, in other words, tempts all within earshot of it, and though Christ alone is required to answer, the speeches are for all of us to hear. In a certain sense, we too are placed in the wilderness. The purpose is plain: we are to hear temptation just as Jesus does; we are to register its impact and wrestle with it—and then judge how well our responses to it match those of the "perfect man." Because he is as yet no *more* than man, the comparison is relevant.[13]

The poem thus sets up an affective pattern: Satan speaks, our responses take shape, and Jesus then audibly denies the tempting tendencies in what Satan has said. Much of the "coldness" we find in Jesus is the difference we can sense between what we might say and what Jesus does say. His responses are more accurate or more thorough than the ones our instincts provide us, and our instincts—at least for those of us who take this difference seriously—are thereby chastened.

Chastening, I should add, differs from outright denunciation, for the "instinct" I assume in my hypothetical reader is Christian, though fallen. If denying the Devil is what is required, then the reader has it in him to survive the test. A simple no, however weak, is enough; though an accurate, eloquent, thorough no is better. This conflict of good against better provides the dramatic interest of *Paradise Regained*. Good against Evil, the nominal conflict, pits the indefatigable winemaker against indefatigable fruitflies; good against better, however, involves the reader directly, pits his own instincts against his own instructed understanding. The reader's feelings provide the poem's most interesting battleground, and it is high time to describe the battle that the poem sets to raging there.

III

As the first temptation begins, Satan appears in the disguise of a humble desert dweller. Milton makes him look enough like Archimago, however, that any reader of Spenser would suspect him at once. There is no question, in other words, whether a trick is in the offing; the question is what the trick will be. Satan's opening words show concern for Christ's welfare:

> Sir, what ill chance hath brought thee to this place
> So far from path or road of men, who pass
> In Troop or Caravan, for single none
> Durst ever, who return'd, and dropt not here
> His Carcass, pin'd with hunger and with drought?   (I, 321–25)

The desolation round about is vividly evoked, and no declarative un-
truth lurks in these lines: Christ *is* by himself, "far" from "paths"; the
danger alluded to is typical of deserts; and the glimpse of carcasses
makes the hunger and drought of the place seem palpable. Satan treats
all this as common ground, drops it, and shifts to being curious about
the man he is addressing. As he does, he gives an impression of prying,
searching for dangerous information.[14] He attended the Baptism, he
says, and is he now addressing the "Son of God" he saw there? He may
be isolated, he explains in an awkward afterthought, but the world's
great events still reach him. When he pauses for a reply, the question
faces us briefly: What should the reply be?

One possibility is silence. The temptation in these words, if any, is
obscure, and it might be best to venture nothing. "You *are* the Son of
God, aren't you?" is the ostensible drift, but though there may be danger in such prying, Jesus can surely say now what John the Baptist and
the Holy Spirit had already proclaimed for all to hear. But wariness is
best, so that if one gives words at all, let them be curt and unhelpful,
some version of "What if I were?"—or, more aggressively, "What are
you doing here alone?" If this will serve, the reply actually given is
nearly as brief, fully as unhelpful, and vastly more precise. "Who
brought me hither," Christ says, "Will bring me hence, no other Guide
I seek" (I, 334–35).

These words bring into focus just what the temptation has been.[15]
Satan was not asking whether this man is the one he saw baptized at the
River Jordan. That part of the speech is distraction, an attempt to mis-
direct attention from the question that matters: *What ill chance hath
brought thee here?* "Ill chance" is the dangerous notion, and all those
concrete details in the opening lines were there to give it resonance.
"Look about," they encourage us, "feel lost"—and since ill chance is a
highly probable cause of being lost in a desert waste, the phrase can easily slip past unnoticed, as a cliché of sorts. If it does, if we do not consciously reject this concept of being lost, then Satan has planted the
seeds of his victory. To receive "ill chance," even unwittingly, is to begin to substitute that concept for providence, to substitute a lie for the
truth, to forget God, and to forget what the poem has explicitly told us:
Jesus is not wandering at all; he is "led / Into this wilderness" by "some
strong motion" (I, 290–91) from the will of God. Satan's shift to curiosity, then, is a diverting tactic, the purpose of which is to deflect attention from this dangerous idea, so that it may settle in the mind beneath
the threshold of conscious thought. Once there, it could influence the
way some other issue is seen, as colored lenses do when one forgets one is

wearing them. Silence or curt unhelpfulness may be adequate, then, but remembering to assert providence is exact. Milton wants us to recognize—and feel—this difference.

By "feel," here, I mean something resembling surprise: there *was* a temptation in that address, though only in retrospect do we see it clearly. The recognition jolts, clarifies, enlightens, and even excites. To understand the temptation just given is to be reminded of what we must remember before all temptations whatever, and thus far the surprise is clarifying and informative. But since it reveals the dangerousness of the wheedling figure in black, the emotional temperature of the poem rises as well. This surprise cannot register unless we want it to, of course. We must cooperate to receive its effect. If we do, however, a livelier sense of the poem's instructiveness and a more urgent appreciation of its action will be our reward.

Satan continues with the temptation as it is recorded in the Bible. In the desert, he says, we "live on tough roots and stubs" and are as "inur'd" to thirst as camels are—but:

> But if thou be the Son of God, Command
> That out of these hard stones be made thee bread;
> So shalt thou save thyself and us relieve
> With Food, whereof we wretched seldom taste.   (I, 339–45)

Again, since temptations against faith are in the offing, Satan's purpose should be clear enough. Turning stones to bread would be acting upon distrust of the situation, and thus would imply mistrust of God's providence. Masking this danger is the diversionary appeal to charity, relief for the misery of the desert dwellers. We know we must refuse the main request, and the diversion is easily enough exploded, too—for where, we might ask, are those desert dwellers he refers to? Answers in this vein would serve, but once again the answer we hear is surprisingly better. "Think'st thou *such force* in Bread?" (I, 347; my emphasis), asks Jesus scornfully, and the jolt here is that tone of scorn. Why scorn? One must not turn stones to bread at Satan's behest, but bread, surely, has "force" enough: one either has it or starves. But scorn for bread, however odd, is the heart of this issue. "Living by faith" has a metaphorical ring, but it is no metaphor. One lives by it literally, even to the extent of starving, if need be, because true life is not here, but beyond. The scorn insists that *bread*, in fact, is the metaphor, since the "life" sustained by bread is a shadow to the substantial life in heaven. We know this, of course, as the "Christians" the poem assumes we are, but how well do we know it? Do we know it well enough *instinctively* to see the irrelevance of bread,

well enough to feel no jolt when bread is reduced to metaphor?[16] If the
scorn strikes us as odd, as I am arguing it does, then we are once again
reminded not only of what we know, but also of how dimly we know it.

Thus ends the temptation, as the Bible records it, but Milton is not
through with it yet. Satan and Jesus exchange lengthy speeches, reviewing the relevant biblical history. As this goes on, the dramatic pressure
lets up, for the recorded temptation has failed, and no new one seems to
be developing now. We may find ourselves relaxing into the role of
more passive spectators, but if we do we shall be unprepared for Satan's
next move. Under the pressure of Christ's firm scrutiny, Satan's compo-
sure dwindles, and his tone becomes a whine. He confesses things, as
though desperate for something to say. "Thou art plact above me, thou
art Lord," he admits; he must endure these reproofs and be glad they
are no harsher. But he insists that he loves the truth he is excluded from,
and so begs Jesus to "permit" him to stay around, so that he may put
questions and learn truth from the answers. The impact of this may
well be irritation, since there is something too pat about it to be sincere,
and if not sincere, it is disgusting, being at once both abject and sneaky.
Without ceasing to whine, Satan turns nasty:

> Thy Father, who is holy, wise and pure,
> Suffers the Hypocrite or Atheous Priest
> To tread his Sacred Courts, and minister
> About his Altar, handling holy things,
> Praying or vowing, and vouchsaf'd his voice
> To *Baalam* Reprobate, a Prophet yet
> Inspir'd; disdain not such access to me.   (I, 486–92)

Christ responds, as Milton notes carefully, "with unalter'd brow": "do
as thou find'st / Permission from above," he says evenly, "thou canst
not more" (I, 493–96).

To reflect upon this moment is to become aware, again in retrospect, that a dangerous temptation has come and gone. When Satan
begs Jesus to permit his staying by, he suggests, indirectly, that Jesus
can do otherwise: he may banish Satan from his presence, for he has the
power of doing so. These last lines of his are nasty because they impute
capriciousness to God, and if God's justice is slovenly, so the argument
goes, Satan may claim his just share of the general laxness. This is sly of
Satan, and cheaply snide as well. Cheap snideness in a whining tone is
not easy to endure, especially when one has power to silence it. Were
Christ to crush Satan in righteous anger at this slur upon God's justice,
or turn his back in righteous disgust and put Satan "behind" him then

and there, one could not blame him—but Paradise would not then be regained. Christ's mission requires extraordinary precision: he cannot reverse the Fall unless he withstands the full force of Satan's wiles, whatever their form, with a capacity no greater than human. His standing fast before all onslaughts is the one antidote to the active choice by which Adam embraced damnation; his refusing to exceed human capacity is the one antidote to Adam's failure to use the fullness of his. Should Jesus refuse further access to Satan, he would fail in the first of these; should he invoke a power beyond the human to silence him—even to silence wicked reflections on God the Father—he would fail in the second. Merely to do nothing is enough here, but to do nothing *with brow unaltered* is self-control that is heroic indeed.

In Milton's account, then, the temptation of the stones involves three temptations, each one an opportunity for substitution: "ill chance" for providence, bread for the life of the spirit, and mistimed zeal for patience. Each opportunity is presented indirectly, so that one is more apt to sense its danger vaguely than know instinctively what the precise danger is. The moments are set up in a way that gives us a chance to respond to them ourselves before hearing the response of the perfect man. "Our" responses, I am arguing, match the vagueness with which we sense the danger. They would be adequate responses, but when we test them against the precision of Jesus, we may feel how far short of *full* human capacity our mere adequacies are. In this subjective drama, I think, lie the poem's most interesting effects: the excitement that comes from clarification of the issues and from fresh recognition of what we already know, and the chastisement that comes from the distance we can feel between ourselves and our Savior—when "good enough" seems good enough no longer, because one now knows the "much better" that one *ought* to have remembered to attain. This is a drama of the reader's feelings, not a drama of external characters— subjective drama that requires willing involvement on the reader's part. The opportunity for this involvement is set up in the first temptation; the willingness to *stay* involved is tested in the second.

IV

In the second set of temptations, the pattern of reader's response I have been describing continues, but with one important difference. In the first series, the temptations were indirect; in this one, they are straightforward. The question now is not whether Jesus can be distracted but whether he has an appetite he cannot control, be it for food, riches, glory, power, or eloquence. And since Satan now works directly on human appetites, the gap between "our" responses and those we hear from Jesus is no longer defined by forgetfulness; it is defined by sheer inability. Most of us cannot fully assent to so *complete* a disdain of these appetites as Jesus can show, and because we cannot, his heroism of denial must seem heartless, prissy, or downright cold.

As an example, let us look at how Jesus deals with a temptation to relieve the miseries of the Chosen People. "Reduc't a province under Roman yoke," as Satan says, the Kingdom of Judah "obeys Tiberius" and suffers violations of the Temple, "affronts" to the Law, and "abominations" of the kind Judah suffered under Antiochus (III, 157–63). Antiochus, however, was overthrown, and surely the time has arrived for the reign of King Jesus:

> Zeal and duty are not slow,
> But on Occasion's forelock watchful wait.
> They themselves rather are occasion best,
> Zeal of thy Father's house, Duty to free
> Thy Country from her Heathen servitude;
> So shalt thou best fullfil, best verify
> The Prophets old, who sung thy endless reign,
> The happier reign the sooner it begins.   (III, 172–79)

Can Jesus' passion for human justice be so tempted that he will seize the day before his proper time? Of course not: it is not up to him *or* to Satan to determine what "best" will fulfill the prophecies of old. "All things are best fulfill'd in their due time" (III, 182), he says in reply, and thus, it would seem, duty has outranked "zeal." Later, however, one wonders whether Jesus feels any zeal at all. Still pressing this issue, Satan has offered the military strength of Parthia: properly employed by an active king, this strength will free the Chosen People at last. Jesus seems not to care. "As for those captive Tribes," he answers, "themselves were they / Who wrought their own captivity, fell off / From God to worship Calves" (III, 414–16)—and so their slavery might as well continue as not:

> Should I of these the liberty regard,
> Who freed, as to their ancient Patrimony,
> Unhumbl'd, unrepentant, unreform'd,
> Headlong would follow, and to thir Gods perhaps
> Of *Bethel* and of *Dan?* No, let them serve
> Thir enemies, who serve Idols with God.   (III, 427–32)

Throughout these temptations, such thoroughness is typical. His first answer, the refusal to seize the time, is perfectly sufficient; this second one, though correct as well, seems gratuitous, and being gratuitous, it seems heartless, too. Milton must have known what effect he was getting, for he gets it too consistently and too often not to have known.

Lawrence Hyman makes an interesting point about the passage we have in hand. "Zeal," he says, is a virtue—if the world of our virtues is the world of the Old Testament. Indeed, all of the Devil's offerings—military strength, imperial organization, eloquence, secular learning—are genuine gifts in a pagan or pre-Christian world. The coming of Christ invalidates them all, of course, but the new values Christ brings in, unfortunately, do not and cannot make emotional sense to the rest of us. This passage we have studied enacts this problem: the reader understands the disdain Christ shows, but he knows in his heart that he cannot go and do likewise. "No matter how much he understands," Hyman says, he cannot "give up his humanity also."[17] Milton, then, has created an interesting situation: Jesus is the perfection of human nature, but, as it turns out, perfected human nature is depressingly different from what "humanity" actually means to us. This situation is typical of all the temptations in the second series.

This second series of temptations takes up most of Book II, all of Book III, and half of Book IV—which is to say that it dominates the poem. It makes its single point relentlessly. For the attentive reader, who has been drawn into the excitement of the first temptation sequence, this very relentlessness presents a problem. To continue to engage the poem with the attention it demands is to continue to face these unsurprising, unpleasant revelations. In a word, the poem becomes an endurance test.

Good poems are not endurance tests, of course, but to recognize that aspect in this one is to get at the heart of its design. Endurance tests are themselves temptations, for they tempt one to give them up. Giving up, in this case, would be ceasing to pay attention to the poem, disengaging from it, justifying oneself, perhaps, by declaring Milton wrong or impossibly demanding and by flying to some "warmer" view of the salvationary moment. I am proposing that Milton has designed this temptation deliberately, and that he wants his reader to face it, reject it, and continue to endure.

The point of continuing is not fully evident until the conclusion of the third temptation, but a hint at this point comes in before the long endurance test begins. Milton sets up a parallel between the enduring "we" must do and the enduring of the poem's only other mortals, Simon, Andrew, and Mary. The hundred lines that begin Book II give us a glimpse of their plight, and the experience we see them undergo has a bearing on our own. Simon and Andrew lost track of Jesus when he disappeared into the wilderness, and as Book II begins, they, having searched for him all over the Holy Land, bewail their failure to find him. To them, this failure is the failure of all their hopes, a disappointment both painful and unexplained:

> Alas, from what high hope to what relapse
> Unlook'd for are we fall'n!
>   . . . .
>   soon our joy is turn'd
> Into perplexity and new amaze:
> For whither is he gone, what accident
> Hath rapt him from us?
>   . . . .
>   God of *Israel*,
> Send thy Messiah forth, the time is come;
> Behold the Kings of th'Earth how they oppress
> Thy chosen, to what height thir pow'r unjust
> They have exalted, and behind them cast
> All fear of thee; arise and vindicate
> Thy Glory, free thy people from thir yoke!   (II, 30–48)

As we see, the apostles have not "given up their humanity," and they express it movingly. But their cry of disappointment, having reached its climax here, collapses into a different mood entirely:

> But let us wait; thus far he hath perform'd,
>   . . . .
> Let us be glad of this, and all our fears
> Lay on his Providence; he will not fail.   (II, 49–54)

This sudden shift causes surprise, and "to the extent that we find their resignation surprising," writes Stanley Fish, "it presents us with the same problem that the disappearance of Jesus presents to them. It is not on its face sufficient to the occasion; and our experience of its insufficiency is very much like our experience of the Son's conduct in the temptation scenes."[18]

This analysis points up two important aspects of this moment. The first, its "insufficiency," is perfectly plain. Their outcry had been appropriate for the zeal they bore and continue to bear. "Appropriate," indeed, is too weak a word: it was *inevitable*, for how else should true zeal speak, in its frustration? Yet their mood changes instantly, and for no discernible reason. It is a moment of simple discontinuity, then, an effect seemingly without a cause. The second aspect, the resemblance of all this to our own experience, can be extended into a comparison with the effects of the first set of temptations. The fervor the apostles were expressing is good; the patience it collapses into—which does not follow and is a surprise—is better, and we know it is better the moment we see it. In both these aspects, this episode, carefully inserted here, shows us what we need to understand about endurance before our own endurance test begins.

Endurance, as it turns out, is a mode of faith. Faith surmounts frustrations not by explaining them or assuaging them but by enduring them in the fullness of what they are—and dismissing them. The outcomes of faith, in other words, do not follow the logic of ordinary knowledge and desire; they come as surprises, moments of discontinuity. In retrospect, these outcomes are obvious, but *only* in retrospect: one endures things as they are, and then finds oddly and suddenly that things as they were—indeed, as they *had* to be—are no more. It was a kindly gesture on Milton's part, therefore, to begin the second series of temptations with Simon and Andrew. In their frustrations, we find the image of our own. If apostles cannot understand, we cannot, and if they must endure the insufficiency of their humanity, so must we. Enduring their predictable failure, they arrive at an *un*necessary, *un*predictable success. The second temptation sequence presents us with our own failures, all of them necessary and predictable. As one enticement follows another, conclusive evidence mounts up to prove that we cannot cross the gap between fallen and perfected humanity—that we can never be good enough for Jesus. "What dost thou in this World?" asks Satan in exasperation when all enticements have failed (IV, 372). At this point we too may wonder, but the unnecessary, unpredictable sequel to it all is that our Savior and we are actually—nay, obviously—one. The reader senses this oneness from the outcome of the third temptation, and this moment which makes it obvious is also, as it happens, the poem's most conspicuous discontinuity.

V

Reminded by the jolts of the first sequence, depressed by the rigors of the second, the reader finds a different kind of involvement in the third. Since trickery and direct enticement have failed, Satan turns now to naked force and terror. God never required mere human nature to stand up before supernatural force and terror: that was made plain in *Paradise Lost.*[19] This last temptation, therefore, is not for the reader to share with Jesus, and so the reader's involvement must change. Speeches, so prominent up to now, become brief. Narrative becomes the important thing, and the narrator addresses Jesus as "thou," a sure sign that the poem no longer places us as though beside him. But if our activity must change, it need not cease: where before we had been engaging with the impact of speeches, we now may turn to the interpretation of narrative, for Milton's narrating leaves things unsaid and puzzles to solve. Taking on these puzzles will lead us to the poem's most heartening insights.

Satan begins with a crude attempt to soften Jesus up. Leaving Jesus in the wilderness without shelter, he causes a storm to buffet him for an entire night:

> ill wast thou shrouded then,
> O patient Son of God, yet only stood'st
> Unshaken; nor yet stay'd the terror there.
> Infernal Ghosts, and Hellish Furies, round
> Environ'd thee, some howl'd, some yell'd, some shriek'd,
> Some bent at thee thir fiery darts, while thou
> Satt'st unappall'd in calm and sinless peace.   (IV, 419–25)

As the presence of "thou" indicates, we are now spectators, not participants, with little to do but feel sympathy for the fortitude Christ displays. But how to interpret this fortitude? What, precisely, is meant by "sinless peace"? Here we have scope for our own activity. The temptation is to gloss sinless as "fearless," since Jesus endures without fear a storm meant to frighten him. But if we engage this problem and reflect on this, we cannot equate fear with sin:[20] sinful acts often proceed from fear, but one can fear—as we would ourselves in a storm like this—yet still refuse to deny God. A better gloss, then, brings in cause: "peaceful *because* sinless," but once we think of cause, a better gloss yet would be "sinless because *peaceful*." In this last gloss is a reminder that the one sin available to the Son of God, and available to no one else, is using God's sovereign power before the appointed time. If the point of endurance is that we must all stand and wait, standing and waiting is particularly important in one who has the power to do otherwise. Satan can "pervert God's plan" even here, by inducing Jesus to act prematurely.[21] "Sinless because peaceful" points to Christ's refusal to be anxious or irritated, his calm determination to suffer all and do nothing, the positive side of that same imperturbable thoroughness which makes him so distant in the second set of temptations. Christ is enduring, now, and we can recognize in him the same stance that we see in Simon and Andrew—and in ourselves, for that matter: one endures what is, and waits. It is an interesting reversal. Now that Christ is transcendent, undergoing difficulties appropriate only to the Son of God—just now, as he rises above us in capacity—the emotional gap between him and us becomes narrower instead of wider. What matters now is the likeness we share with him; differences fade away.

The scene on the spire confirms all this. Satan snatches Jesus up, transports him through air, and sets him down atop the tallest tower of the Temple of Jerusalem:

> There stand, if thou wilt stand; to stand upright
> Will ask thee skill; I to thy Father's house
> Have brought thee, and highest plac't, highest is best. (IV, 551–53)

Satan is witty: *stand, upright, thy Father's house,* even *highest,* are terms of glory in the language of the spirit; their significant meanings are spiritual. But Satan has created a situation in which they all make sense as merely local and physical terms as well, and the cheaper meanings mock and parody the grander ones–if one's attitude, like Satan's, is "scorn." For this, it turns out, is the ultimate test: material reality is pitted against the reality of the spirit; something so mundane as the force of gravity is brought in to destroy God's essence in the Son.[22] To avert this, Jesus can give up his status as merely man, renounce his physical limits, and save his life by asserting his divinity; and this, of course, would be acting on his own, the very thing he has been avoiding all along. On the other hand, he may surrender to gravity and fall off the spire, presumptuously confident that his Father will save him. But presumption is sin, and the Son of God would thereby be tainted. The situation is Satan's masterpiece.

Neither alternative occurs, but just what does happen is the poem's deepest mystery. This is what we are told: Jesus is about to be set on the spire, and ten lines later Jesus speaks: "Also it is written, / Tempt not the Lord thy God; he said and stood." Satan now falls, both literally and figuratively (IV, 560–61 and ff.), and that is all we know. Milton leaves us with the most important interpretive puzzle in the poem.

Now, all along the poem has been showing us that truth appears only in retrospection. What does retrospection tell us here? Exactly what happened may be a mystery, but the following points are beyond dispute: (1) this is the climactic moment: all temptations end here; (2) we know this only in retrospect, for it is not in our power to predict climactic moments; (3) this temptation is ended, as are all temptations, by "standing"; (4) standing required an effort of some kind, though just what effort is not clear;[23] (5) this ability to stand was beyond the limits of merely human possibility, so that (6) whatever happened, the energy to stand came from beyond, and the event that took place is discontinuous with the conditions of the situation that brought it forth. The pattern is familiar: endurance is required beyond the capacity for it; the effort is made anyway; the effort succeeds, not by the logic of the situation that required it, but by a better logic that comes as a surprise and mystery. The difference here is that Jesus, not some lesser being, is the human figure at the center.

Thus if the experience itself is obscure, its moral is plain. Even the Son of God must face a moment when he can do no more. Despite the vast, persisting differences between perfected and fallen human nature, all men share the fundamental insufficiency. Endurance has limits, and not even perfect man can endure all perfectly; the forces of evil will find a way to push any man beyond his capacities. But if resistance ultimately cannot succeed, the point of it, oddly, is not success. Making the attempt is what counts, and the attempt once made, God does the rest. The attempt is not *truly* made until one resolves to endure beyond one's known capacity and thus refuses to evade one's certain failure. It is at this point that endurance becomes faith. The odd thing about faith is that once it is answered, its success seems as inevitable as its failure had seemed before. It is an odd experience, then, but it is the experience that links the person who has had it with the apostles and with Jesus himself—the experience that constitutes salvation, the experience by which one may recognize that he or she belongs to the invisible church of God. *Paradise Regained* is cold because Milton wanted it to present this experience, and this experience cannot come cheaply.

VI

Casting his eye upon the "unhospitable barrenness" of *Paradise Regained*, "its generous portion of didactic tedium, and the dramatic failure of its static contest," Howard Schultz declared those problems irrelevant for a proper reading of the poem. We must see it as "a parable for the church," he said, not as a "manual for holy living."[24] This is a useful idea, but it requires refinement. In her answer to it, Barbara Lewalski said that if *Paradise Regained* is no "manual" of ethics, its emphasis surely is "moral and individual," not corporate. The church for which it is a "parable," furthermore, must be "the whole community of the saved,"[25] a community defined by ethics, not sacraments, by a shared quality of will, not by ritual, doctrine, or ecclesiastical polity. One can resolve this dispute quite simply, however, for the "church" Milton recognized was the "invisible" church, a church based on the individual relations between its members and God. A "parable" for such a church can be nothing less than an image of what that relation ought to be. And *Paradise Regained* was written to make this image plain.

Milton's image, of course, had plenty of rivals. Conservative churchmen saw the church establishment and its priests as intermediaries between man and God. Calvinists, on the other hand, saw no intermediary at all, and because God simply saved whom he would, no human effort could seem significant to them. For Milton, and for a good many like-minded radicals, neither picture would do: "Men and women were not saved through the church, and were not preordained to salvation by an irreversible divine decree thanks to Christ's imputed righteousness. God foresaw that they would save themselves by their own efforts."[26] What *kind* of effort, however, was another question, and on this question Milton differed from most of his radical associates. Their image of this effort is warm; Milton's is cold. This difference appears plainly in a sermon by William Dell. Dell was an important figure of the Commonwealth period, and one with whom Milton agreed on most issues. Both men were anticlerical and anti-Catholic; both supported Cromwell, even after he dismissed his parliaments; both wanted to establish local universities and end the monopoly of Oxford and Cambridge. Dell, himself the head of a Cambridge college, denounced mere "humane learning" and classical studies much as Milton had Jesus do in *Paradise Regained*. Both believed, furthermore, that men could be one with Christ in this world, not merely in the next, so that both believed that achieving that oneness must free even worldly deeds from the taint of sin.[27] Both, in other words, were thoroughgoing radicals in social and religious beliefs alike, so that the vast difference between them, when it comes to man's relation to God, is instructive indeed.

"If *Christ* be present in our *hearts* by *faith*," says Dell in a sermon of 1653, "his works will be undoubtedly manifest in our *lives*": he means this almost literally. Christ was a man "whose *business, imployment* and *Kingdom* lies with the Poor, Lame, Blind, and all sorts of Afflicted, Sorrowfull and distressed persons," he continues. If Christ dwells within us, then, we shall be likewise:

This *Gospel* is preached to the *Poor*, that is, to the *Poor* in *Spirit*; and these are *such*, who do not love, nor desire, nor delight in *present* things, but are so *afflicted* and *oppressed* in their heart & consciences with the sense of *sin* and *wrath*, that they regard not the *world*, nor the *Riches*, *Pleasures*, and *Honors* of it, but *all* they mind, or care for, is *Jesus Christ*, and in *Him*, the *love* of God, and the *Remission* of sin, and gift of the Spirit.[28]

So afflicted are they, in other words, that they hate the world as instinctively as Jesus hates it in *Paradise Regained*. Dell does not allow for a gap between the affections of the true Christian and those of his Savior.

Those who hang back, who cannot hate the world as easily as Jesus does, may count themselves damned. It does not seem that Dell would greatly have minded if this judgment included most of his listeners.

Now Dell's image of the relation of man to Christ is what one would call "warm." It is intimate, total, even automatic. Milton's idea, as we have seen, is "cold": not intimate, but distant; not total, but distressingly partial; so far from automatic that our strivings toward our Savior seem bound to fail. With this difference go several others. Dell's true Christian is overwhelmed by his sense of sin, whereas Milton's Christian feels uncomfortably inadequate—a feeling in some ways similar, but on the whole importantly different. For on Dell's account, man in his own nature can do nothing good: if his works are good, he has performed them not as himself but as a limb of Christ. With Milton, on the other hand, a person's own energy can do well, even if not well enough. Dell's Christian glories in being one of a small, separated, and persecuted minority; Milton's is any reader who genuinely wants to love God. As a member of a sacred minority, infallible in his attachment to Christ, Dell's Christian is a radical activist, and the measure of his faith is his excitement, his delight in the trouble his activity creates. "Where ever the *word* comes in truth," says Dell, "there are alwayes *troubles* and *uproares;* but where the *world* is *quiet,* that for *certain* is not the *true word* of God."[29] Milton, radical though he was, came finally to think that excitement and faith were vastly different experiences. For him, the Christian's grand achievement was to suppress excitement, to learn to stand and wait. In sum, then, although Dell's image of man and Christ is warm and intimate, it also entails contempt (if not hatred) for most of one's fellow men, endless strife (though holy and for the Lord), sturdy but narrow confidence in self, and the conviction that human energy, of itself, is worthless. Milton's image, though distant, chilly, and troubling, does not exclude one's fellow men; it makes Christian strife a matter of endurance, not aggression; it places the confidence of faith outside of self; and it finds value in human energy, insufficient as that energy may be.

Paradise Regained is cold, then, because Milton chose to exchange intimacy for responsibility, the power to act for the power to endure, automatic sanctity for a sanctity dignified by effort—even failing effort. Jesus "will have *all* those whom his Father hath given him," Dell said, and Milton agreed. But Milton would have added this proviso: those whom his Father hath given him must still take the trouble to *be* given, and this requires a steady, strenuous, but quiet commitment to

God—something that resembles balancing on a spire and waiting for God to act.[30] Excitement and warmth, for all the pleasure and confidence they give, also suffocate. Milton makes Jesus distant because he believes that people must have room to breathe, space of their own through which to reach toward God. The energy they spend reaching must be their own, and the figure to whom they must reach, distant as he is, expends this same energy and no other—on their behalf. Not to be intimate, not to be assured, not to feel oneself a limb of God may all be "chilling" experiences for the would-be faithful, but they are bracing, not numbing, if properly understood.

University of Washington

NOTES

1. "The Life of Mr. John Milton," prefaced to Phillips' edition of Milton's *Letters of State* (1694), reprinted in *John Milton: Complete Poems and Major Prose*, ed. Merritt Y. Hughes (New York, 1957), p. 1036. All quotations from Milton's works are taken from this edition.

2. The phrase is used by Ralph W. Rader, "Fact, Theory and Literary Explanation," *Critical Inquiry*, I (1974), 253.

3. Readers familiar with recent criticism will recognize how closely this approach resembles that of Stanley Fish. In *Surprised by Sin* (New York, 1967), Fish takes the irreducible problem of *Paradise Lost*, as Waldock and others understood it, and declares that problem to be the poem's most important point. Needless to say, I am indebted to this procedure, as I am also indebted to his specific way of undertaking it, the analysis of the "reader's" response. Fish has written on *Paradise Regained* as well, again analyzing the reader's response, and many of his conclusions anticipate mine. But we are addressing different formulations of the "problem" in that work: his calls attention specifically to the "inactivity" of its hero, while mine deals with the less specific matter of the poem's overall demeanor toward its readers—in a word, the poem's "coldness." The conclusions we come to differ considerably, but I regard mine as complements to his, not as refutations of them. See "Inaction and Silence: The Reader in *Paradise Regained*," in *Calm of Mind: Tercentenary Essays on "Paradise Regained" and "Samson Agonistes" in Honor of John S. Dieckhoff*, ed. Joseph Anthony Wittreich, Jr. (Cleveland, 1971), pp. 25–47.

4. Bentley's note to *PL* X, 182, in his edition of 1732, reprinted on p. 1 of Dunster's edition of *Paradise Regained* (1795); this edition is reprinted in *Milton's "Paradise Regained": Two Eighteenth-Century Critiques*, ed. Joseph Anthony Wittreich, Jr. (Gainesville, Fla., 1971). Samuel Johnson, Thomas Thyer, and William Warburton agreed with Bentley; Dunster quotes them, pp. 1–3.

5. Dunster edition of *PR*, pp. 3, 2.

6. "The Typology of *Paradise Regained*," *MP*, LIII (1956), reprinted in *Milton: Modern Essays in Criticism*, ed. Arthur E. Barker (New York, 1965), pp. 439–40.

7. *The Paradise Within: Studies in Vaughan, Traherne and Milton* (New Haven, 1964), p. 190.

8. *"Paradise Regained": The Tradition and the Poem* (Baltimore, 1947), p. 40.

9. "The Better Fortitude," in *The Living Milton*, ed. Frank Kermode (London, 1960), p. 134.

10. Fish, *Surprised by Sin*, p. 6.

11. Hughes ed., p. 727.

12. Rader's article, cited in n. 2, takes the latter position and attacks Stanley Fish as a proponent of the former. Fish's "Facts and Fictions: A Reply to Ralph Rader" appears in *Critical Inquiry*, I (1975), 883–91, and is answered in turn by Rader in the same issue.

13. The question of Christ's nature is thoroughly discussed in Barbara K. Lewalski, *Milton's Brief Epic: The Genre, Meaning, and Art of "Paradise Regained,"* (Providence, R.I., 1966), pp. 133–63. My conclusions about where to find the "drama" of the poem differ from hers, but we agree that Christ must be—at this point—acting within and not beyond the capacities of men.

14. Pope, *The Tradition and the Poem*, pp. 31 ff., thinks that this is Satan's purpose not only here, but throughout the poem. While I agree with A. S. P. Woodhouse ("Theme and Pattern in *Paradise Regained*," *UTQ*, XXV [1956], 167–82) that this purpose does not explain Satan's activity, Pope's argument is testimony to the impression Satan sometimes gives.

15. See Arnold Stein, *Heroic Knowledge* (Minneapolis, 1957), p. 11: "the answers not only expose the intentions of Satan, but they undermine his pitfalls and play cat-and-mouse with his motives, checkmating or taunting the secret motive still several removes from sight."

16. Luke iv, 4, says "And Jesus answered him, saying, It is written, That man shall not live by bread alone, but every word of God"; Matthew iv, 4, has it as "every word that proceedeth out of the mouth of God." Neither Gospel records the instructive scorn that Milton puts into his version.

17. "The Reader's Attitude in *Paradise Regained*," *PMLA*, LXXXV (1970), 497.

18. "Inaction and Silence," p. 30.

19. IX, 344–56.

20. An interesting parallel is Christ's "let this cup pass from me," (Matthew xxvi, 39), his prayer on the morning of the Crucifixion. John Colet, following Jerome, could not believe that the "cup" could refer to his impending death, for that would imply fear. Erasmus answered Colet thus: "If he ever declined death, his love was imperfect; but if he never declined it, why does he ask to be delivered from that which he willed? Surely at that moment he spoke as a man, for men, to men, and in the words of men, expressing man's fears; . . . For a man who is by no process of reasoning unwilling to die may still be terrified by death." His nature, in other words, is subject to fear; his will can overcome the weakness of his nature—as indeed it did. Milton adumbrates this moment here. See *The Correspondence of Erasmus, Letters 1 to 141: 1484 to 1500, The Collected Works of Erasmus*, vol. 1, trans. R. A. B. Mynors and D. F. S. Thomson, annotated by Wallace K. Ferguson (Toronto, 1974), Letter 109, Erasmus to Colet, October 1499, p. 208.

21. See Laurie Zwicky, "Kairos in *Paradise Regained*: The Divine Plan," *ELH*, XXXI (1964), 271–77.

22. As Stein puts it, Satan is now invoking "brute, mechanical . . . momentum" and no longer is tempting the mind (*Heroic Knowledge*, p. 127).

23. William Blake and J. M. W. Turner both illustrated this moment. Blake's Christ "stands atop the spire lightly touching it with a single toe," weight ostentatiously out of

balance, implying an instantaneous miracle as his foot touches the spire—a miracle of "self-annunciation" in which he "recognizes his own divine nature and can exercise that divinity." The majority of critics see this moment as Blake does. Turner has Christ performing "a human balancing feat . . . with one foot on a sharp spire, the other foot apparently behind to balance," arms out, and "weight centered." J. Karl Franson, who describes these illustrations (*Milton Quarterly*, X [1976], 48–53), thinks that Turner's version implies that "no miracle occurs." It would be more accurate, I think, to say that no miracle has occurred *just yet:* the Turner version suggests a moment of supreme human effort—a perceptible moment of struggle, however short—just before God's power and its miracle are manifest. Turner's view is not widely held, but I prefer it. The text supports his as much as Blake's.

24. "Christ and Antichrist in *Paradise Regained*," PMLA, LXVII (1952), 790.

25. "Theme and Structure in *Paradise Regained*," SP, LVII (1960), 188.

26. Christopher Hill, *Milton and the English Revolution* (New York, 1977), p. 272.

27. For the like-mindedness of Milton and Dell, see ibid., pp. 103–04, 219–20, 190, 149, 424–25, 109, 309, 312–13.

28. *The Stumbling-Stone* . . . (London, 1653), pp. 5–7.

29. Ibid., pp. 18–19.

30. The whole poem, in a way, is a commentary on God's declaration in *Paradise Lost*, III, 173–75: "Man shall not quite be lost, but sav'd who will, / Yet not of will in him, but grace in me / Freely voutsaf'd." Salvation requires grace as its efficient cause, the power that actually does the saving, and it requires the human endeavor of reaching up to God to set grace in motion. If we see Christ as actually balancing on the spire, he becomes the emblem of this entire process. His ability to balance is not sufficient unto his standing, but he endeavors, and God does the rest.

THE PHOENIX AND THE SUN
IN *SAMSON AGONISTES*

Anthony Low

R E A D E R S O F Milton learn to expect an unusual richness of meaning and depth of allusiveness; few passages in his mature poems do not involve multiple allusions to his predecessors as well as to other passages in Milton's own works. The New Critics have taught us to read poetry as if it were a series of self-sufficient Grecian urns, but Milton's poems often are more like symphonies, skillfully built up out of familiar and half-familiar themes to achieve new and harmonious wholes. One example of such harmonious complexity is the second semichorus near the end of *Samson Agonistes*, which culminates in the image of the phoenix. The profusion of images in this semichorus, complex in itself, also echoes the tradition, echoes Milton's other works, and compresses many if not most of the important motifs in the play:

> But he though blind of sight,
> Despis'd and thought extinguish't quite,
> With inward eyes illuminated
> His fierie vertue rouz'd
> From under ashes into sudden flame,
> And as an ev'ning Dragon came,
> Assailant on the perched roosts,
> And nests in order rang'd
> Of tame villatic Fowl; but as an Eagle
> His cloudless thunder bolted on thir heads.
> So vertue giv'n for lost,
> Deprest, and overthrown, as seem'd,
> Like that self-begott'n bird
> In the *Arabian* woods embost,
> That no second knows nor third,
> And lay e're while a Holocaust,
> From out her ashie womb now teem'd,
> Revives, reflourishes, then vigorous most
> When most unactive deem'd,
> And though her body die, her fame survives,
> A secular bird ages of lives.   (1687–1707)[1]

219

The semichorus, which relies on Milton's use of light-dark imagery, a common running motif in his poetry, also refers back to the elaborate imagery of seeing and blindness developed earlier. Not only are Samson's former physical sight and spiritual blindness, his later physical blindness and spiritual sight evoked, but at the same time his new vision is contrasted with the total blindness, deafness, and insensateness of the Philistines, who go down into darkness as Samson rises out of it:

> So fond are mortal men
> Fall'n into wrath divine,
> As thir own ruin on themselves to invite,
> Insensate left, or to sense reprobate,
> And with blindness internal struck.   (1682–86)

The movement of the two semichoruses is from the insensate Philistines, falling into darkness, to the reborn Samson, rising out of ashes and blindness into "sudden flame." The contrast is not only between light and dark, seeing and blindness, but between dynamic downward and upward movements, symbolizing spiritual change.[2]

The second semichorus also recalls the theme of sacrifice. Samson as the phoenix is a "Holocaust," a burnt offering to God. The play takes place against a constant background of references to sacrifice: the burnt offering of Samson's parents when the angel foretells his birth (26), the sacrifice the Philistines plan to offer to Dagon (436), Manoa's suggestion that Samson propitiate God with offerings after he is ransomed (519), the sacrifices the Public Officer wants Samson to participate in (1312), and the sacrifices at the feast itself (1612–13). The Philistines propose to offer Samson's humiliation as a sacrifice in honor of Dagon, but instead at the moment of triumph he becomes a ransoming victim offered up to the true God of Israel. As such he unknowingly becomes a type of Christ, the perfect victim.

Samson is first compared to "an ev'ning Dragon." As Lee Sheridan Cox points out, Milton must have been thinking not merely of a serpent, but of the winged monster of legend.[3] His dragon is like Spenser's in The Faerie Queene (I.xii) or like the "huge dragon" he himself describes in The Reason of Church Government as the antagonist of St. George, a "mighty saile-winged monster," "breathing out wast, and desolation to the land."[4] The image of a flying dragon suits the exalted mood of the Chorus and accords with the other images. So do the dragon's traditional ability to breathe out fire and destruction and, as Cox points out, the original meaning of dragon: "the seeing one."[5] Samson now is one who sees spiritually, as he brings down destruction upon the blind Philistines.

Samson is also like an eagle. A bird of prey, thus suited to destroying the hapless Philistines, the eagle is also the bird of Jove who brings down "cloudless thunder" on their heads. Samson as eagle reinforces the theme of the Hebrew champion as God's minister of vengeance and justice.[6] And as critics point out, the eagle (like the dragon) is a bird who is supremely sighted. In the well-known passage from *Areopagitica*, which also evokes a revivified Samson, Milton recalls the tradition that only the eagle can look directly on the midday sun:

Methinks I see in my mind a noble and puissant Nation rousing herself like a strong man after sleep, and shaking her invincible locks: Methinks I see her as an Eagle muing her mighty youth, and kindling her undazl'd eyes at the full midday beam; purging and unscaling her long abused sight at the fountain it self of heav'nly radiance; while the whole noise of timorous and flocking birds, with those also that love the twilight, flutter about, amaz'd at what she means.[7]

Samson not only falls like a thunderbolt on the paralyzed Philistines, he also rises in triumph like an eagle; he renews his sight and his youthful vigor, under a sun that stands at noon over the temple of Dagon.

The third and culminating comparison is to the Arabian phoenix. Like Samson, this mythical bird is unique and stands alone. Like the dragon and the eagle, it is winged to swoop down or soar up. Most important, it is a symbol of rebirth. In its context the image suggests a rebirth of Samson's strength, courage, and ability to play once more an active hero's part. The Chorus evokes immortality through posthumous fame and influence on others, a meaning Milton might have found in Henry Peacham's *Minerva Britanna* (1612), in an emblem addressed to Robert Cecil, Earl of Salisbury:

> You, you (Great Lord) this wondrous *Phoenix* are,
> Who wast your selfe in Zeale, and whot desire,
> Of Countries good, till in the end your care
> Shall worke your end, as doth this Phoenix fire.
>> But while you are consuming in the same,
>> You breede a second, your immortall Fame.[8]

Most important, the phoenix is a typological emblem, a symbol of both Christ's Resurrection and the immortality of the soul. The latter is perhaps the commonest meaning of the emblem among Christian writers. Nowhere in *Samson* is personal immortality explicitly referred to, though it is several times hinted at; but, as I argue elsewhere, Samson's immortality is implicitly assumed by the Christian playwright and his

presumedly Christian audience.[9] The afterlife cannot be referred to or
the play would lose its tragic force as well as its historical probability,
but Milton reveals in the *Christian Doctrine* his belief that salvation
was possible to the Hebrew forerunners of Christ by faith in the
Father.[10] When the Chorus evokes the phoenix it may be thinking chiefly
of Samson's fame, but Milton's reader, with his greater revealed knowledge, is expected to see further.

Perhaps the phoenix as well as the dragon is anticipated at the beginning of the semichorus. It too, "thought extinguish't quite," rouses
its fiery virtue "From under ashes into sudden flame." The passage
seems deliberately blurred; one image fuses with another and what we
usually like to call "vehicle" and "tenor" merge inextricably:

> But he though blind of sight,
> Despis'd and thought extinguish't quite,
> With inward eyes illuminated
> His fiery vertue rouz'd
> From under ashes into sudden flame.

Samson, literally blind, is metaphorically extinguished, and the two
statements are put on the same level. Or is the "he" that seemed extinguished the metaphorical dragon or phoenix? The blurring of distinctions does not confuse the meaning but knits the images more closely
together. In a sense, the three images become one. Something similar
occurs toward the end of the passage, where long grammatical suspension leaves unclear whether virtue, the phoenix, or Samson dies in body
but lives on in fame.

What gives this semichorus its greatest resonance is yet another
link between image systems, noticed, so far as I am aware, only in a
very brief comment by Albert L. Cirillo.[11] This is the traditional link between the phoenix and the sun. Milton does not make the connection explicit at this point, yet the solar implications of the phoenix were as well
known to contemporary readers as, say, Helen of Troy's destructive
beauty. When Milton's Raphael descends toward the Garden of Eden in
Paradise Lost,

> to all the Fowles he seems
> A *Phœnix*, gaz'd by all, as that sole Bird
> When to enshrine his reliques in the Sun's
> Bright Temple, to Ægyptian *Theb's* he flies.   (V, 271–74)

The tradition that the phoenix deposits the ashes of its former self at the
temple of the sun is ancient and widespread, though usually Heliopolis

rather than Thebes is mentioned. Kester Svendsen cites Bartholomew, Batman, Maplet, La Primaudaye, and Swan, to whom we may add Herodotus (*The Persian Wars*, II.73), Pliny (*Natural History*, X.2), and Ovid (*Metamorphoses*, XV, 391–402). As Arthur Golding has it in 1567:

> And flying through the suttle aire he gettes to
> > Phebus Towne,
> And there before the temple doore dooth lay his
> > burthen downe.   (447–48)[12]

A connection between the phoenix and the sun is also suggested in Milton's *Epitaphium Damonis*. Engraved on one of Manso's cups is a picture of the phoenix waiting for the coming of dawn:

> Has inter Phœnix divina avis, unica terris
> Cæruleùm fulgens diversicoloribus alis
> Auroram vitreis surgentem respicit undis.   (187–89)

[Among (the trees) the phoenix, the divine bird, unique on earth, gleams cerulean with varicolored wings, and watches Aurora rising over the glassy waters.]

Coming as it does just before the turn in the poem, this image may symbolize both Damon's youthful hopes, cut off before their realization, and his expected resurrection. Kathleen Hartwell cites a similar passage in Lactantius and another in Claudian. Both are variants of the phoenix's traditional relationship with the sun. Here is Claudian's *Epigram de Phoenice:*

> Hic sedet et blando Solem clangore salutat
> debilior miscetque preces ac supplice cantu
> praestatura novas vires incendia poscit.[13]   (45–47)

[He sits on this (pyre) and as he grows weaker greets the sun with a sweet cry; offering prayers and supplications, he begs that those fires will give him renewed strength.]

Thomas Browne, postulating an even closer relationship between the phoenix and the sun, writes in *Pseudodoxia Epidemica:* "Others have spoken Emblematically and Hieroglyphically; and so did the Egyptians, unto whom the Phoenix was the Hieroglyphick of the Sun" (III.xii).[14]

A still more interesting connection between the phoenix and the sun runs through the tradition: a widespread belief that the flames that destroy the old phoenix are kindled by the sun and that the sun is thus the agent of its rebirth. Pliny writes that the phoenix is first reborn as a worm or maggot, like other creatures that the sun conceives: "ex ossibus deinde et medullis eius nasci primo ceu vermiculum" ["Then from its bones and marrow is born first a sort of maggot"].[15] This theory, not often repeated by literary as distinct from scientific phoenixologists, may have given rise to the idea of the phoenix being born of the sun's rays. Geoffrey Whitney, in his popular book *A Choice of Emblemes* (1586), writes:

> The Phœnix rare, with fethers freshe of hewe,
> *Arabias* righte, and sacred to the Sonne:
> Whome, other birdes with wonder seeme to vewe,
> Dothe live untill a thousande yeares bee ronne:
>   Then makes a pile: which, when with Sonne it burnes,
>   Shee flies therein, and so to ashes turnes.[16]

Whitney's phoenix, sacred to the sun, dies and is reborn on a pyre kindled by the sun. In Henry Peacham's emblem poem, part of which was quoted earlier, the sun both kindles the flames and breeds the new phoenix out of the ashes:

> Th' Arabian *Phoenix* heere, of golden plumes,
> And bicie brest, upon a sacred pile
> Of sweetest odors, thus himselfe consumes;
> By force of *Phoebus* fiery beames, the while,
>   From foorth the ashes of the former dead,
>   A faire, or fairer, by and by is bred.[17]

The phoenix pictured in the *Symbolorum ac Emblematum Ethico* of Joachim Camerarius is seen standing in the flames with wings and breasts raised toward the sun, which shoots down its rays from the upper left.[18] A similar woodcut accompanies Peacham's poem; in this picture the sun and its rays are more prominent than the fire, which as yet only plays about the phoenix's legs.[19]

Francis Quarles, in an emblem on Job xiii, 24, introduces a phoenix that dies and is reborn not on a funeral pyre but by directly confronting the heavenly luminaries that are emblems of God's countenance:

> Unscreen those heavenly lamps, or tell me why
> Thou shad'st thy face; perhaps Thou think'st no eye
> Can view those flames, and not drop down and die.
>
> If that be all, shine forth and draw Thee nigher;
> Let me behold and die, for my desire
> Is, phoenix-like, to perish in that fire.[20]

Quarles's usage, however, is conceited rather than conventional.

Milton undoubtedly was familiar with most, perhaps even all, of the writers who have been cited. If any doubt remains, it may be dispelled by referring to a passage from *Britannia's Pastorals* (I.4) by William Browne of Tavistock, which describes the birth of Truth in terms of the death and rebirth of the phoenix:

> As that Arabian bird (whom all admire)
> Her exequies prepar'd and funeral fire,
> Burnt in a flame conceived from the sun,
> And nourished with slips of cinnamon,
> Out of her ashes hath a second birth,
> And flies abroad, a wonderment on earth. . . .[21]

In the margin opposite "that Arabian bird" is written in Milton's hand "The Phœnix."[22]

True, Milton does not refer explicitly to the sun-phoenix tradition in *Samson Agonistes*. But certainly he knew it and could assume his audience knew it, from the emblem books, the bestiaries, or the major classical sources. The Chorus uses the phoenix image without being fully aware of its most important implications for a Christian audience, resurrection and personal immortality, but Milton's readers were bound, and presumably intended, to think of these additional implications. Moreover, as many of the most important image complexes in the play converge on this semichorus and the phoenix image, they reinforce and elucidate the ties between the phoenix and the sun, as Samson dies and is reborn under the blaze of noon.

Critics point to a connection between the biblical Samson story and ancient solar myths.[23] Samson's Hebrew name *Shimshon* is related to *shemesh*, the sun. His long locks correspond to the sun's rays, and their shearing by Dalila resembles the sun's eclipse or setting. Just as in the traditional solar myths the sun emerges once more out of darkness from the underworld, so as Samson's locks grow back he regains his strength and vitality. Milton, familiar with these connections, used the myth in *Samson Agonistes* much as he used similar myths elsewhere. The solar myth would presumably have had, in his eyes, a relationship to the Samson story like that of the mythical pagan paradises to Eden in *Paradise Lost*. Both are mere empty dreams of the pagans, yet both shadow forth the truth and provide sources of vivid imagery that can be assimilated to the truth through poetry. The connection between Samson and the sun that Milton makes in *Areopagitica* is echoed by an even more explicit connection in *The Reason of Church Government*:

I cannot better liken the state and person of a King then to that mighty Nazarite *Samson*; who . . . grows up to a noble strength and perfection with those his illustrious and *sunny locks* the laws waving and curling about his god like shoulders. . . . They wickedly shaving off all those *bright* and waighty tresses of his laws . . . *put out* the fair, and farre-sighted *eyes* of his natural discerning. . . . Till he . . . nourish again his puissant hair, the *golden beames* of Law and Right; and *they sternly shook, thunder* with ruin upon the heads of those his evil counsellors.[24]

Perhaps too the title "Samson pursophorus" in the outlines for tragedies suggests more than a play centering, as critics assume, on the foxes that set fire to the Philistine crops.[25]

The culminating image complex in the second semichorus, which relies so heavily on tradition, relies also on earlier images in *Samson* itself. The play significantly begins with the blind Samson led toward a choice of "Sun or shade" (3). As he emerges from the close, dark air of the prison, he feels for the first time since his fall "amends, / The breath of Heav'n fresh-blowing, pure and sweet, / With day-spring born" (9–11). Comfort comes with the sun's rising, though he cannot see it. He remembers the prophecy of his birth:

> from Heaven foretold
> Twice by an Angel, who at last in sight
> Of both my Parents all in flames ascended
> From off the Altar, where an Off'ring burn'd,
> As in a fiery column charioting
> His Godlike presence.   (23–28)

Roger Wilkenfeld connects the passage with the second semichorus on account of its similar imagery.[26] Thus the play begins linking Samson with images of sun and flame while it presents him as a man cut off from light, eclipsed, extinguished:

> O dark, dark, dark, amid the blaze of noon,
> Irrecoverably dark, total Eclipse
> Without all hope of day!
> O first created Beam, and thou great Word,
> Let there be light, and light was over all;
> Why am I thus bereav'd thy prime decree?
> The Sun to me is dark
> And silent as the Moon,
> When she deserts the night
> Hid in her vacant interlunar cave.   (80–89)

In *Paradise Lost*, Satan undergoes an eclipse, but his path and Samson's diverge from that point. While Satan, standing beneath the midday sun, curses its beams, Samson at noon finds reconciliation with the Father.

Samson's opening soliloquy develops a close connection between light and life. Light "necessary is to life," "almost life it self" (90–91); "Light is in the Soul" (92). If only its organs were not the eyes, he would not now find himself "exil'd from light; / As in the land of darkness" (98–99). Thus he powerfully laments his blindness, at the beginning of the play both physical and spiritual. Exiled from light and the Father of light, cut off from the sun, he is himself like an eclipsed sun, shorn of its beams. Entering, the Chorus laments:

> Which shall I first bewail,
> Thy Bondage or lost Sight,
> Prison within Prison,
> Inseparably dark?
>
> · · · · · · ·
>
> Shut up from outward light
> To incorporate with gloomy night;
> For inward light alas
> Puts forth no visual beam.   (151–54, 160–63)

The Chorus ironically reverses Milton's lifelong view that inward light is better than outward. Later Samson will be transformed, but in his near despair, closed within himself, he is like an eclipsed sun that can put forth no "visual beam."

At the battle of Ramath-Lechi, Samson burst his imprisoning cords like "threds / Toucht with the flame" (261–62). Milton found the image in Judges, but it proved well suited to his play. A little later, Milton modifies a familiar biblical phrase, "The fool hath said in his heart, There is no God," to say that fools and atheists "walk obscure" (296). To deny God is to be cut off from the sun and from light, just as in *Comus:* "He that hides a dark soul, and foul thoughts / Benighted walks under the mid-day Sun; / Himself is his own dungeon" (382–84).

After his victory at Ramath-Lechi, Samson puffed himself up and behaved as if his strength were his own, not a divine gift. Before his downfall, "famous now and blaz'd" (528), he walked about like a petty god. The primary meaning of "blaz'd" is "heralded" or "made known"; but the word also suggests a fire or a sun out of control. Samson still enjoys his sunlike powers, but (as in several solar myths) he is beginning to abuse them. The play's fire imagery, Cox points out, sometimes suggests falsity or evil, when it is associated with the Philistines or (as here) when Samson abuses his gift.[27]

After Samson describes the hubris that preceded his fall, the Chorus, in what has seemed a digression, praises him for his abstemiousness, for avoiding wine and drinking only "from the cool Crystalline stream" (546). The water Samson drinks, while cool, is linked with the sun:

> Where ever fountain or fresh current flow'd
> Against the Eastern ray, translucent, pure,
> With touch ætherial of Heav'ns fiery rod
> I drank, from the clear milkie juice allaying
> Thirst, and refresht; nor envy'd them the grape
> Whose heads that turbulent liquor fills with fumes.   (547–52)

In *Elegia Sexta*, Milton repeatedly associates Apollo with Bacchus and wine-drinking poets, not with the followers of Homer who drink water and commit themselves to heroic verse. In *Samson* there has been a transformation: the sun is a patron of water drinkers. The change is anticipated in the invocation to Book III of *Paradise Lost*, which associates the springs of inspiration with the sun and light. Of course, Apollo and the muses were closely linked in Classical tradition, and both sun and water are familiar Christian symbols of God's graciousness to man.

These sun images shine from Samson's past; in his present he is still eclipsed. During Manoa's visit he reaches his darkest psychological state and expects to plunge still further into darkness:

> these dark orbs no more shall treat with light,
> Nor th' other light of life continue long,
> But yield to double darkness nigh at hand.   (591–93)

He is wrong; he will go to his end not in darkness but in a metaphorical blaze of light. But that cannot yet be known. The Chorus, lamenting his fall and that of other great men, uses solar imagery to describe their downfall:

> Yet toward these thus dignifi'd, thou oft
> Amidst thir highth of noon,
> Changest thy countenance, and thy hand with no regard
> Of highest favours past.   (682–85)

"Amidst thir highth of noon": the sun, at its highest point, is suddenly thrown down or eclipsed.

At the exit of Harapha, the Chorus fears trouble if the disgruntled giant reports Samson's conduct to the Philistine lords. Ironically, although their fears are false, their words seem to anticipate the catastrophe: "He's gone, and who knows how he may report / Thy words by adding fuel to the flame?" (1350–51). If the image of a fire being fueled foreshadows the conclusion only dimly, the Chorus's last words are more direct:

> Go, and the Holy One
> Of *Israel* be thy guide.
>
> .   .   .   .
>
> Send thee the Angel of thy Birth, to stand
> Fast by thy side, who from thy Fathers field
> Rode up in flames after his message told
> Of thy conception, and be now a shield
> Of fire.   (1427–35)

The prayer will be answered. The great event in the temple, while not just what the Chorus expects, fulfills this petition to the letter.

The Messenger, after giving his disjointed report of the catastrophe, says that he entered the city gates "with Sun-rise" (1597). He reports that Samson was brought into the temple as "Feast and noon grew high" (1612). Samson's death and the destruction of the temple take place as the sun reaches its peak, under that blaze of noon invoked in Samson's first complaint. The two semichoruses follow immediately on the Messenger's description. The first pictures the Philistines preferring their drunken idolatry to God "In *Silo* his bright Sanctuary" (1674). So, blind and insensate, they go down into darkness as Samson had earlier expected to do. But Samson rises out of darkness, from under the ashes of shame and defeat, like a dragon, an eagle, or the phoenix: a bird of the sun or the rekindled sun itself. He leaves the memory of his great acts to "inflame" the breasts of Israel's youth (1739). Samson himself, unknown to his friends in the play but known to Milton's presumed Christian audience, soars up at his death like the angel charioting up in the column of fire, like the eagle, like the phoenix, to join not merely the noonday sun but that "greater Sun" who is the source of all light.

Samson assumes at his death two additional qualities of the phoenix. Throughout the play he is a center of attention, held up to the "scorn and gaze" of his enemies (34), to the Chorus a "mirror of our fickle state" (164), "to visitants a gaze" (567), the "Image" of God's strength (706), a public "spectacle" in the temple (1604). A major aspect of his mission in life was to serve as an image or exemplum that would lead the Jews out of bondage to Philistia and its idols toward national freedom and true worship. For a long time the real nature of his deeds escaped the perception of both friends and foes. At first they ignored his example or admired him wrongly, then after his fall gazed only to pity or mock him. But in the temple of Dagon Samson performs a "great event" (1756) that can no longer be ignored or misunderstood by either Philistine or Jew.[28] At that instant he is the cynosure of all eyes. Like the eagle of *Areopagitica*, he is surrounded by "the whole noise of timorous and flocking birds . . . amaz'd at what she means." He is a phoenix, traditionally portrayed as a gaze and wonderment, as in Whitney and Browne of Tavistock. Like Milton's Raphael, who in phoenix form is surrounded by lesser birds, Samson is "gaz'd by all" (V, 272).

Albert L. Cirillo notes that in *Paradise Lost* Raphael appears like a phoenix over Eden at noon, when the sun is at its height, and that a tradition connects the phoenix with noon and the birth of the Platonic "great year."[29] As Pliny writes in the *Natural History*: "Manilius also states that the period of the Great Year coincides with the life of this bird, and that the same indications of the seasons and stars return again, and that this begins about noon on the day on which the sun enters the sign of the Ram."[30] This tradition may explain why Milton calls the phoenix in *Samson* a "secular bird." Born in Aries, the first sign of spring, the phoenix signals the beginning of a new age. So too the deed of Samson, if only the Jews can "Find courage to lay hold on this occasion" (1716). If a new age fails to dawn, it will be their failure, not his. Milton knew, of course, from his vantage outside the play, that the birth would prove abortive, as it would prove on two similar occasions in England. But he also believed that the new age would eventually dawn with the coming of that greater Phoenix of whom Samson was only a type, and, moreover, that a new birth would occur in the hearts of those who in future would emulate Samson (1738–40). Success or failure of the Jews or of individuals among them is no longer Samson's responsibility. Having fulfilled his task he rests from his labors. Like the phoenix, he has died and been reborn, and has risen into the heavens to join the noonday sun.

New York University

NOTES

1. All Milton quotations are from *The Works of John Milton*, ed. Frank A. Patterson et al. (New York, 1931–40), hereafter cited as CM.

2. See my *The Blaze of Noon: A Reading of "Samson Agonistes"* (New York: 1974), pp. 90–117.

3. "The 'Ev'ning Dragon' in *Samson Agonistes*: A Reappraisal," *MLN*, LXXVI (1961), 577–84; other critics and editors disagree.

4. CM, III, 275.

5. Cox, "The 'Ev'ning Dragon,'" p. 583.

6. See *Blaze of Noon*, pp. 185–205.

7. CM, IV, 344.

8. See the Scolar Press facsimile (1969), p. 19. Capitals are normalized as italics.

9. *Blaze of Noon*, passim.

10. CM, XV, 403–05.

11. "Time, Light, and the Phoenix," in *Calm of Mind*, ed. J. A. Wittreich, Jr. (Cleveland, 1971), pp. 227–28. In spite of the title, Cirillo devotes only a paragraph to the phoenix.

12. Kester Svendsen, *Milton and Science* (Cambridge, Mass., 1956), pp. 146–49; Ovid, *Metamorphoses*, trans. Golding, ed. J. F. Nims (New York, 1965).

13. Hartwell, *Lactantius and Milton* (Cambridge, Mass., 1929), p. 130.

14. *The Works of Sir Thomas Browne*, ed. Geoffrey Keynes (Chicago, 1964), II, 194.

15. *Natural History* (X.2), ed. H. Rackham, Loeb Classic Library (Cambridge, Mass., 1940), III, 294.

16. (Menston, Yorkshire, 1969), p. 177. Capitals are regularized as italics in this and the next quotation.

17. Scolar Press facsimile, p. 19.

18. Reproduced in *John Milton: Complete Poems and Major Prose*, ed. Merritt Y. Hughes (New York, 1957), p. 548.

19. Scolar Press facsimile, p. 19.

20. *Seventeenth-Century Prose and Poetry*, ed. Alexander M. Witherspoon and Frank J. Warnke (New York, 1963), p. 832.

21. *Poems of William Browne of Tavistock*, ed. Gordon Goodwin, The Muses' Library (London, n.d.), I, 110.

22. CM, XVIII, 338.

23. Kenneth Fell, "From Myth to Martyrdom: Towards a View of Milton's *Samson Agonistes*," *English Studies*, XXXIV (1953), 145–47; Barbara Harrell Carson, "Milton's Samson as *Parvus Sol*," *ELN*, V (1968), 171–76; Samuel S. Stollman, "Samson's 'Sunny Locks the Laws': An Hebraic Metaphor," *Seventeenth-Century News*, XVI (1968), 71–72.

24. CM, III, 276 (italics added).

25. Trinity College Manuscript; CM, XVIII, 236.

26. "Act and Emblem: The Conclusion of *Samson Agonistes*," *ELH*, XXXII (1965), 160–68.

27. "Natural Science and Figurative Design in *Samson Agonistes*," *ELH*, XXXV (1968), 54. Cox briefly discusses "fire imagery" in a survey of elemental imagery with different emphases from mine.

28. See *Blaze of Noon*, pp. 90–117.

29. "Noon-Midnight and the Temporal Structure of *Paradise Lost*," *ELH*, XXIX (1962), 372–95.

30. Pliny, p. 295.

"WISDOM BY ADVERSITY": DAVIDIC TRAITS IN MILTON'S *SAMSON*

Miriam Muskin

S AMSON AGONISTES, Milton's moving drama about the hero from the tribe of Dan, contains many elements that puzzle critical readers as much as the biblical Samson's riddles perplexed the Philistines.[1] Difficulties abound in a literary creation that places a Hebrew story in a Greek structure for the perusal of a Christian audience. Not the least of the perplexing problems centers on the material Milton has injected into his drama, his own inventions which cannot be found in the saga recorded in the Book of Judges. These inventions, in turn, affect three interlocking puzzles involving the hero, the moral drama, and the overall direction of the poem.

One such invention, Samson's encounter with the giant Harapha, while obviously missing from the account in Judges, draws heavily upon an equally turbulent tale found in the Book of Samuel—the David-Goliath battle. Milton makes this comparison explicit by describing Harapha's armor in terms that parallel the description of Goliath in 1 Samuel xvii, 5–7, and by stating that he is the "Father of five Sons / All of Gigantic size, *Goliah* chief" (1248–49).[2] Samson, too, is depicted in terms that parallel the biblical account of David's duel with Goliath. Like David, who met Goliath unarmed except for his slingshot and endured the taunts of the giant (1 Samuel xvii, 43–44), Samson faces an opponent who abuses him with contemptuous remarks (1106–07), and is willing to venture against him though armed "only with an Oak'n staff."[3] Although we know Milton did not hesitate to utilize the characteristics of one biblical figure to enhance another, as in *Paradise Lost*, Book V, where Adam's conduct parallels that of Abraham,[4] nonetheless some riddles remain. On the one hand, we must wonder why Milton would introduce material about David, one of Israel's noblest spiritual and political leaders, in a story about Samson, Israel's brawniest but morally weakest champion. On the other, we must question how this material would resolve the puzzles about a hero who differs sharply from his namesake in the Bible; about a moral drama that centers on the sin and repentance of a man who has a weakness for women and enjoys fighting Philistines; and about the overall direction of a work that, unlike *Paradise Lost* and *Paradise Regained*, lacks any specifically Christian message.

The answers to these conundrums suggested by many scholars involve theology and are predicated upon the view that, since Milton can be termed the Christian poet par excellence, the hero, moral drama, and overall direction of *Samson* must be placed within the same Christian tradition as the two epics. In this view, Milton's inventions serve only to help transform Samson into a Christian hero, the moral drama into a Christian theme, and the overall direction of the play into a Christian tragedy which complements the epics. In the opinion of John M. Steadman, for example, since both David and Samson are mentioned in the Epistle to the Hebrews as heroes of faith, Milton has utilized the encounter with Harapha to emphasize this Christian aspect of his own hero.[5] Northrop Frye similarly equates Harapha with the Goliath of the David story, but he suggests that Milton's invention emphasizes that his hero is a dramatic prototype of Christ, an analogy which can be felt during the colloquy with Harapha when Samson asserts himself as a champion of God.[6] Though Frye believes the drama should be interpreted by the same theological principles that apply to the epics, he notes that Milton's poem about a savage hero does seem an anomaly, that if it did not exist "we could say with some confidence that Milton could never have chosen Samson for a hero."[7]

When viewed in the context of the epics, Milton's decision to relate the turbulent tale of a hero like Samson does appear baffling and incomprehensible. In addition, should we accept the assumption that the hero, moral drama, and overall direction of *Samson* follow the pattern of the other major poetry, then our own "riddling days" may never be past. A possible solution may be found, however, if, rather than attempting to squeeze *Samson* into a traditional Christian mold, the reader looks at it instead from a historical perspective. To understand what appeal a rough champion could have for a blind poet beyond mutual blindness, we need to go back to the rough days of Milton's own hard-hitting prose during the Puritan experiment when he praised fighters against Philistines. To appreciate the moral drama with its prophetic, Old Testament emphasis, we need to return to the intense scripturalism of both Milton and his fellow militant Puritans during the struggles of the Puritan Revolution. And to recognize the overall direction of a work which markedly differs from the epics, we need to reenter a world in which ancient Israel's story had become England's experience, a world in which the example of Hebrew heroes became precedent for political action, a world inhabited by Milton, the Puritan revolutionist, from 1640 to 1660. By examining the hero, moral drama, and overall direction of the poem from the perspective of that world, we may best decipher the riddles that *Samson* poses.

Milton's *Samson* was formed, grew, and developed out of the scripturalism that marked the Puritan movement. Three aspects of that scripturalism seem to apply to his conception of his hero. First, Milton, no less than other Puritans, regarded both Testaments as equally sacred. When he argued in *The Reason of Church-Government*, the anti-prelatical tract that attacks Old Testament ceremonial law, that the "sacred Bible may be our light," his reference is not to the New Dispensation but to Israel's history which he revered, believing that Israel alone had communicated directly with God.[8] This reverence, however, was combined not only with his theology but also with his politics. Like his fellow Puritans, Milton utilized his scripturalism for a practical end and bent the Bible to serve political purposes. The regicide pamphlets, for example, cite those portions of Israelite history which could justify regicide and republican government. During the years spent fighting Charles, he derived much of his ammunition from the appropriate stories in Judges, Samuel, and Kings. Those sections which proved relevant to his cause were mustered into service and treated with the respect accorded honored allies. In this company could be found a dynamic hero such as Samson, whose struggle resembles England's own strenuous fight for liberty against enslavement by Cavalier "Philistines."

Milton, however, possessed one further belief about Scripture which he recognized went against much Protestant opinion. In his view, all Old Testament heroes without exception deserved to be venerated. He therefore felt it incumbent to defend them whenever they were attacked for seeming to have human frailties and feet of clay.[9] He maintained unequivocally that Israel's heroes were "unquestionably holy teachers and lights of our faith."[10] This position, however, does not explain why he did not portray Samson in the same colors provided by his sacred source. Perhaps the answer lies in that source. Samson hardly constitutes a typical biblical hero. In all of Hebrew Scripture, only one other hero, Samuel, is a Nazarite from birth, and no other hero ever was endowed with prodigious strength which was diverted by physical passions and baser instincts. Nevertheless, Samson did have one redeeming feature: he never forgot that his strength came from God (Judges xvi, 17). Possibly the root of Milton's portrayal can be found in this redeeming feature. Whenever he defended God's chosen instruments, he looked for their justifying qualities. In other instances, Scripture provided him with ample evidence to show that the maligned were, in fact, "holy teachers"; but Samson proved an exception. Though his story provided one indication that he was worthy of defense, this needed to be supplemented in order to raise a purely physical into a truly spiritual hero of Israel.

The manner in which Milton supplemented his hero's qualities, endowing him with a noble conscience, deep piety, integrity, and intelligence, has been a source of critical controversy. It is difficult, however, to harmonize suggestions that Samson has been transformed from a rugged Hebrew character into a passive Christian hero of faith or a tragic Christ figure with the fact that Milton has not altered the setting as given in Judges, but, instead, has retained most of the details supplied in his source. To solve the dilemma, numerous other analogues and parallels have been mentioned.[11] Yet in all the Hebrew Bible, from Moses through the great prophets, only one person has both the weaknesses of the original Samson and the strengths which Milton has provided. The only character who sins and repents, has a failing for the fair sex, fights Philistines, endures being a man alone, outlawed, and persecuted by his own people, and yet at the same time is a man of rare nobility, integrity, and prayer, is David. Perhaps the unusual manner in which Samson and David were viewed by both militant Puritans and Milton himself during the revolutionary period may explain why Milton would enhance his hero with Davidic traits.

Puritans' attitudes toward the two biblical heroes are related to their scripturalism, which resulted in a propensity to identify themselves with ancient Israel. Early in the development of the Puritan movement they discovered the parallels between the religious and political situations in England and in biblical Israel. In Old Testament history, they found recorded the struggles of a people fighting against wicked kings so that they could establish a government true to God's worship. Since this seemed a perfect mirror of their own situation, they turned to Hebrew Scripture to learn how to act, how to achieve their goals. At some point in their struggle, analogy led to identity whereby they equated ancient Israel—the people of God—with English Puritans who likewise held a special relationship with the Deity. Richard Hooker, at the turn of the century in his classic defense of the Church of England, accused his Puritan foes of viewing themselves as "new Israelites" who would "under the conduct of other Joshuas, Samsons, and Gideons, perform a work no less miraculous in casting out violently the wicked from the earth."[12] By the Civil War period, it had become a commonplace, reiterated by countless preachers and laymen alike, to call England "Israel," to think of London as Jerusalem and the English Puritans as Israelites, and to refer to Parliament by such titles as "the Worthies of our Israel," the "Elders," or the "Heads of our Tribes." In this atmosphere, opponents were dubbed "these *British Amalekites*" or "those uncircumcised *Philistines*," with all the unsavory associations that the names of the biblical enemies of Israel had acquired.[13]

As revolutionists, Puritans found themselves pitted against a legitimate government and desired, therefore, to find arguments that would legitimize their own actions. In addition to searching for precedents in historic English law, it was natural for people who regarded themselves as "Israel" to turn to Old Testament history and seek in the authority of sacred Scripture a warrant to undermine the authority of the king. That their arguments from Scripture were both effective and widespread was noted by a Royalist like Edward Clarendon, who was appalled that Puritan preachers used Old Testament texts for "seditious sermons," claiming that it was un-Christian for them to do so and lamenting, "It would fill a volume to insert all the impious madness of this kind."[14] This "impious" appeal to Scripture, however, served Puritan activists in their attempts both to justify their movement and to inspire zealous participation in it. The pamphlet war, in which Milton participated, was waged to convince the public that the Puritan point of view had the authority of Holy Writ. Included in the ammunition derived from Scripture were parallels between the English people and Israel's blinded fighter against the Philistines and between England's government and Israel's most beloved king.

Although specific comparisons to Samson did not appear often in Puritan discourse, on those occasions when the Danite hero was referred to Puritans tended to present him as a symbol of their own countrymen. Both before and during the Civil War, prominent Puritan preachers and speakers alluded to the biblical Samson to symbolize the ordinary citizenry of England who constituted the strength of their nation. In 1625, the brilliant Puritan divine, John Preston, asked to address the House of Commons at a time of crisis because of the plague, compared the zealous among his countrymen to "the haire from *Sampsons* head, wherein the strength of every Countrey and Nation, and every Citie and Towne consists."[15] Later in the century, as the Civil War drew near, details of the Samson saga seemed a perfect parallel to the situation of the Puritans engaged in a bitter religious controversy. To a Puritan such as Nathaniel Fiennes, one of the "root and branch" men in Commons, his enemies, the bishops, were Philistines who would treat his fellow countrymen as Samson, so that "having put *out our Eyes,*

. . . they may afterwards make us *Grind,* and reduce us unto what Slavery they please."[16] To Edmund Staunton, speaking in the midst of the war, the comparison remained apt. Enemies who attempted "to blind the eyes of the people" were considered "Philistim-like," while the common folk who resisted acted the role of Samson, "for the people are the *Sampson,* the strength of a Nation."[17]

Whereas a hero such as Samson provided a parallel for the common people, the biblical David, in the extensive treatment given to him by the fiery preachers, supplied a model of proper leadership for king, or Parliament, or both. Disgust with Charles at the outset of the Civil War caused members of the Puritan clergy to call upon Parliament to emulate David's courage and competence. With tensions rising in the months before the outbreak of hostilities, Thomas Case, preaching at Westminster before Commons, encouraged Parliament by telling them that in defending God's *"English Jerusalem, He hath made him that was weak* among you *as David,"* and foretold that the Puritans would defeat "those *uncircumcised Philistins . . .* who hath not ceas'd to blaspheme and scatter the *Armies* of the *living God"* because "God hath honoured you with little lesse than a *miraculous effusion* of *his Spirit,* heightning your Spirits, and strengthening your hands to *David-like prowesse."*[18] Case also suggested that Parliament utilize David as their "pattern" in the important Puritan task of renewing their *"Covenant* with God."[19] In the same period, Edmund Calamy, a Presbyterian minister who frequently was called upon to address the Long Parliament, cited a number of incidents from David's life as examples for Parliamentary behavior.[20] During the early months of the war, however, it seemed to some divines that Parliament's duty required that they act the role of David's minister, Joab, who had given sound advice to his king during the period of civil war (the Absalom rebellion) in Israel. Joab had counseled David that "your *Absolom* and your *Adonijah,* you may love them wel, but not better then your own peace, your owne people. If the Queene of your bosome stand in competition with your Kingdome, your people, you must not love her better then us." Such advice needed to be "applyed to our *David,"* whose duty as king required that he command "reasonable things."[21] As the Civil War advanced, the unreasonableness of Charles caused the renowned preacher Stephen Marshall, who at the beginning of the troubles had suggested David as "an example fit for a *King* and *Parliament* to follow," to lament that in fact England lacked a king who would be their David.[22]

If, for the Puritan polemicist, a Samson could characterize the common people, and a David could provide both a standard with

which to measure the fallible Charles and a symbol for their own determination to conquer the *"uncircumcised Philistins,"* for Milton the biblical heroes represented, in addition, many of his own personal ideas.
Like his fellow Puritans, Milton read Hebrew history as a mirror of his
own time, claiming that by "not shutting wilfully our eyes, we may see
the like story brought to pass in our own Land."[23] Similarly, his treatment of Samson and David paralleled Puritan usage in that his prose
tracts contain very few references to Samson but a host of allusions to
the "sweet singer of Israel."[24] In the early prose tracts, moreover, in good
Puritan fashion, Milton utilized Samson to characterize the English nation or compared him to Charles, who embodied in his own person the
totality of the entire people. In *Areopagitica*, for example, Milton referred to the English people as "a noble and puissant Nation rousing
herself like a strong man after sleep," while in both *Reason of Church-
Government* and *Eikonoklastes* he likened Charles to "that mighty
Nazarite *Samson*," with the condition that the king avoid shaving the
"Nazarites lock," which he defined in *Church-Government* as "the
golden beames of Law and Right."[25] Milton's handling of Samson, however, underwent a subtle shift when he wrote *A Defence of the People of
England*, a shift which may be connected to his affinity for and ideas
about the other fighter against Philistines, Israel's great poet-king.

Milton's own "portion in David" paralleled his participation in the
Puritan Revolution during the turbulent years from 1640 to 1660. Few
acts of that revolution evoked as much emotional response as the trial
and execution of Charles I. With the beheading of Charles, January 30,
1648/9, a gasp of horror went up throughout royalist Europe. Milton's
involvement in the controversy resulted from the decision of Charles II,
who was then at the Hague, to commission Claudius Salmasius, one of
Europe's most respected scholars, to write a defense of Charles I and
England's monarchy while sympathy for his father was at its height.
Salmasius set to work, and by November 1649 his *Defensio Regia pro
Carolo I* had been published and distributed on the Continent and
readied for mass importation into England.[26] The new republic tried to
keep the book from reaching English shores, but without success, and
on Tuesday, January 8, 1649/50, the Council of State ordered "that Mr.
Milton do prepare something in answer to the Book of Salmasius, and
when he hath done it bring it to the Council."[27] Though Milton already
had shown his skill as a proregicide polemicist in *The Tenure of Kings*
and *Eikonoklastes*, the council order nonetheless represented a difficult
challenge. As his nephew Edward Phillips later recalled, Salmasius was
"the great Kill-cow of *Christendom*," and to defy "a Man so Famous"

required as much bravery as attacking a veritable Goliath. Indeed, "there could no where have been found a Champion that durst lift up the Pen against so formidable an Adversary, had not our little *English David* had the Courage."[28]

In many respects, Phillips' reference to his uncle as "our little *English David*" can describe not only Milton's valor in the Salmasius dispute, but also his lifelong veneration of Israel's fearless poet, warrior, leader, and champion of God's cause. As early as his antiprelatical tracts, he spoke with admiration of the "incomparable" "kinds of Lyrick poesy" found "throughout the law and prophets,"[29] and in *Paradise Regained* he bestowed his highest praise upon "Hebrew Songs" such as "Psalms" and "Hymns" in which "God is prais'd aright" (IV, 331–50). In 1648 and again in 1653 he undertook to translate some of the Psalms— Psalms lxxx–lxxxviii in April 1648 and Psalms i–viii in August 1653. Though no record has been left to indicate why Milton decided to paraphrase these particular Psalms when he did, the attempt itself indicates a feeling of affinity with Israel's divinely inspired poets.[30]

In similar fashion, Milton found David's abilities as a warrior to be an apt example for contemporary action. In *The Tenure*, he paralleled the rebellion against Saul with England's and Scotland's against Charles and commented that when David had once taken up arms he never again trusted Saul, whereby his "sanctify'd prudence might be alone sufficient, not to warrant us only, but to instruct us."[31] Despite his total distrust of Charles and English monarchy and his expressed republican convictions, Milton never failed to admire David's leadership ability not just as warrior, but as king. Naturally, whenever he contrasted Charles to David, the latter appeared in glowing colors; but when he noted that Charles had plagiarized David's Psalms, and wittily claimed "had he borrow'd *Davids* heart, it had bin much the holier theft," he sincerely meant that David possessed the kind of heart a true leader of England required.[32] Such a heart developed under "suffering without just cause," whereby David "learnt that meekness and that wisdom by adversity, which made him much the fitter man to raigne."[33] In addition, David ruled under a constitutional monarchy in which the ultimate power resided in the people, so that he did not reign until he "*first made a Covnant with the Elders of Israel, and so was by them anointed King, 1 Chron.* 11."[34] But, above all, Israel's leader was God's champion, a man totally imbued with the presence of the Divine. To Milton, it was sacrilegious on the part of Salmasius to "speak of David especially as one to be abhorred." Indignantly, he questioned how Salmasius dare compare Charles to David, "one full of superstitious fancies . . . with a king and a reverent prophet of God, a fool with a wise man, a coward with a hero, a sinner with a saint?"[35]

Although Milton, by using the biblical yardstick, insisted that Charles could never be compared to David, he did not mean that David's achievement was beyond human attainment. On the contrary, as he noted in *Christian Doctrine*, David's actions proved he was, above all, a mortal being, exemplifying the man who sins and repents.[36] In addition, as Israel's history indicated, David could provide his people with the type of leadership his nation needed. Though Charles, in Milton's estimation, personally lacked these Davidic qualities, he did, by virtue of his office, represent the English nation: as noted above, Milton had at first likened Charles to Samson, who symbolized the nation. In the midst of the regicide controversy, however, as it became apparent that England required strong leadership, Milton's idea of Samson began to change. This can be seen in his answer to Salmasius, where he employed the "heroic Samson" as an example for the right "to kill those masters who were tyrants over his country, even though most of her citizens did not balk at slavery."[37] Samson here symbolizes not the nation but the nation's leader, willing to lead even when not followed.

Milton initially held the same views as other Puritans about both Samson and David, especially during the early years of the fight against the Royalists, when Samson symbolized the folk and David the ideal leader. The shift in his handling of Samson evidenced in *A Defence of the People of England*, whereby the brawny Danite acquired Davidic nobility, may represent a merging of the two heroes in Milton's mind. This new conception of Samson seems to have arisen under the pressure of events following the beheading of Charles, when Milton believed England needed a leader who, like David, could learn "wisdom by adversity," could understand the secret of genuine repentance, and could provide the heroic qualities necessary to rescue England from Philistine slavery. Perhaps Milton's application of Davidic leadership qualities to Samson at this juncture of English history may be the clue to understanding not just the character of the dramatic Samson, but also the nature of the moral drama in *Samson Agonistes*.

The riddle of the moral drama has sent critics searching in many different directions. Obviously, Milton could not have depended upon the account in the Book of Judges to supply his hero with any inner spiritual struggle, since the author of the biblical story silently passes over Samson's remorse, acceptance of guilt, and repentance. Since Milton's hero, in contrast, is engaged in such an inner struggle, the nature and source of that struggle have elicited numerous suggestions.[38] Solving the riddle, however, depends on recognizing two prime elements. On the one hand, we need to realize how Davidic traits not only can ennoble Samson but also can make him the kind of hero who can learn "wisdom by adversity." On the other, we need to understand why Milton would consider the Hebraic concept of genuine repentance to be of pivotal importance. A careful analysis of the poem will show how Milton has incorporated a Davidic approach to sin, repentance, and collective piety in Samson's story, and a careful consideration of the revolutionary period will determine how such themes became incorporated in the Puritan program and in Milton's thinking.

The themes of sin and repentance are interwoven in David's history. The Book of Samuel records that David's tragic grandeur consists partly in his ability to recognize how heinous was his crime, to feel complete mortification, to accept unequivocal blame, and to repent. Milton appears similarly to have elevated his Samson with these sentiments. From his initial speech in the prologos, "Whom have I to complain of but my self?" (46), we recognize that Samson is willing to some extent to accept the blame for his current debasement. Actual awareness of the extent of his guilt, however, is not evidenced until Manoa confronts him with it (433–47), charging that Samson is responsible for causing Dagon to be magnified and God blasphemed. Manoa, of course, bears no resemblance to the prophet Nathan, but, in this instance, he serves a similar function. By painting a picture of the repercussions of Samson's sin, he elicits the immediate mortified response, "Father, I do acknowledge and confess" (448). A humbled Samson admits he has sinned against God, just as a humble David admitted, "I have sinned against the Lord" (2 Samuel xii, 13).

A humbled Samson does more, however, than just acknowledge sin. In this admission, he indicates that, like David, he understands the relationship between sin and God, a relationship which Milton himself emphasized when, in his argument with Salmasius, he explicated the words of David in Psalm li, "Against thee only have I sinned." Pointing out that it is nonsense to assume that David's crimes were not crimes against his fellow man, Milton insisted that the verse means, rather, that God in particular is sinned against in all sins against God's creatures.[39] In such a situation, David's only hope was to turn to God in penitence and implore his mercy. Similarly, Samson's betraying to Dalila the source of his strength might be thought of as sin against himself, since he certainly betrays himself, or as sin against Israel, since he no longer can defend his people, but he correctly terms it a sin against God. Like David, Samson knew that sin against God's creatures involves sin against God the Creator; and, like David, he knew that the only amendment was to beseech pardon from the one against whom he had sinned.

Pardon for Samson, as for David, results from the Hebraic scheme of repentance, which involves as its first step recognition of man's free will. Samson's question as to whom he can blame except himself (46) underscores the fact that no one has forced him to sin, no devil has interfered with his free will. Similarly, no one can make him repent, though Manoa's Nathan-like comments prod him into feeling the full consequences of his act and admitting his guilt (448–59). When he meets Dalila, however, and confronts her claim of penance (735–39), Samson begins to understand what true repentance really means. Milton distinguished sharply between the false and true repentance illustrated in Hebrew Scripture, between a "worldly repentance" and a "conscientious" one.[40] Readers tend to forget, because of the skill with which Dalila argues, that her "wedlock-trechery" consisted of gouging out Samson's eyes. Although she did not personally perform the deed, she served as an accessory, and though she claims she did not know her betrayal would bring physical harm, as her argument shifts it reveals that she values gold more than Samson. Her "feign'd remorse" (752) likewise indicates she now wants the best of two worlds: Philistine fame and a Hebrew lover. Samson's recognition that Dalila is "Not truly penitent" (754) indicates not only that he can distinguish between the two types of repentance, but also that he already has taken a second step in his return to God. This step involves what the prophet Isaiah, in his summary of the stages of "return" (i, 16–17), terms "put away the evil." Samson, in turning his back on Dalila, has left evil behind him and is prepared to move up to Isaiah's third step, "Learn to do well," which implies not just the negation of evil but acceptance of the challenge to action. Harapha supplies the challenge, and Samson responds with David-like confidence because he knows his biblical lesson. Those who turn back to God, as David did, will find his "ear is ever open; and his eye / Gracious to re-admit the suppliant" (1172–73).

As a suppliant seeking God's gracious mercy, David was intensely aware, not only of the unworthiness of a sinner standing before a righteous Judge, sentiments so poignantly expressed in his Psalms, but also of his own creaturely reliance upon his God. This sense of dependence extended throughout his life, from the time he was a persecuted outlaw until he became a mighty monarch. In his rebuke to Michal, Saul's daughter who had been his first love but later "despised him in her heart" (2 Samuel vi, 16), David coupled pride in his royal estate with a

humble recognition of his own insignificance in the glorious presence of
the Supreme King. Retorting to Michal that before the Lord he willingly would debase himself and make himself lowly in his own sight (2
Samuel vi, 21–22), David has not forgotten that the source of his own
royal power is the ruler of both heaven and earth. Similarly, during the
Absalom rebellion when his fortunes had reached low ebb, David accepted the curses of Shimei with humility as the will of God (2 Samuel
xvi, 5–14). The author of Judges likewise implies that Samson, too, recognizes that the source of his might and strength resides in the power of
the Almighty, but the biblical tales hardly convey the picture of a personality possessing the quality of humility. Milton's hero, in contrast,
displays a Davidic appreciation of his own human frailty, of his ability
to learn "wisdom by adversity." He not only can state that God sent
Dalila to debase him and aggravate his folly (999–1000), but he likewise
can acknowledge that God has inflicted such indignities upon him
"Justly" (1168–71).

The strength of David, however, resided not only in his ability to
feel humility and to turn humbly to the path of repentance but also in
his talent to inspire his countrymen with his own religious personality
and to stamp his passionate faith in the power of penitence upon their
collective conscience. The idea that the Israelites collectively possessed
an identifiable personality is fundamental in Hebrew Scripture. Its
pages present a picture of a God-intoxicated covenant community who
collectively can both rise to lofty heights and sink to abysmal depths,
who know their responsibilities to God, who are constantly backsliding
but who can be guided upward again under the impetus of inspired
leadership. David supplied that leadership. Throughout a life spent in
the public arena, he instinctively knew how to interact with his people
and elicit their allegiance to his ideals. His sense of responsibility never
wavered, and even when he was exiled among the Philistines he used his
time to fight the enemies of Israel (1 Samuel, chap. xxvii). As monarch,
he considered it a prime task to dispense justice (2 Samuel viii, 15), and
throughout the vicissitudes of his life his unswerving dedication to his
people elicited their loyalty, affection, and strong emotional ties. As a
result, during the Absalom rebellion, when a grief-stricken David fled
Jerusalem and ascended the Mount of Olives, weeping as he went, his
tears, his suffering, and his mourning were mirrored in the eyes of his
countrymen who wept with him (2 Samuel xv, 30).

In Milton's hands, the Chorus of Danites represent a community
with an identifiable personality. Like the countless models he found in
Hebrew Scripture, his Danites follow the cyclic pattern of the biblical

Israelites. As a people in covenant, a "holy nation," they actively strive to fulfill God's word, seek justice, and pursue righteousness, but the temptations to yield to sin are many. They fall from their task, rebel against God and his appointed leaders, and are punished for their disobedience through loss of liberty. Made aware of their sins, they repent, turn back to God, reestablish the covenant, and regain God's blessings.

The Chorus, however, is not merely a typical Israelite community; it is Samson's own community. As such, it responds to Samson in a fashion similar to the way David's countrymen responded to him. Though it follows the typical Israelite cycle of waywardness and ever recurring return, the Chorus basically moves with rather than against Samson. It responds to the ideals he holds: his sense of responsibility to the community he has been chosen to save, his search for justice in human affairs, and his awareness of his duty to obey God's word. It shares his concern for divine justice (667–704) and objects to a world in which "Just or unjust, . . . both come to evil end" (703–04), though its remonstrance is predicated on the conviction that somehow the ways of God must be just.[41] In addition, the Chorus responds to Samson's bitter experience. Like the countrymen who wept with David, the Danites come to Samson as his "friends and neighbours" and, in the larger sense, his brethren, to bring "Counsel or Consolation" as "Salve to thy Sores" (180–84). Because they come, because they stay and learn to empathize with Samson's grief, the beautiful lyric prayer of supplication bursts from their lips beseeching God to deal with Samson with the compassion they themselves feel.

With the plea for Samson comes the realization of how deeply the community can respond to its fallen hero. But Milton likewise has presented a hero who responds to his community. Samson's rededication to his mission does not occur within the lonely recesses of his soul, but arises from his interaction with his community. When they react to his failure by wavering in faith (454–56), he realizes that his responsibility is not private, but public. At the same time he does not forget that the community has failed him. In its review of collective sin under other judges (277–89), the Chorus supplies Samson with the historic perspective of its own failure, while Samson's comment about loving ease more than liberty (270–71) likewise refers to the lesson of Israel's history. Though Milton does not supply a direct allusion, Samson's passionate protest is in harmony with prophetic teaching on liberty, beginning with Moses' castigation of the Israelites' yearning for Egyptian fleshpots, and it may also include Milton's opinion about his own elect nation.

This prophetic view, that bondage is punishment for "Nations grown corrupt" who do not listen to "thir Deliverer," is Samson's response to his brethren (265–76, 1211–16), repeated to emphasize why "*Israel* still serves." Yet Milton's Samson, with Davidic sensitivity, knows that the God who punishes is the God who pardons when individual or nation turns to him in sincere repentance. He likewise recognizes that God can, and will, deliver the single individual or the entire community if they are true to him. This recognition also comes to the Danite community (1268–76) as they see Samson's spirits reviving. They now are prepared to stand by their deliverer, even to go with him if he wants, as Samson's farewell indicates (1413–15), and are united with him in prayer that the "Holy One / Of *Israel*" will remain "Fast by thy side" (1427–40). The direct consequence of their return to God is the return of liberty through the destruction of the enemy. The reference to this destruction in the unrestrained outburst of the Semichorus (1669–86), reminiscent not only of Old Testament victory odes but also of Puritan sermons following the routing of the Royalists at Marston Moor or Naseby,[42] reflects their intense sense of relief. David has killed Goliath for them; one man has destroyed the enemy force, cast down the mighty ones, and eradicated the wicked from the earth. In calmer mood, their passions spent, they realize that by means of repentance they too have been rejoined to God and have thereby regained honor and freedom (1714–15).

The path to honor and freedom followed by the Danites likewise was espoused by militant Puritans in their attempts to rid themselves of the yoke of Cavalier "Philistines." Like Samson's and David's countrymen, Puritans viewed their own nation as a corporate entity which could sin, repent, and enter into fellowship with God. During the war years, the idea developed that England, like biblical Israel, could enter into a covenant with God involving national election coupled with national responsibility. To demonstrate that it was worthy to have been chosen for such a covenant, the nation was expected to fulfill moral and spiritual obligations. As the Civil War approached, a preacher like Stephen Marshall found comfort in the idea that a covenant nation, selected by God, could anticipate his divine protection against its enemies, as Israel's history demonstrated. At the same time, however, a covenant represented a challenge by its demand "to be a holy people, a *Ieshurun, a righteous Nation.*"[43] A nation in covenant that did not fulfill its obligations would be guilty of a heinous crime since, as Thomas Case explained from the example of Hosea, a covenant nation enjoyed a conjugal relationship with God. Though other nations may sin, they cannot commit adultery; they may rebel against God, but they cannot be guilty of whoring. Only an Israel or an England, bound to God by the covenant, could attain the highest marital bliss or commit the most depraved sin.[44]

Thus a national covenant, as it came to be understood during the years of Puritan dominance, included fundamental biblical character-istics: fulfillment of the covenant required activism; disobedience in-volved national sin, for which the remedy was national repentance; and fidelity implied the possibility of attaining national blessings. Puritan preachers tended to play on all themes simultaneously, buttressing their arguments with ample illustrations from Israel's story.

Activism involved righteousness, which required the same kind of public action demanded in David's day. Though such Puritan mentors as Luther and Calvin had spoken of a Pauline righteousness of faith, a passive inner righteousness that has no connection with political action, it was the passionate pleas of the prophets of Israel for the execution of justice which now reverberated in Puritan ears. From Jeremiah, Wil-liam Greenhill, for example, learned that Jerusalem had been destroyed because public justice was neglected. In the same manner, England could anticipate national "ruine" unless it concentrated on national justice.[45] To avert such ruin, Puritans advocated zealous action in both civil and religious affairs. "*David*," according to Thomas Wilson, "was zealous for Gods house; for *Zion*, as well as *Ierusalem*; for religion, as well as righteousnesse."[46] Possibly, as Arthur Salwey suggested, "in matters civill we have sometimes a latitude," but in religion "it is a very evill thing to be either a *Neuter*, . . . or a Waverer."[47] Even worse, for Puritans in the midst of a battle for survival, those who were not willing to take sides, those who, in Marshall's famous words, "stand *neuters*," would be cursed as the men of Meroz during Deborah's war for Israel.[48]

To avoid being "neuter," Puritans insisted upon the Hebrew idea of covenant. By ratifying the Solemn League and Covenant with Scot-land in 1643, and later renewing it, the entire nation could be held re-sponsible for its collective actions and punished for collective guilt. As a result, Puritans explained disasters during the Civil War in terms of na-tional sin. Although Calvinism stressed personal faith and salvation, the covenant focus during the war caused Puritans to shift their emphasis from individual sin and election to national guilt and corporate re-demption. A nation that broke her covenant could anticipate curses, wrath, destruction, the miseries of war, and, even worse, desertion by God; but comfort could be found in the knowledge that just as "the sinne and punishment are Nationall, so must the amendment be."[49]

The "amendment," "return O Israel," turn to God and repent,

echoed from countless pulpits during the revolution and interregnum. Immersed in a struggle to fashion a nation in accordance with what they conceived to be the will of God, Puritan divines looked for direction in the parallels they found in sacred writ, comparing always their present condition to that of the days of judges or kings when Israel's sins caused God's wrath, but when repentance brought healing from the Lord.[50] Though opponents objected that Old Testament repentance had been superseded by New Testament Christian liberty and faith, for those busy building a covenanted community, trust in the remedial powers of repentance fit the facts as they saw them.

The belief that the nation could sin, repent, and reap the resultant blessings was coupled with the conviction that this scheme likewise applied to the individual. Though sin caused man's relationship with his Creator to be torn asunder, the breach could be repaired by the biblical expedient of *"turning to God by new obedience."*[51] The Hebrew Bible, as in the classic case of David, showed that man could choose not only to sin, but also to repent, and that repentance provided the effectual method of attaining divine pardon; but the biblical man's freedom to choose either course hardly could be followed directly by adherents of Calvinism.[52] Despite the acceptance of covenant theology, with its free choice of accepting or rejecting a contract with God, most Puritans also believed that man had lost the freedom Adam originally possessed and could not repent without divine assistance.[53]

Repentance without free will robs much of the Old Testament doctrine of its moral force. Yet, despite the fact that free will was ostensibly denied, repentance was taught from Hebrew Scripture using texts and phrasing which frequently produced the Hebraic conclusion that "repentance is not onely a *duty*, but a *happinesse*. It is a *happinesse* that there is such a gate as repentance to get into heaven by."[54] Praise for the powers of repentance arose repeatedly from Puritan pulpits during the war years, presented by divines who had a "Text for it" that the very instant a person turned from sin, as in the case of David, God would turn as well.[55]

If militant Puritans could find a "Text for it" and incorporate an Old Testament approach to sin, repentance, and collective piety for the purpose of turning England into a new Israel and the English into a new chosen people, Milton could do so too. Convinced that England, like Israel, had been chosen as a "speciall mark" of God's favor, he thought of England as another Zion, of London as a biblical city of refuge, of the English people as God's prophets, and of a special covenant existing between God and England for the reformation of the English church, as it had between God and Israel for reform in religion and government during the biblical period.[56]

Milton's familiarity with covenant concepts is attested to in his prose. Though the theological term "covenant of grace" usually applied to an individual, Milton believed that the nation, too, could enter into such a covenant and make a public vow as a single entity.[57] During the war years, his support of the Solemn League and Covenant reflected his conviction that a national covenant was the proper course of action for an elect nation.[58] Like other Puritans, he believed that a national covenant required not only biblical activism but also a corporate type of sin and punishment, repentance and reward. Just as these ideas were intertwined in Puritan pronouncements, they likewise were interwoven in Milton's lengthy prose arguments and the brief poetic pieces produced during the years of Puritan dominance. His demand for the active achievement of justice, his fight for what he conceived to be a righteous form of government, was predicated on his belief that England, collectively, would deserve God's punishment or reward depending upon its own choice of action.

In Milton's view, a covenant not founded upon justice was a contradiction in terms. In his argument against Charles, he pointed out that a covenant that would exempt the king from justice would be an offense "against the Law of God" as well as against the laws of the country, because God's law demands equal justice for all.[59] Taking his example from Israel's history, Milton maintained that God's chosen, even when they were only a remnant, as were those who supported Parliament in the regicide controversy, had the duty "to stand upright and stedfast in his cause" by defending "truth and public libertie."[60] That defense, as Milton later reiterated in his tract against Salmasius, had to be carried out with prophetic zeal so that the epithets of "Enthusiasts," "Inspired," and "Prophets," cast by their enemies, could be accepted with pride by those engaged in the Lord's battle.[61] For Milton, no less than for Marshall, "neuters" were unacceptable and righteousness was mandatory for a nation in league with God.

Milton's plea for justice, which he stressed in his paraphrase of Psalm lxxxii in 1648, was linked to his acceptance of the Old Testament idea that nations, no less than individuals, are responsible for their conduct. The group of Psalms he chose to translate in 1648 emphasize the relationship between God and his people, including the fact that Israel's iniquities evoked God's displeasure. Twelve years later, the iniquities of England and "her perverse inhabitants" aroused Milton's own passionate condemnation.[62] This theme of national sin is reiterated in *The History of Britain*, which Milton published in 1670. Tracing the account of God's other chosen people, the English, Milton repeatedly shows how their transgressions were responsible for their failures. Failure, however, could have been averted if Parliament, as representative of the entire nation, had turned back to the paths of justice and implemented a truly free commonwealth.[63]

Turning back, repenting and starting anew, which had been demonstrated in the "godly and repentant ages of the Jewes," was something Milton believed during the entire period of Puritan rule could be accomplished by Parliament.[64] Milton took literally—and claimed politicians should do the same—those passages in Hebrew Scripture which stated that national obedience to God's commandments was rewarded with prosperity, good fortune, and victory.[65] England, in his view, could achieve those blessings God had once promised Israel, if its leaders remained true to their covenant responsibilities, if they followed the "righteousness" that "exalts a nation," and if they repented of their evil ways.

While Milton thought in terms of the salvation of the English people through collective action, like most Puritans he believed that man's propensity for sin could prevent the achievement of the utopian ideal. Writing after the failure of the Commonwealth, Milton realized that the catalogue of sins he enumerated for fifth-century Britain applied equally to his own generation, standing as an insurmountable barrier between dream and reality.[66] These sins, Milton insisted, were man's own responsibility, because even though God tempts the righteous to prove man, he never tempts "one in the sense of enticing or persuading him to sin."[67] All sin, however, which man commits, no matter of what nature, ultimately is sin against God. In his argument with Salmasius he made this point by explicating Psalm li, emphasizing that this was David's sin.[68] In the picture of David "repenting in bitter grief and tears" and receiving God's pardon and "wondrous mercy," which he drew for Salmasius, Milton caught the essence of the concept of repentance and reconciliation presented in the Hebrew Bible. Though in other contexts he expressed the traditional Christian view that repentance represents "the Gift of God" through "the Son,"[69] the effect of reading Scripture through the spectacles of an England-Israel analogy permitted him, as it did other Puritans, to assimilate the lesson of David's sin and repentance and apply it to both his politics and his art.

Since the Bible suggested that two different types of repentance were possible—one false and the other true—Milton concluded that false repentance arose from a fear of punishment.[70] Politically, this meant that Charles I, who liked to compare his penitence to that of David, in actual fact proved as short "of true penitence" as a Cain, Pharaoh, or Ahab because his repentance was based upon "feare, and nothing els," making it a "worldly repentance not a conscientious" one.[71] "Conscientious" repentance, on the other hand, arose despite punishment in those who, of their own free will, chose to turn away from evil. Though in his insistence on free will Milton differed from many Puritans, he maintained that the "striking exhortations to penitence" found in Hebrew Scripture "would be pointless" unless they were addressed to man "gifted with some powers of judgment and with free will." Scripture thus showed the link between the justice of God's ways and man's capacity to repent based on his ability to choose right from wrong.[72] With that ability, like David, each man could follow the progressive steps of repentance derived from scriptural texts, which included "recognition of sin, contrition, confession, abandonment of evil and conversion to good."[73]

Those steps which Milton used to guide the repentant hero of *Samson Agonistes* back to his God and his people likewise assist the reader to understand the overall direction of the work. In the final act, standing in the midst of the hated Philistines, Samson not only quit himself like Samson but also set the scene for the final riddle of the drama. How tragic is his tragedy? Is it dark, bleak, and unduly pessimistic?[74] Is it an exercise in futility, since Milton knew that the Danites had vanished from history, that the Israelites did not take the opportunity to obtain freedom mentioned in Manoa's concluding remarks (1714–16), and that the second Israel—the Puritans—would not have a second chance to remedy their own dismal failure?[75] Or is Milton's drama a tragedy of victory in death, of suffering through martyrdom, to which Samson "Bore witness gloriously"?[76] The contradictory alternatives probably can be resolved best by one last look at the source for Milton's fearless fighters against Philistines—the Hebrew Bible. In that Bible, the tribe of Dan forms part of the greater community, Israel. True, Dan ceases to exist as an independent unit, but just as the individual has a life beyond himself as part of his community, so, too, the tribe's destiny is linked to and inseparable from that of the nation. Samson dies as an individual, but his story remains as part of the legacy of the nation—a nation which, as Milton knew, perpetually perseveres. He had come to this conclusion in examining the question of God's existence and the truth of Scripture. The affirmative answer lies in the existence of the Jews through the "constant flux of history," providing "living proof of the existence of God and the truth of the scriptures."[77] The truth to be found within that Scripture insists that whenever God's chosen instrument, a David or a Samson, or the nation itself, is estranged from him through sin, then God turns his back ("Oft he seems to hide his face" [1749]), but following their sincere repentance he "unexpectedly returns" (1750) because his people have returned. Never a final answer, only a partial one, since the cycle will begin again; nonetheless this offers a glimmer of hope, a cautious note of optimism in the midst of the bleak human condition that somehow, even when we fail as the English did in 1660, "All is best" because we, like a Davidic Samson, can learn "wisdom by adversity" and can start again on the long road to return, which in God's own time will become permanent.[78]

Cleveland State University

NOTES

1. See for example William R. Parker, *Milton* (Oxford, 1968), II, 903–17; "The Date of *Samson Agonistes*," *PQ*, XXVIII (1949), 145–66; and "The Date of *Samson Agonistes* Again," in *Calm of Mind*, ed. Joseph A. Wittreich, Jr. (Cleveland, 1971), pp. 163–74, for a review of some of *Samson*'s puzzling elements such as the date when the drama was composed, why rhyme is included, and why Milton selected Greek tragedy as a model. These puzzles are, however, beyond the scope of this paper.

2. *Samson Agonistes*, in *The Works of John Milton*, ed. Frank A. Patterson et al. (New York, 1931–40), I, pt. 2, 381. Parenthetic references to Milton's poetry are to this edition, referred to hereafter as CM.

3. John M. Steadman, "Milton's Harapha and Goliath," *JEGP*, LX (1961), 786–95, provides a detailed account of the many points of comparison between the David-Goliath duel as recorded in 1 Samuel, chap. xvii, and the Samson-Harapha encounter.

4. For critics who have noted this paralleling device in *Paradise Lost*, see James H. Sims, *The Bible in Milton's Epics* (Gainesville, Fla., 1962), pp. 202–04, 210; Jason P. Rosenblatt, "Celestial Entertainment in Eden: Book V of *Paradise Lost*," *Harvard Theological Review*, LXII (1969), 411–13, 427; and Mother Mary Christopher Pecheux, "Abraham, Adam, and the Theme of Exile in *Paradise Lost*," *PMLA*, LXXX (1965), 365, 368.

5. "Milton's Harapha," pp. 789–94.

6. "Agon and Logos," in *The Prison and the Pinnacle*, ed. Balachandra Rajan (Toronto, 1973), pp. 144, 140.

7. Ibid., p. 153.

8. *The Complete Prose Works of John Milton*, ed. Don M. Wolfe et al. (New Haven, 1953–), I, 798, referred to hereafter as YP. In *A Defence of the People of England*, YP, IV, 383–84, Milton argues that direct appeal to God was available only in the Hebrew state.

9. *Christian Doctrine*, YP, VI, 762–64.

10. Ibid., p. 366.

11. See Anthony Low, "Tragic Pattern in *Samson Agonistes*," *TSLL*, XI (1969),

923, for suggestions of other Hebrew heroes, including Moses. See Harold Fisch, *Jerusalem and Albion* (New York, 1964), pp. 145–47; Murray Roston, *Biblical Drama in England* (Evanston, Ill., 1968), pp. 164–73; and Ann Gossman, "Samson, Job, and 'the Exercise of Saints,'" *ES*, XLV (1964), 212–24, for a parallel to Job. Resemblances cited include Job's sufferings, dramatic form, and theme; but since Job is a rich country farmer who suffers without cause, he could not be considered an active, dynamic hero and would hardly fit the *Samson* setting.

12. *Of the Laws of Ecclesiastical Polity,* in *The Works of That Learned and Judicious Divine, Mr. Richard Hooker,* ed. John Keble, 3rd ed. (Oxford, 1845), I, 188–89.

13. Calybute Downing, *A Sermon Preached to the Renowned Company of the Artillery* (London, 1641), sig. F2 and F2ᵛ. The term *Philistines* for the Royalists was popular among Puritans.

14. *The History of the Rebellion and Civil Wars in England* (Oxford, 1843), pp. 297–98.

15. *A Sermon Preached at a General Fast,* in *The Saints Qualification,* ed. Richard Sibbes and John Davenport, 2nd ed. (London, 1634), p. 287.

16. "Mr. Nathaniel Fiennes His Speech," in *Historical Collections of Private Passages of State,* ed. John Rushworth, 2nd ed. (London, 1721), IV, 180.

17. *Rupes Israelis: The Rock of Israel* (London, 1644), p. 10.

18. *Two Sermons Lately Preached at Westminster* (London, 1641), "The Epistle Dedicatory," sig. A2ᵛ and A3.

19. Ibid., "The Second Sermon," p. 49.

20. *Gods Free Mercy to England* (London, 1642), pp. 34–35.

21. W[alter] Bridges, *Ioabs Counsell and King Davids Seasonable Hearing It* (London, 1643), pp. 20–22.

22. *A Peace-Offering to God* (London, 1641), p. 49; *A Sacred Panegyrick* (London, 1644), p. 5. For Marshall's popularity, see David Masson, *The Life of John Milton,* rev. ed. (1875–94; rpt. Gloucester, Mass., 1965), II, 519, and Hugh Trevor-Roper, *The Crisis of the Seventeenth Century* (New York, 1968), p. 297. Marshall was the first of the five writers whose initials made up the pen name "Smectymnuus."

23. *Eikonoklastes,* YP, III, 510.

24. In *An Index to the Columbia Edition,* II, 1721, excluding *Samson Agonistes,* only eight references to Samson are listed. In contrast, the *Index,* I, 429–31, contains almost two full pages of references to David, with over seventy listings from the prose alone.

25. *Areopagitica,* YP, II, 558; *Church-Government,* YP, I, 858–59; *Eikonoklastes,* YP, III, 545–46.

26. Masson, *Life,* IV, 162–66. The date of publication of *Regia* is disputed. For differing views, see Masson, IV, 151, n. 1; J. Milton French, ed., *The Life Records of John Milton* (New Brunswick, N.J., 1949–58), II, 246; Parker, *Milton,* II, 962, n. 36; and Don M. Wolfe, "Introduction," *Defence,* YP, IV, 5.

27. Masson, *Life,* IV, 151; *Life Records,* ed. French, II, 286.

28. *The Life of Mr. John Milton,* in *The Early Lives of Milton,* ed. Helen Darbishire (1932; rpt. St. Claire Shores, Mich., 1972). p. 70.

29. *Church-Government,* YP, I, 816.

30. In the first group, Psalms lxxx–lxxxviii, only Psalm lxxxvi is ascribed to David. Psalms lxxx–lxxxiii each bear the title "Psalm of Asaph," who was a contemporary of David's. Psalms lxxxiv, lxxxv, lxxxvii, and lxxxviii are Korahite Psalms. Psalms i–viii traditionally are all ascribed to David. For 17th-century arguments on whether, despite the inscriptions, David wrote all the Psalms, see George Wither, *A Preparation to the Psalter*

(London, 1619), pp. 32–33, reproduced in *Publications of the Spenser Society*, 37 (Manchester, 1884). For modern critics who relate Milton's choice of Psalms to the England-Israel analogy, see Michael Fixler, *Milton and the Kingdoms of God* (Evanston, Ill., 1964), pp. 143–44, and Carolyn P. Collette, "Milton's Psalm Translations: Petition and Praise," *ELR*, II (1972), 249.

31. *The Tenure of Kings and Magistrates*, YP, III, 240.

32. *Eikonoklastes*, YP, III, 547.

33. Ibid., p. 571.

34. *Tenure*, YP, III, 207.

35. *Defence*, YP, IV, 408.

36. YP, VI, 469.

37. *Defence*, YP, IV, 402.

38. Most suggestions relate to traditional Christian themes such as faith, patience, regeneration, and God's grace. See John M. Steadman, "'Faithful Champion': The Theological Basis of Milton's Hero of Faith," *Anglia*, LXXVII (1959), 12–28; Marcia Landy, "Character Portrayal in *Samson Agonistes*," *TSLL*, VII (1965), 239–53; and A. S. P. Woodhouse, "Tragic Effect in *Samson Agonistes*," *UTQ*, XXVIII (1958–59), 218–19.

39. *Defence*, YP, IV, 361–62.

40. *Eikonoklastes*, YP, III, 373.

41. Arnold Stein, *Heroic Knowledge* (1957; rpt. Hamden, Conn., 1965), p. 165, argues that the Chorus's statement against divine justice could only be made "if it is answerable," if, within the context of the drama, God is concerned with human justice.

42. See John Owen, *Eben-ezer*, in *A Complete Collection of the Sermons of the Reverend and Learned John Owen, D.D.*, ed. John Nesbitt et al. (London, 1721), pp. 245, 248, 254, 259. The sermon, preached following the defeat in August 1648 of the Royalists in Essex at Colchester, uses biblical phraseology to recall other great Puritan victories such as the defeat of Charles at Naseby in June 1645. The title is an allusion to the defeat of the Philistines, 1 Samuel vii, 12.

43. *A Sermon Preached Before the Honourable House of Commons, . . . November 17, 1640* (London, 1641), pp. 13, 17, 25–28.

44. *Spirituall Whoredome* (London, 1647), pp. 3–6.

45. *The Axe at the Root* (London, 1643), p. 22.

46. *Davids Zeale for Zion* (London, 1641), p. 14.

47. *Halting Stigmatiz'd* (London, 1644), p. 8.

48. *Meroz Cursed* (London, 1641), p. 22.

49. Bridges, *Ioabs Counsell*, p. 7.

50. See, for example, Herbert Palmer, *The Glasse of Gods Providence Towards His Faithfull Ones* (London, 1644), pp. 63–65.

51. Thomas Hooker, "A True Sight of Sin," in *The Puritans*, ed. Perry Miller and Thomas H. Johnson, rev. ed. (New York, 1963), I, 296; Edmund Calamy, *Englands Antidote, Against the Plaque of Civil Warre* (London, 1645), pp. 37–43.

52. Early General Baptists such as John Smyth returned to the concept of free will by abandoning the Calvinist interpretation of predestination and original sin. See William Haller, *The Rise of Puritanism* (1938; rpt. New York, 1957), pp. 203–05.

53. See Calamy, *Englands Looking-Glasse* (London, 1642), pp. 61–62.

54. Calamy, *Englands Antidote*, p. 20.

55. Ibid., pp. 23, 28. See also William Spurstowe, *Englands Patterne and Duty* (London, 1643), pp. 21, 24, and Thomas Gataker, *Gods Eye on His Israel* (London, 1644), p. 74.

56. Seriatim: *Eikonoklastes*, YP, III, 348–49, and *Animadversions*, YP, I, 704; *Areopagitica*, YP, II, 552–53, 554, and *Defence*, YP, IV, 459; *Eikonoklastes*, p. 494.

57. *Christian Doctrine*, YP, VI, 607–08, 680.

58. Masson, *Life*, III, 12, 56. For Milton's defense of the Solemn League and Covenant, see *Eikonoklastes*, YP, III, 493–96.

59. *Eikonoklastes*, YP, III, 594. See also *Tetrachordon*, YP, II, 624.

60. *Eikonoklastes*, YP, III, 348.

61. *Defence*, YP, IV, 459.

62. *The Readie and Easie Way to Establish a Free Commonwealth*, CM, VI, 148–49.

63. See *The History of Britain*, YP, V, 129, 139; and *Character of the Long Parliament*, YP, V, 442, 444, 446. See also the Digression, V, 443, 445, 447, 449, 451, and *Readie and Easie Way*, CM, VI, 112.

64. See *An Apology Against a Pamphlet*, YP, I, 878, and *Readie and Easie Way*, CM, VI, 113.

65. *Christian Doctrine*, YP, VI, 804.

66. *History*, YP, V, 139–40, and *Character*, V, 442.

67. *Christian Doctrine*, YP, VI, 338. See also pp. 334–37 on man's responsibility for his own sins.

68. *Defence*, YP, IV, 361–62.

69. *Christian Doctrine*, YP, VI, 464, 466.

70. Ibid., p. 458.

71. *Eikonoklastes*, YP, III, 554, 373.

72. *Christian Doctrine*, YP, VI, 459, 190–91. See also pp. 396–98 and 457. For early advocacy of free will, see *Areopagitica*, YP, II, 515.

73. *Christian Doctrine*, YP, VI, 468.

74. See Parker, *Milton*, II, 910.

75. See Frye, "Agon and Logos," pp. 157–58.

76. See Woodhouse, "Tragic Effect," pp. 220–21.

77. *Christian Doctrine*, YP, VI, 132.

78. Material in this essay forms part of my doctoral dissertation at Case Western Reserve University. I acknowledge with pleasure suggestions and criticism given to me by James G. Taaffe and Robert Ornstein.